THE GRAIN
RACES

The Baltic background

Viking *lying in Mariehamn with a deep laden* galeas *alongside her.*

THE GRAIN
RACES

The Baltic background

Basil Greenhill
& John Hackman

CONWAY
MARITIME PRESS

In grateful memory of Sjöfartsrådet Edgar Erikson, Shipowner, Gentleman and Friend.

First published in 1986 by Conway Maritime Press Ltd, 24 Bride Lane, Fleet Street, London EC4Y 8DR.

ISBN 0 85177 415 6

Typesetting and page make-up by C R Barber and Partners (Highlands) Ltd.

Printed and bound in Great Britain by R J Acford, Chichester.

Contents

Notes

Åland Family Names

The use of patronymics by Ålanders is sometimes confusing to outsiders, and even, in the context of family history, to Ålanders themselves. Gustaf Erikson's ancestors were the Melanders of Granboda in Lemland but his father signed himself Gustaf Adolf Eriksson. Gustaf Erikson was registered in the parish records as Gustaf Adolf Mauritz Gustafsson but for years was known as Gustaf Adolf Eriksson. In due course, to shorten and simplify his name for foreigners, he dropped both the middle name and the second 's' in Eriksson and became known throughout the world as Gustaf Erikson.

The arbitrary nature of the system is shown by the following true story. Karl Karlsson, a 'jungman' in the four-masted barquentine *Mozart* in 1928 was surprised to find there was no mail waiting for him on the vessel's arrival in Australia. His disappointment was remedied when he discovered that letters addressed to Karl Kåhre were meant for him. His family had decided that the patronymic Karlsson was too commonly used and made identification difficult, but they had failed to tell Karl of the change.

Place Names

Place names have been given in Finnish. Where there is also a Swedish name this follows in brackets.

Pronunciation of Swedish words in Åland

å is pronounced like the *a* in *small* (thus Åland is Awland)

ä is pronounced like the *e* in *nest*

ö is pronounced like the *ea* in *heard*

j is prounced like *y*

w at the beginning of a word is prounced like *v*

v at the beginning of a word is sometimes pronounced like *w*

g is often silent but at the beginning of a word is *y* as in *yeast*

sk is prounced as *sh*

Foreword

I am very glad that my friends Basil Greenhill, and John Hackman of the Åbo Akademi, have written this extensive account of the history of Åland seafaring, and particularly of the shipowning activities of my family. Our seafaring story goes back to the middle of the last century and beyond. This book shows how the enterprise of my grandparents (on my father's side) led to my father's brilliant success as the last owner of a great fleet of big merchant sailing ships in Europe. They were known throughout the world as the vessels which sailed in the annual 'Grain Race' as the newspapers called it, from Australia to Europe and this led to my father being dubbed 'the sailing vessel king' by those same newspapers.

After my father's death in 1947 I became managing owner of the *Passat*, *Pamir* and the *Viking* as well as the laid-up *Moshulu* and *Archibald Russell*. After the last voyages of the first three, with grain from Australia to England in 1949, it was clear that it was absolutely impossible to sail them profitably any more. Costs, wages (especially following the introduction of the compulsory three watch system), and insurance, were all much higher than before the war. Freights had not increased in proportion to costs, so I sold the *Pamir* and *Passat* to German owners. *Pamir* was tragically lost with almost all her crew and cadets. *Passat* has been preserved and can be seen at Travemünde, though she has been much changed since her days as a Grain Racer, as has *Viking* which now lies in Göteborg. *Moshulu*, which I sold to Norwegian owners, is now a restaurant in Philadelphia. She, too, has been greatly altered. *Archibald Russell*, which had spent the war laid up at Goole on the Humber in Britain, I had to sell to Tyneside shipbreakers.

Only the *Pommern* remained and my family and I presented her to the town of Mariehamn. There she lies today, moored alongside the Åland Maritime Museum in the Western Harbour. She is the only big steel merchant sailing vessel in the world which has survived unaltered from her sailing days. Like the seventeenth century warship *Wasa* in Stockholm, the *Victory* in Portsmouth, the frigate *Constitution* in Boston, the first modern passenger steamship *The Great Britain* (launched in 1843 and now restored in Bristol), and the little barque *Sigyn* in Åbo, she is a monument of international importance.

Today we are passing through the greatest crisis that the merchant shipping nations of the Western world have ever seen. It is very difficult to predict what the outcome will be. But in these difficult times I have been delighted to make the records of the Erikson family and companies available to Basil Greenhill and John Hackman and to give them every encouragement and support in writing this book.

25th of May

Edgar Erikson

25 MAY 1985. EDGAR ERIKSON.

Introduction

The Great Britain, *the world's first big iron ship, designed by Brunel and launched in 1843, now restored and preserved in the dock in which she was built in Bristol. She is four feet shorter overall, but four feet broader in the beam than the* Parma, *the largest of the Grain Racers.*
SS *Great Britain* Project

Another book about Gustaf Erikson's fleet of big merchant sailing vessels? There are several reasons why such a book is desirable. Widespread interest in sailing ships in Europe and America today is reflected in literally scores of schemes for youth training through sail. It is expressed in ships restored and ships preserved, at their best as artefacts of human culture in good museum tradition, with properly managed and financed conservation and maintenance, at their worst as 'Micky Mouse' attractions. It is demonstrated by the media and public's enthusiasm for Tall Ships races and by the eagerness of civic authorities in Scandinavia and North America, and increasingly Britain, to acquire or construct 'town ships', vessels which become a symbol of a community's maritime past. In Britain *The Great Britain* in Bristol is an excellent example of this kind of development and has the advantage of being owned and managed by an independent trust, dedicated to her proper restoration and conservation. The fascination extends to the building of copies of historic vessels, or vessel types (with widely varying accuracy) and to the building of new vessels with sails for limited commercial purposes, such as cruising, where the canvas provides a profitable element of novelty in a highly competitive market.

The interest in old sailing vessels is largely romantic. It can be argued that this captivation is the product of societies that are rich enough not to have to depend in the slightest on working merchant sailing vessels. These ships were not romantic, but vehicles built to earn money carrying goods, operating in societies not developed enough to have any means of sea transport more efficient, societies which accepted as normal, living and working conditions which would be considered quite intolerable today.

Though there is complete discontinuity in terms of economic necessity, technical limitation and social background between today's training ships and cruise vessels and the real working sailing vessels of the past, it is doubtful if this late twentieth century interest in sail would exist had it not been for the survival of the merchant sailing vessel into the middle, indeed into the second half, of this century. If such vessels had not lasted just into the beginning of the era of mass communication through the media it is doubtful if there would be much interest in sailing vessels now. The fascination is the stronger because it has its roots in reality still within living memory.

Working sailing vessels survived in various forms in different parts of the world, but were always associated with communities which were in varying degrees underdeveloped. Latterly the vessels were almost always old and were not susceptible to further book depreciation. North Devon in the 1930s was still a remote and deeply rural area of Britain where working schooners and ketches survived by the score. Sailing vessels worked from the Bay of Fundy area of Eastern Canada, from Newfoundland, and from some places in Maine and elsewhere in New England – areas which had ceased to be part of the mainstream of North American life. There were many sailing vessels working on the Italian coast, amongst the Greek and Turkish islands and among the islands of Denmark. A considerable fleet of locally built large wooden square-rigged vessels worked in the Bay of Bengal. But the most conspicuous of these survivors, and the only vessels to compete in the general world freight market, were the big iron and steel square-rigged sailing vessels which still operated from the Åland Islands of Finland, run latterly, as other local owners migrated to Helsinki or turned to investment in other forms of tonnage, almost entirely by Gustaf Erikson. Finland was then a relatively poor country, dependent on forestry, marginal farming and to some degree on sailing vessels.

Because these spectacular anachronisms regularly discharged cargoes in the principal British and western European ports they attracted media attention on a large scale. They were the subject of numerous books written by passengers or temporary crew members who had sailed in one of them on a single passage, or at the most a round voyage. At least eighteen of these narratives were published in English and others in German and Swedish. In addition there are the authoritative general studies by W L A Derby and Georg Kåhre and, at a later date,

the autobiographical narrative of an Åland seaman, Elis Karlsson. It was the survival of these Åland vessels and the publicity which attended them, which, more than any other single factor, was responsible for the interest in sailing vessels in Europe and America today.

When Ray Blackmore, managing director of Conway Maritime Press, (publisher of the English language version of Georg Kåhre's history of the Erikson fleet entitled *The Last Tall Ships*), asked us if we would prepare a further study of the history of the Erikson vessels we were happy to accept the commission for a number of reasons. Finland, and especially Åland, is a country we both in our very different ways know well and the record perhaps needs some slight readjustment of emphasis. It is possible, even from *The Last Tall Ships*, to get an impression of Gustaf Erikson as a barefoot boy who made good. He was not that, but a product of a relatively prosperous background, and his life's work was an extension of family traditions going back for three generations.

John Hackman's study of contemporary records has shown that Gustaf Erikson's birthplace has in the past been wrongly recorded – although only by a matter of a few hundred yards – and that the names and dates of the ships on which he served in his youth given in *The Last Tall Ships* are not entirely accurate. More important is the impression conveyed by some writers that the Grain Race and all that was associated with it was a low profit, frequently loss-making affair and that the ships were operated for reasons largely of sentiment. There was an element of the latter, but it was not indulged at the expense of the hard facts of shipowning economics. There were bad years – 1930 was perhaps the worst – but for most of the time the last of the big sailing ships were bringing in very adequate returns on investment and at times making relatively large profits. The case of the *Parma* which paid for herself and made a net profit in her first year of operation for Åland and British owners is documented here in detail and there is a general examination of the economics of the Erikson fleet's operations, with conclusions supported by Gustaf Erikson's own letters to the master of the *Ponape*.

Even reputable merchant shipping historians have seen the Erikson shipping enterprise in isolation as purely a phenomenon of one man's idiosyncratic business genius. It was nothing of the sort. It emerged naturally as a result of Åland and Finland's very late development, and was embedded in the deep tradition of a whole society. More important and

interesting still is the whole story of Åland society and how it has emerged, as a result of the slow and infinitely arduous accumulation of capital by previous generations through sailing ships, into a highly prosperous modern community today. Åland, in 1935 the last society in Europe to be entirely dependent for its livelihood on the operation of big merchant sailing vessels in world trade, is now rich and modern, and an important part of the wider economy of an exceedingly prosperous Finland which has a growth rate higher than that of Japan.

This is, of course, a micro study. Åland shipowning activities in the great days of wooden sailing ships in the last century were indeed on a small scale in comparison with those of, for example, some Canadian communities of roughly the same population. But the subject is unusual in that of the many rural areas of Europe and North America which dragged themselves up by their bootlaces in the late nineteenth century, using wooden sailing ships in world trade to generate capital, Åland has not reverted, as so many of these areas have, into a relatively poor backwater. Nor has it been industrialised, or turned into an area virtually

Edgar Erikson, Solveig Erikson, and Ann Giffard on board the Finnish coastal patrol vessel Telkkä *in the Åland Sea in September 1979.*
Basil Greenhill

entirely dependent on tourism (important though tourism is) like many parts of Britain and North America which were once deeply involved in shipping. Åland shipowners made the great transition to big iron and steel sailing vessels and eventually to steamers and motor ships which so many comparable communities did not make. As a result Åland is now a very prosperous rural community dependent on large scale shipowning. As such in the late 1980s it faces new and perhaps graver problems than ever before.

The plan of this book, an Anglo-Finnish collaboration, as was the operation of Åland shipping in the years of the Grain Race, was developed in discussion between the authors and in consultation with Edgar Erikson in Mariehamn in September 1984. There has been considerable interchange of ideas, and we helped one another mutually in the amendment and correction of drafts. Chapters 1, 2, 5,

6, 10 and 11 were first drafted by Basil Greenhill, the last chapter with considerable help from Captain Karl Kåhre and Dr David Papp. Chapters 3, 4, 7 and 8 were drafted by John Hackman. Chapter 9 was written by Brigadier I R Ferguson-Innes, who in his youth spent a year in *Killoran*, one of the least publicised units of the Erikson fleet – and, regarding the voyage as valuable experience in its own right, he did not write a book about it. Among the many people and institutions who helped him in the preparation of this chapter he was particularly grateful to Mr Lars Grönstrand of Åbo, Finland, and Dr David Papp of the Ålands Sjöfartsmuseum, Mariehamn.

The research which led to the writing of this book was made possible by the enthusiastic co-operation of Gustaf Erikson's elder son, Edgar Erikson, until his death in early 1986 the doyen of Åland shipowners and businessmen. He placed the enormous and comprehensive archive of the family's business transactions freely at our disposal and helped in many other ways with facilities for research and illustration, with personal reminiscence, and with his recollections of the general trends of business development over the years. This book, which would certainly never have been written had we not had Edgar Erikson's support, has with his death become a memorial to him. We are also most grateful to Solveig Erikson, his wife.

To Captain Karl Kåhre, Dr David Papp, Hilding and Marja Lundqvist, Lars Grönstrand, Stig Lundqvist, the late Captain Karl V Karlsson, Edward Wennström, Captain Göte Sundberg and many others too numerous to mention we also extend our most grateful thanks, as we do to Ann Giffard for her careful checking of typescripts and proofs and for the index. In the traditional phrase, the good things in this book are theirs, its faults ours.

Basil Greenhill,
Boetheric.

John Hackman,
Turku (Åbo).

September 1984–September 1985.

Chapter 1

ÅLAND TODAY

A very special luncheon is still held every month at the Åland Nautical Club in Mariehamn on Fasta Åland. This is one of the Swedish-speaking Åland Islands, which form the most outlying westerly part of Finland's archipelagos. Fasta Åland lies right in the middle of the mouth of *Bottniska Viken*, the Gulf of Bothnia or 'the Bottom Bay', the great arm of the Baltic Sea which stretches north of the sixtieth parallel of latitude, north of Stockholm and Helsinki, almost to the Arctic Circle. It is almost exactly half way between Stockholm and Turku (Åbo), the nearest town on the Finnish mainland. Here in the long dining room of the *Restaurang Nautical*, with its magnificent view over Mariehamn's Western Harbour and the four-masted barque *Pommern*, moored just below, a remarkable group of men gather to eat salt beef and potatoes at what they call the Buffalo Lunch.

The Buffalo Lunch at the Åland Nautical Club. The president of the Åland Cape Horners, Captain Karl Kåhre, is giving the address.
Ålands Sjöfartsmuseum

I have been privileged, as an honorary life member of their club, to be present at a number of these lunches. Looking around the table on these occasions I have been struck by the appearance of my companions. They are almost all of uniformly fair complexion – most have clear blue eyes and those who are not now grey or white-haired are blond. Whether short or tall, they all look powerfully built. The illusion of uniformity is enhanced by their dress; nearly all wear double-breasted blue blazers with brass buttons, either plain or embossed with the initials G.E., and grey cloth trousers. When they leave the club after the brief formal speeches and announcements by their president, Captain Karl Kåhre, and the toast (what they drink depends very much on how far they have to travel in this society which does not tolerate the mixing of alcohol and

driving), they put on blue peaked caps with shiny black nebs. They speak quietly to one another during lunch; for those who live in the distant communities of the Åland archipelago this is a monthly treat, a time to visit town and see old friends.

These men are the Cape Horners, who in their youth worked as seamen, stewards and mates on the last big European merchant sailing ships which by going about their business on the seas of the world earned a living for their crews, masters, shareholders, and, more peripherally, for brokers, chandlers, ship repairers, insurers and many others. It is astounding that in the mid 1980s there are nearly two hundred Cape Horners in Åland, of whom fifty or so will normally be present at each of the monthly lunches.

At the time of writing there are only two men left in Åland who were masters of merchant sailing vessels

Above: 'a normal job for a working man in this particular society', Captain Abrahamson (in bowler hat) and the crew of the Åland barque Schwanden.
Karl Karlsson

Below: 'just work and to hell with the rest', Karl Kåhre, left, as a boy at the double wheel of the four-masted barquentine Mozart in the Southern Ocean.
Karl Kåhre

on passages round Cape Horn in the 1920s and 1930s, for, by the nature of things, the masters were the oldest men on board these vessels. They are known as 'Albatrosses' by their fellow Cape Horners. Although not all of the crews were employed on passages which took them round Cape Horn, the other trades which employed the last merchant sailing vessels, the Baltic timber trade and the Atlantic trade, imposed the same way of life on the professional seaman and called for the same, or even greater, skills.

The Cape Horners do not see their years under sail through a haze of romantic nostalgia, though they are quite happy to allow other people to do so. A seaman's life in an Åland sailing vessel in the 1920s was not one of heroic adventure, whatever some contemporary foreign writers may have made of it. It was a normal job, for a working man in this particular society. For the more ambitious, intent on higher rewards as mates and, in due course, as masters of powered vessels, working in sailing ships was a necessary preliminary because Finnish nationals were obliged to have sail experience before they could take full professional qualifications. In the words of Captain Karl Kåhre, 'For me and the others who made five round voyages to Australia and back round Cape Horn it is mostly remembered as a period of normal work to get the practice for our master's ticket,

Jane Banks of Fowey, a schooner built at Porthmadog in 1878, which sailed to Newfoundland, the Mediterranean, the Black Sea and the West Indies as late as the 1920s, was still working without an engine in the British home trade in the 1930s. She was sold to Estonian owners for the timber trade and lost in the Gulf of Finland in the 1940s.
Graham Gullick

nothing special about that, just work, and to hell with the rest . . .'

Every year a few Cape Horners die, a few become too old to make the journey to Mariehamn, and so gradually the monthly gathering becomes smaller. There are those who would like to see it perpetuated by yachtsmen, by lovers of the Tall Ships and by the sons and daughters of these men. But to perpetuate the gathering in this way would be to change its whole nature. It is a unique social event, a get-together indigenous to the society which owned and manned the last big merchant sailing vessels to be engaged in the general business of the world's maritime carrying trades.

It may come as a surprise to many people that there were many other merchant sailing vessels still at sea in the 1920s and the early 1930s besides those of Åland. There was a fleet of German four-masted barques engaged in subsidised trade from Europe to the west coast of South America. Over a hundred schooners and ketches, more than forty of them from north Devon were still making money for their owners in the home trade of the British Isles as late as 1939. There were big four-, five-, and even six-masted schooners sailing in the United States' and Canada's east coast trade and from ports on the Pacific coast; east coast schooners frequently made trans-Atlantic passages. There were scores of merchant sailing vessels of various kinds at work in the Mediterranean. A fleet of anachronistic Indian square-rigged sailing ships worked in the Bay of Bengal, they were little different in hull form and rigging from the vessels which carried the world's trade in the 1850s.

But the Åland vessels were unique in that they had among their numbers almost every type of merchant sailing vessel. There were small wooden schooners; big wooden schooners built in North America or copied from North American models; venerable wooden barques like the merchant vessels of the 1860s and almost new wooden barques which were indistinguishable from the old vessels; barquentines, including an old English tea clipper, and big steel barques and four-masted barques most of which, though the variety of their occupations was steadily contracting due to developments in world trade, were sailed anywhere there was money to be made carrying cargo.

In the end the big ships settled down mainly to the business of carrying Australia's wheat crop from the ports of the State of South Australia to Britain and western Europe. In this trade, as the world's last big steel square-rigged sailing vessels, they stood out spectacularly among the world's shipping and attracted a great deal of attention in the press and on the radio. Their passage times on the trip to Britain via Cape Horn were the subject of widespread interest and even of bets. The vessel which made the fastest passage was hailed as the 'winner of the Grain Race', though in fact the passages did not really constitute a race because the vessels were of widely differing size, age, and origin, there was no system of handicapping, and they sailed at different times and into different seasonal weather systems.

The men who gather each month in the Åland Nautical Club are the last survivors of those who manned these ships – in their youth they were hard-worked men in hard-worked vessels. When the last of them has gone there will be a complete break with the past. These men were moulded by their experience in real working sailing ships and this gives them a unique link with earlier centuries. Their monthly

On board the American four-masted schooner Helen Barnet Gring *which sailed throughout the 1930s, crossing the Atlantic from Nova Scotia to Liverpool in 1937.*
Francis Bowker

gathering is thus a very special occasion and it would be quite wrong to try to perpetuate a shadow of it when they are all dead.

When the lunch is over the guests emerge into an Åland which is completely different to that they knew in their days in sail. Then it was a backward rural part of an underdeveloped country. Today it is one of the most prosperous rural communities in northern Europe. Some 25,000 people live on a labyrinth of over 6000 islands, many linked nowadays by bridges, chain ferries, or regular long distance truck-carrying ferry services, some of which take several hours to reach outlying parts of the archipelago. The Ålander's are a minority within a minority – a self-contained, self-perpetuating enclave inside the minority of roughly 300,000 (6.3 per cent of the total population of 4 million) Finnish citizens whose mother tongue is not Finnish but Swedish. The Ålanders comprise, perhaps, one of the most privileged minorities in Europe. How this should have come about requires some explanation, which

means going back into the history of Finland.

The origins of this community are different from the enclaves of Swedish-speaking people who live on Finland's mainland whose ancestors migrated to Finland from Sweden at various stages between the thirteenth century almost to the present day. Åland, though the origins of its people are complex, was settled in the main by Swedish-speaking people from the area around Lake Mälaren, just west of Stockholm, in about 600 AD during the period of great movements of people in northern Europe which archaeologists call the Migration Period.

The Ålanders have always been a little apart from the tides of history which have washed over them and retreated again. From the 1200s to 1809 Finland was a part of Sweden, not a colony, not a dependent territory, but part of metropolitan Sweden. Sweden in the late eighteenth century, was a territory comprising both much of what we now call Sweden and what is now modern Finland, with Stockholm,

The five-masted schooner Rebecca Palmer, *built at Rockland, Maine, USA, in 1901, sailed in that year from Fowey for New York with 2700 tons of china clay. Four- and five-masted schooners similar to the* Rebecca Palmer *were still sailing from American ports in the 1930s.*
Fred Kitto

An Indian brigantine entering Colombo Harbour in 1952. She may well have been the world's last square-rigged merchant sailing ship at sea without an engine.
Basil Greenhill

the capital of the whole, in about its middle. The exact boundaries moved back and forth over the years as Sweden's fortunes waxed and waned in its long wars with its neighbours to the south and the west and with Russia to the east. Åland was overrun by the Russians more than once; large numbers of its population had to migrate to the land west of the Gulf of Bothnia, only to return again to their ravaged fields and burned farms as the flow of war and peace allowed them to do so.

In 1808, during the Napoleonic wars, the Russians successfully invaded Swedish territory east of the Gulf of Bothnia. The Ålanders put up their own unofficial civilian resistance, using what we would now call guerilla tactics. So successful were they that the Russians were driven out of the archipelago and had to bring in new forces before they could occupy the islands permanently.

In 1809 the war ended and a treaty was signed at Fredrikshamn (Hamina). The subsequent Russian rule in Finland was an extraordinary phenomenon. Generally speaking in all other territories absorbed by Russian expansion over the centuries, Russian

law, language and social customs had been imposed and their people tied to the Russian economy. For complex reasons Finland was not integrated into the Russian system to anything like the same extent as, for instance, Poland. Finland became a Grand Duchy with the reigning Czar as Grand Duke. Serfdom was not imposed and existing laws remained in force. In the area as a whole, Swedish and slowly and increasingly Finnish were the official languages, though in Åland only Swedish was (and is) spoken.

A sizeable merchant shipping industry developed, with vessels owned in and sailing from the coastal towns in the Gulf of Bothnia and to a lesser extent from the towns of the coast of the Gulf of Finland. These vessels became in effect, the Russian merchant fleet, for Russia had no significant merchant shipping industry operated by Russian speaking people. The seamen, mates and masters, of the Finnish vessels brought back news of what was happening in the outside world, so that the coastal communities were better informed of what was going on in the West than almost any other people in the Russian sphere of influence.

Under Russia, Finland actually enjoyed a longer period of peace than at almost any previous time in her recorded history. It was broken only once during the Crimean War, which began in 1854. In the course of raiding coastal towns and destroying merchant ships, the British attacked the great fortress of Bomarsund which lay at the heart of the labyrinthine Åland archipelago. The Russians had been building this fortress for twenty years or more. The contract and supply opportunities the construction work provided were to prove of great importance to Åland's subsequent history, particularly the development of her sailing fleets. After a very stalwart defence against French and British bombardment the fort was surrendered. It was never to be rebuilt and Russian troops and ships were not to return there.

It was the threat to Kronstadt, the stronghold at the mouth of the River Neva which protected the capital, St Petersburg, which finally persuaded the Russians to accept peace in 1856. The end of the war saw Åland remaining part of the Grand Duchy of Finland, but formally neutralised in the Peace Treaty signed in Paris in 1856.

The Administration of Finland learned to live alongside the Russians, and to keep a check on elements, which by seeking more liberty, might incur the wrath of the Russian autocracy and lose the liberty they already had. Under the liberal regime (for Finland) of the Czars Alexander 1st and Nicholas 1st commerce, shipping and industry developed in Finland as it never had done when it was part of Sweden. Intellectuals in Finland pondered on their identity – their sentiments can be summed up in the following phrase, 'we are no longer Swedes, we do not want to become Russians, let us be Finns'. A national consciousness began to develop and in due course a strong material culture expressed in the fine arts emerged and Finnish began to flower as a literary language. The history of the nineteenth and early twentieth centuries in Finland is largely the complex story of the development of political, national and artistic consciousness among the Finnish-speaking majority of the population.

However, the Ålanders played little or no part in these developments. They remained very poor until well into the second half of the nineteenth century, and being conscious they were descendents of the first

The ruins of the central fort of Bomarsund.
Basil Greenhill

Ålanders, felt themselves separate from the Swedish and Finnish-speaking people of the mainland, maintaining a cool detachment from them.

The Åland Islands lie in an area of the Baltic where the land is rising out of the sea at an average rate, say, of a foot and a half per century, often more. As much of the fertile, cultivable land is not far above sea level, it follows that fifteen hundred years ago there was not very much fertile land for settlement. As a Swedish-speaking people with virtually no Finnish-speaking elements in the society the Ålanders played no part in the development of a Finnish language culture. It was not surprising, therefore, that when Finland declared itself independent of Russia after the Bolshevik Revolution in 1917 and after Russia recognised that independence in 1918 the Ålanders should have sought union with Sweden – independence for very small units was not a fashionable idea in those days.

Several years of dispute were ended when the Council of the League of Nations ruled that Finland should be granted sovereignty over Åland provided that the islands remained neutral, that their people were given a high degree of autonomy, and they were secured and guaranteed 'their Swedish language, culture and local traditions'. Over the last sixty-five years successive Finnish governments have honoured this undertaking.

The present constitution of the Åland Islands is based on the Finnish parliament's Autonomy Act of 1951 which cannot be amended without the agreement of Åland's provincial parliament. Åland, subject to the unity of Finland as a state, has a high degree of autonomy. The islands' parliament has the

Traditional wooden boats are being built in Åland again,
for recreational sailing. This is a storbåt *in Mariehamn's*
Eastern Harbour.
Basil Greenhill

Captain Göte Sundberg's öka *at Bolstaholm. Captain*
Sundberg is director of the Ålands Sjöfartsmuseum.
Basil Greenhill

right to levy its own taxes and its legislation is subject to the veto of the president of Finland only if the parliament has exceeded its legal powers under the constitution, or if the security of the realm is endangered. Matters which primarily affect the Ålanders only, for example, police, education, local commerce and industry are their responsibility and to a degree they operate as a quasi-independent unit within Finland. Åland regional citizenship is confined to those who have lived for an unbroken period of five years in the islands and without this there is no right to vote, to purchase land or to carry on business.

The neutrality of the islands stretches back to the Crimean War and the destruction of Bomarsund. It carries a very important consequence today – Ålanders are not subject to Finnish military service. Åland has its own flag which can be flown anywhere in Åland (but not as a national flag on Åland merchant ships, which must fly the blue cross on a white ground of Finland). The Autonomy Act is currently under a review which may lead in due course to further

Fishing huts in Geta Community in the early 1900s.
Ålands Sjöfartsmuseum

developments in the islands' quasi-independent status.

Finnish governments have treated this cultural, and to a degree ethnic, minority with liberality and model punctiliousness. Gradually a separate Åland culture has emerged. The society and the people have characteristics which differ from those of their great neighbours on either side of the Gulf of Bothnia, even the Swedish dialect spoken is peculiar to Åland. This is not surprising in view of the fact the size of the archipelago's population has remained more or less static for hundreds of years and it is contained within the clearly marked geographical confines of an archipelago. Many Åland farmers can trace back their ancestors, who lived on the same land, for many generations, some as far as four centuries.

Moreover, these are people of the sixtieth parallel of latitude. In most areas in the northern half of the world the sixtieth parallel marks territory uninhabitable by the human race except with a high degree of support from the south. West Siberia, the Sea of Ohotsk, Alaska, the Yukon, Hudson Bay and the southern tip of Greenland are all areas in which life can not comfortably be conducted without the benefits of a good deal of modern technology. Although the penetration of the Baltic Sea into the continental land mass ameliorates the climate, conditions are still extremely rigorous. This self-contained population, which retained its cultural and ethnic identity for so long, inevitably revealed an indigenous characteristic – it became a people of the sea, and it is the sea which has given the Ålander's their modern prosperity over the last century.

Even today, life on the outlying islands is relatively hard and the people who live there are tough and self-dependent, both physically and mentally. The low temperatures, the snow, frozen seas, and sub-Arctic darkness of the long winter months all make life harder. This is a dimension missing in Nova Scotia, Newfoundland, and particularly on the outlying islands off their coasts, where conditions are otherwise somewhat comparable. For the generations of people who grew up on Åland's small farms before the advent of diesel snow-ploughs, ice-breaking truck-carrying ferries, packaged foods, and telephones, life was very hard indeed. Natural selection and the inherited practical traditions of peasant farmer–seafarers produced an exceptionally hardy, resourceful, self-reliant, individualistic, yet gentle people. The men who gather in the Nautical Club each month were the last generation to grow up in the full rigours of the old way of life.

Men, women and children haul in the nets in the inshore fishery in the early 1900s.
Ålands Sjöfartsmuseum

By all the rules of late twentieth century economics Åland should now be an impoverished backwater, subject to steady depopulation – it is not. Life has changed. Marginal peasant farming is no longer the norm. Sheep are no longer taken in the *storbåt* (farm boat) to the outer skerries, to the strange, beautiful, wild world of the *skärgård* (literally the skerry yard) where they survived the summer grazing off the leaves of the hardy bushes and sparse grass. Farmers no longer tend their inshore nets from the *eka* or *öka*, (the two-transom clinker-built boats, stable, seaworthy, capacious, and easy to handle, which every farm had when the Cape Horners were young) or fish from the *skötbät*. Many of the outlying farms are now the second homes of prosperous families who are based on Mariehamn, or perhaps even in Stockholm. These families are usually the descendants of the peasant farmers of seventy years ago. But the Ålanders still go to sea, now not only the men, but the women too. They work on the modern equivalent of the old Baltic traders – the great truck-carrying ferries. The thunder of their engines can be heard almost all the time on some of the islands as they shuttle back and forth endlessly day and night between Helsinki, Turku (Åbo), Mariehamn and Stockholm.

Åland is divided administratively into fifteen 'communities' or 'parishes' and since their names will recur many times in this book it would be as well to rehearse them briefly now. In the far west is Eckerö, the nearest point to the Swedish mainland and therefore the historic stopping place on the route from the west across the sea to mainland Finland, and on to St Petersburg. This was the post route, an important historic Russian link with the west, which was hazardous when conducted, as it used to be, in farm boats, and extremely arduous in the winter. To the east of Eckerö is Hammarland and to the north is Geta Community, which has the highest land in Åland, then Finström with one of the finest medieval churches in all Fenno-Scandia and Jomala which contains the 'new town' of Mariehamn (founded by Czar Alexander II in 1861 and named after his wife, Marie Alexandvovna).

All of these areas, like Sund and Saltvik in the east, are part of Fasta Åland, the main land mass. Although they are, in a sense, mainland communities, the sea penetrates everywhere, into what before the land rise was a series of separate scattered small islands (their harbours are the old shipbuilding and shipping

'the great truck-carrying ferries . . . shuttle back and forth endlessly' – ferries passing in a narrow channel off western Lemland.
Basil Greenhill

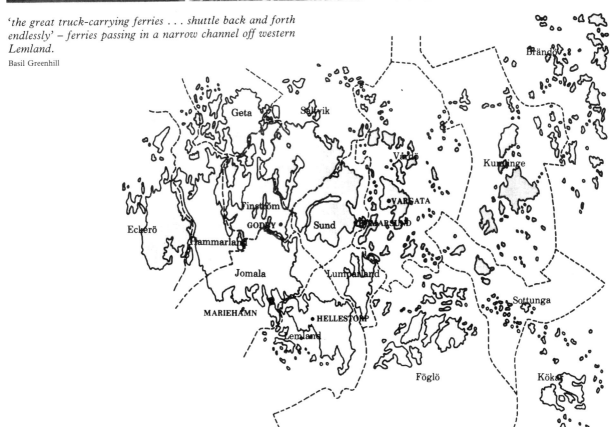

Map of the Åland Islands showing the fifteen communities

The shallow valleys, which themselves were navigable channels two or three hundred years ago, run down to plunge into deep water to make the funnel-shaped viks. This is Båthusviken, the harbour of Vargata in Wårdö.
Basil Greenhill

'The whole place is a labyrinth of islands and skerries' – boathouses on Östra Simskäla.
Basil Greenhill

areas). Each community has its own islands and Eckerö is joined to the others only by a bridge. Lemland and Lumparland to the south are separate islands, though only just divided from one another by the narrow Lumparsund; each has its own fringe of islands. The prosperity of Åland as a modern society began with shipowning ventures in Lemland and in Wårdö, further east still. Wårdö is essentially an island community, as is Föglö to the south. Further to the east, out across the open stretch of water called the Delet, are Kumlinge, Sottunga, Brändö and remote Kökar, where there was little forest, relatively small populations, and difficult communications with the bigger islands to the west. These communities provided manpower but played little part in the social and economic changes which turned Åland in a century from a country of hardy independent peasant farmers into a prosperous modern community.

In the summer Åland can be breathtakingly beautiful. The predominant colours of the granite are varying shades of red and pink. The sea is everywhere, in the most unexpected places, apparently far inland. The brackish, lightly salt water of the Baltic gleams between the dark woods which are carpeted with wild flowers in the spring. The land

is still rising out of the sea and what once were scattered tiny islands, separated by wide shallow channels, are now big islands, with little wooded hills and fertile valleys where the shallow channels were only a few centuries ago. In the years of the Vikings and the Hansa cogs, Åland was on the principal trade route between north west Europe and the Middle East by way of Gotland, the Gulf of Finland, Lake Ladoga and the Russian rivers. Some of the old trade routes through the islands followed channels where tractors now plough rich soil.

The shallow valleys run down to plunge into the deeper water and make long, often funnel-shaped harbours, *viks*, which in turn open out on to the deeper channels which still separate the 6000 islands. These channels are sometimes only a few hundred metres wide, but they are still deep enough to take big ships. The whole area is a labyrinth of islands and skerries, rocks and red granite reefs rising straight out of deep water. To sail these waters outside the well marked and much used ferry and small craft channels requires intimate local knowledge.

Generally, in pre-industrial societies, those who cannot hold their own are pushed by one set of forces or another to the sea. Here on the marginal land of the rocky coasts, not fertile enough to live by farming alone, they have to take to seafaring to survive. Often the men of the sea are despised by the more prosperous people of the land and the two groups become alienated, suspicious and fearful of one another. Sometimes, as in New England and maritime Canada, seafaring may prove, for a while, a highly prosperous business for the lucky, the entrepreneurially venturesome and hardworking. In New England the generation of capital was expressed in high standards of living and towns with streets of captains' and shipowners' houses, which are still an architectural delight today. Then with the acquisition of financial power the marginal communities by the sea may become respected and develop links with the wider world – but these very links mean the end of seafaring. In the United States after the Civil War, with the opening up of the continent by railroads and with developing industrialisation, money and men turned from the sea to industry, railroads, real estate and the West. Like the United States, but a little later, Canada turned her back on the sea and men of enterprise looked to the developing land. The old sea port towns, Yarmouth, Charlottetown, Digby, St John, became depressed backwaters.

None of this happened in Åland – the normal rules were reversed. The Ålanders by necessity were always a people of the sea and were not pushed to the islands by the pressures of more dynamic or powerful migrating groups. Once there, to live, even to farm, you had to be a boatman – everyone was involved with the sea in one way or another. The Ålander's generated capital through the carrying trade, but this was reinvested in shipping and there was no flight into land based investment, partly because ships operated with the ancestral skill of the Ålanders are usually profitable, partly because the circumstances did not offer opportunities for lucrative investment ashore. Nor has seafaring at any time been regarded in Åland society as anything but an esteemed occupation, a way of life followed by part-time farmers, by their sons and even their wives and daughters. The seaman was regarded as a normal citizen and accepted and treated as such. The successful men, the masters with shares in vessels, were highly respected members of society. The Baltic freezes, thus traditionally in the days of the wooden sailing ships many of the crew members stayed ashore in winter while their vessels were laid up in the *viks* of the islands, and they worked either on their own land or on the land of other farmers. In this way their contact with the normal life ashore was constantly renewed. In Åland the seafarer has never been alienated from the rest of society.

When the monthly Cape Horners' lunch is over some of the men go downstairs to the Åland Maritime Museum which is in the same building as the Nautical Club. Here they can tread the poop, or the bridge, once again, for full-sized examples of both exist in this, the world's finest regional merchant shipping museum. They can admire the world's finest collection of portraits of merchant ships (all Åland vessels) and the best collection of figureheads from the last big windjammers. They can enter the complete saloon of the steel four-masted barque *Herzogin Cecilie*, salved from her wreck, or the forecastle taken from the Åland-built wooden barque *Helmi* when she was broken up. Everywhere they look there are the everyday artefacts of merchant seafaring in the world's richest collection of its kind. Through the windows the towering masts and long yards of the *Pommern* dominate the view of the Western Harbour. Here she has lain, beautifully maintained and unchanged, since she came in from the sea in August 1939. She is the world's only big

The Pommern, *the world's only unchanged big square-rigged merchant sailing vessel, lies alongside the Maritime Museum and Nautical Club in Mariehamn.*
Basil Greenhill

square-rigged sailing ship which remains today exactly as she was when she made her last passage from Australia to England round Cape Horn with a full cargo of Australian grain.

Further down the harbour are the ferry terminals. All the time huge ships are coming and going. The last word in modernity, they have a first line life of only about five years before they begin to be relegated to second line service. As I write a new generation of ferries is coming into service. *Mariella*, built by Wärtsilä at Turku (Åbo) is 36,400 gross registered tons, 582.6 feet long and 95 feet in the beam. She carries 2500 passengers, all with berths, 600 cars and lorries and a crew of 450. All waste material, from kitchens, shops and lavatories is first treated aboard and then transferred ashore in containers. The hull is designed to provide minimal wash – wash is a serious problem in some of the very narrow deepwater channels between the islands, through which these huge ferries must go on their regular routes. Stabilising fins and trimming tanks have been fitted

Mariella is the latest of the great Baltic ferries, owned and registered in Mariehamn.
SF Line, Mariehamn

The 'new town' of Mariehamn lies between the Western and Eastern harbours. The Pommern, *with the Nautical Club on the shore beside her, is almost in the centre of the photograph.*
Basil Greenhill

to make the journey across the open sea between Stockholm and Helsinki as comfortable as possible. She has first class ice-breaking capacity and the most modern navigation equipment – her bridge is more like the flight deck of a jumbo jet aircraft than a traditional ship's bridge. She shuttles between Sweden and Finland at 22 knots, driven by 28,000 horsepower with no less than 36,000 horsepower available for more difficult conditions. In her limited life as a first line ship she has to make a profit on an investment of 400 million finnmarks, (about 60 million pounds sterling). *Mariella* is owned by the S. F. Line of Mariehamn, of which the chairman is maritime counsellor (*sjöfartsrådet*) Stig Lundqvist. He is a son of Hugo Lundqvist (who owned, among other vessels, the four-masted barquentine *Mozart*, the four-masted barque *Ponape*, the barques *Plus*, *Prompt*, *Thekla*, and *Zaritza* and the schooner *Hildur*) and grandson of Mathias Lundqvist junior, of Wårdö Community, owner and manager of a large fleet of big iron and steel sailing vessels. Mathias Lundqvist was the first man ever to be bestowed the honour of the title of maritime counsellor by the Finnish government. He is the great-grandson of the first Mathias Lundqvist, of Lemland Community, who was one of the three or four men who began large scale shipowning ventures in Åland soon after the Crimean War. He is also chairman of the Lundqvist Rederierna, the cargo shipowning company which, among other vessels, owns the tanker *Anni*, a quarter million ton VLCC which is Finland's largest merchant ship.

The operations of the Sally Line of Mariehamn, one of Finland's largest shipowning concerns, include tankers, ferry services, and international cruise services. Through complex ramifications under the parent company in Mariehamn their business extends to embrace companies in Britain, Germany, Sweden, the Cayman Islands and Panama. This vast international business was founded and developed by Algot Johansson with twenty 100th shares, a total investment of about £400, in the steel four-masted barque *Parma* in 1931.

The Birka Line, which specialises in the cruise business from Sweden to the Åland Islands, also operates a new vessel, the *Birka Princess*, comparable in size and sophistication (and in cost) to the *Mariella*. The chairman of the Birka Line is Björn Erikson, grandson of Gustaf Erikson, the last of the great sailing ship owners and the principal owner of such tonnage in the days of the Grain Races. Over the years Gustaf Erikson was owner or principal shareholder and manager of no less than forty-six sailing and auxiliary motor vessels, and was still operating big sailing vessels at the time of his death in 1947. Björn Erikson's father was Edgar Erikson, chairman of the Rederiaktiebolaget (shipowning company) Gustaf Erikson, which operates some dozen or more specialised refrigerated ships and vessels built to carry forest products. Edgar Erikson was the doyen of Åland shipowners and his immediate family group are the biggest shareholders in tonnage. In 1980 the Erikson family holding was valued at about 86,000 gross registered tons, a value of about 39 million pounds.

In 1985, despite the world shipping depression, the Rederi Gustaf Erikson took delivery from the shipyard at Rauma (Raumo) on the Finnish mainland, of the motor ship *Degerö*, a three deck stern-loading roll-on roll-off vessel with an additional pallet handling, side loading, capability. She is 9200 tons deadweight and 441.5 feet overall. She has a lane length of nearly a mile and great flexibility and capability in the handling of various types of cargo. She represents a highly sophisticated modern vessel for use in medium range trade, including the historic Baltic timber trade to western Europe, as it is nowadays conducted. Other Åland shipping companies also trace their origin to the groups of shareholders who owned sailing vessels in the days of the Grain Races and before. The Asta Company, for instance, has its origins in the fleet of Arthur Andersson which included the four-masted schooner *Atlas*, the iron barque *Oaklands*, the iron barque *Transocean* and the wooden barquentine *Lenita*.

Ships are sold and new ships built. An Ålander resident in the United States has placed an order for two big four-masted motor schooners, designed by the Finnish shipbuilding firm of Wärtsilä, for employment in the Carribean cruise business. Some vessels owned and managed in Mariehamn are registered under flags of convenience because of the high cost of manning with Finnish nationals. So the total tonnage owned in Mariehamn varies all the time, but usually represents between a quarter and a third of the total tonnage of the merchant ships of Finland. Though there has been no flight of investment from vessel property, even in the world shipping recession of the middle 1980s (the worst since the great depression which began in 1929), the shipping companies have wisely diversified. There is a good deal of cross investment, though the Gustaf Erikson Company remains entirely in the hands of the family, which is also involved in the sports equipment and footwear business in mainland Finland and Canada. The great shipping families also own the bulk of the share capital in the Bank of Åland. In 1980 the shares of the major shipping companies were owned by nearly 4000 Ålanders, spread through the islands. Investment in shipowning therefore persists right through the Åland community.

So much for the modern scene. The quiet, tree lined, streets of Mariehamn, which resembles a small town in New England in appearance, have a unique character. Each summer they are filled with the million holidaymakers who descend on Åland. Finns, Swedes and Germans come for a day on the cruise liners, or for a few days to stay in Mariehamn, or for a week or more to stay in a rented summer house out in the countryside. They bring tents, caravans, yachts and foreign currency in great quantities. The short term cruise business is highly dependent on the duty-free privileges given on board the ferries to those passengers who are out of Sweden for more than twenty-four hours. When they pour ashore in Mariehamn, despite the modernity of the vessel in which they have travelled, despite the admirable facilities which greet them everywhere, they will find that the symbol of Åland is still the sailing ship.

When they cash their travellers cheques at one of the branches of the Ålands Bank they will find models and photographs and paintings of sailing ships used as the principal motif in the interior design. They will find the same in the Hotel Archipelago, where there is, amid many other sailing ship features, an oil painting made from a photograph I took on board the four-masted barque *Viking* when I sailed in her as a

Degerö is a highly sophisticated modern vessel with ice-breaking capacity.
Rederi ab Gustaf Erikson

schoolboy. They will find that the memory of sailing ships, large and small, is perpetuated in modern Åland in shops, in public buildings, in private houses and apartments, indeed everywhere. Even the tourist logo of the islands is a delightful simple wooden model of a brig, the constituent parts of which are cut out of two egg-shaped pieces of wood.

Åland was late in capital generation, late to enter the modern world. Never feudal, never industrial, on the margins of European history, Åland still has a strong character and an atmosphere all of its own, unique, not overburdened with the memories of a sad history. Åland acquired its North American standards of living, its current prosperity, only in the latter part of the twentieth century. It stands on the foundation of capital built up by the operation of merchant sailing ships, and this fact is never forgotten in Åland. The rest of this book is the story of how it happened.

A twentieth century galeas *from Wårdö.*
Original in Seffers in Lövö

Chapter 2

THE GREAT DAYS OF WOODEN SAILING SHIPS

If you visit any of the old towns on the Finnish coast of the Gulf of Bothnia you are quite likely to be told that the town was founded twice. For example, Kokkola (Karleby) situated about two-thirds of the way north up the gulf, is said to have been founded by King Gustaf Adolf II of Sweden in 1620, and then again by the freeing of trade in 1765. This freeing of trade resulted in the beginning of Finnish merchant shipping outside home waters. The products of the Bothnia country were mainly what were known as naval stores, the essential raw materials for the building and maintenance of merchant ships and ships of war.

Probably the most important product was pine tar, an essential preservative of the natural fibre rigging and of the wood of the ships themselves. Pine tar is still widely used in Fenno-Scandia as a wood preservative and the wooden tiled (shingled) roofs of Gotland's wonderful medieval churches are soaked in it in order to conserve them. It is still possible to buy pine tar in Britain and America, and it is used in the treatment of conditions that develop in the hoofs of cattle and of horses. The other main products were hemp for making rope, flax, some of which went into canvas for sails, and timber for shipbuilding and other uses.

Before the freeing of trade, under Swedish law, all these products had to be shipped first to Stockholm or Turku (Åbo) in the small vessels which were all that the Bothnian ports were allowed to sail. In Stockholm, or perhaps whilst in transit before they were ever loaded in the Bothnian ports, the cargoes were acquired by the merchants of the capital city. Here they were transhipped into larger vessels, many of them British, for export to western Europe, in

The Åland jakt Onni, *off the coast of Lemland in 1946.*
Lars Grönstrand

31

particular to north Germany and Britain. This process operated to the great benefit of the bankers and merchants of Stockholm, but not for the profit of the small towns and countryside of Bothnia. So strong was the identification of these products of Bothnia with Stockholm that even today pine tar is known and marketed in Britain as Stockholm tar.

In the middle of the eighteenth century a territorial consciousness emerged in the Finnish coastal towns of eastern Sweden. A notable advance was made when, in 1765–66, the Swedish parliament abolished the restriction on the direct export of Bothnian products to the West. This was a result, largely, of the efforts of the Lutheran minister at Kokkola, Anders Chydenius, who fought against the bitter opposition of Stockholm merchants and bankers. The towns of Pori (Björneborg), Kokkola (Karleby), Vaasa (Wasa) and Oulu (Uleåborg) could now export direct to western Europe using their own ships, though their return cargoes, principally salt, still had to be imported through Stockholm. The freeing of other towns followed.

The effect was dramatic. Only twenty years later in 1783–85 the *Concordia* of Raahe (Brahestad) sailed to Mauritius, Java and Batavia, returning by way of Amsterdam. The Bothnian towns began to build considerable fleets of merchant ships, which were employed in general ocean trade. (These vessels, were, in the next century, to play an important part in the development of the Finnish economy and comprise the greater part of the Russian merchant fleet.) Sweden had treaty relations with the Barbary States of western North Africa and as a result vessels flying the Swedish flag avoided capture by the notorious Barbary pirates. The vessels from the Bothnian towns were able to take advantage of this situation and an extensive Mediterranean trade developed, to be followed in due course by trade with the West Indies.

Recession followed the Russian take-over of the Finnish territories of Sweden in 1809. Merchant shipping revived slowly, partly because Britain had imposed penal duties on imported timber from the Baltic in order to protect the infant Canadian lumber industry, but by the late 1820s the merchant shipping industry of Finland was becoming healthy. Finland was still a nation of farmers, foresters, hunters and, in the coastal regions, seafarers. There was little or no industry ashore, but the inhabitants of the coastal towns had developed great seafaring and managerial skills and merchant shipping became the Grand Duchy's principal generator of capital. Legally this industry was divided into two kinds, what was called 'peasant shipping', (*allmogeseglation* in Swedish, best translated as 'rural shipowning') and the shipping of the recognised towns.

Rural shipowners conducted trade in small vessels (locally built, often by the farmers themselves), from small seaboard communities and rural areas in which there was often not even a village. The rural shipowners' business was centred on trade with Stockholm. In the 1820s Stockholm was visited annually by as many as 350 farm ships from Åland and from the coastal districts and islands around Turku (Åbo), and the city was virtually dependent for its food supplies and firewood on these vessels. Under the Treaty of Fredrikshamn (Hamina) of 1809 commercial relations between the new Grand Duchy and Sweden remained unchanged and thus it was possible for the two countries to continue as trading partners for a long time. Åland shipping was rural and sailing to and from Stockholm was as much a part of life as farming. No Åland vessels sailed beyond the limits of these local, if now technically international trades. Firewood was always the largest export to the insatiable Stockholm market with, in the early nineteenth century, fish, meat, and livestock products. Stockholm would absorb almost anything for sale; most of the butter eaten in Stockholm in the first half of the nineteenth century came from Åland and the islands to the east and Åland cheese was much favoured in Stockholm. Salt, iron, grain, coffee, sugar, spices and tobacco were imported in return, but Swedish money inevitably found its way into Åland. Thus a process of capital generation began which was later to prove very significant. Åland's farm ships also sailed to Helsinki and to Estonia and Latvia.

In the 1820s these ships from rural areas made up forty per cent of the carrying capacity of Finland's merchant shipping. In 1830 a change in Russian law permitted Finnish vessels from rural areas to trade anywhere in the Baltic. At more or less the same time agreement was reached with the Russian authorities under which vessels from the Grand Duchy which entered Russian ports were treated in the same way as vessels from other Russian territories, rather than having to pay the heavier harbour dues imposed on foreign shipping. These two measures opened up the Baltic to ships from Finland's rural areas, and Åland shipping, although still confined to the Baltic, began to grow. Åland vessels sailed to Denmark and Germany as well as to Estonia, transporting their communities' farm and forest products. They became increasingly involved into the carrying trade, the movement of other people's goods, chiefly through the development of a coasting trade to and between the Finnish mainland towns. In the 1840s with the opening up of the sawmill industry on the Swedish coast in the north of the Gulf of Bothnia, Finnish rural vessels joined in the Swedish coastal trade and the number of peasant vessels increased until after the Crimean War.

Bigger vessels were built, able to carry larger cargoes for higher freights. There were two predominant types: firstly, the *jakter* which were cargo smacks with a single mast and bowsprit, setting a big gaffsail, a gaff topsail and one or two headsails, very similar to the smacks which carried much of the home trade cargo of western England and Wales in the last century, and secondly the *galeaser*, a term which changed its meaning as the century wore on. Originally it meant a vessel rigged like a brigantine but with the proportions of her masts those of a ketch.

Later the term came to mean a two-masted schooner with masts usually of equal height, from each of which was set a brailing gaffsail. Many of the older vessels were small, clinker-built, and undecked. Gradually, as farmers became wealthier from sea trading, they began to build schooners and brigs. By 1850, vessels from Åland and rural south-west Finland carried something like 150 cargoes a year from Sweden to Germany, mainly to Lübeck, returning, usually, with cargoes of salt for the owner's own use. The carrying trade became so important to the Åland economy that, according to contemporary reports, agriculture was neglected and with it forestry and rural industry and crafts, for money could be made more quickly and readily upon the sea. By 1854 when the Anglo-French fleet came to destroy the fort

This painting of the Freden *of Brahestad shows the sails and rigging of a mid-nineteenth century* galeas.
Raahe (Brahestad) Museum

of Bomarsund the changes brought about by capital generated from farming and seafaring in the carrying trade were well under way. But as yet, no Åland vessel sailed beyond the Danish Sound and Belts and the Skaw, (the northern tip of Denmark).

It was the recognised seaport towns which continued to increase their participation in the long range carrying trade. At first, after 1809, the Mediterranean trade was risky for Finnish vessels because Russia had no agreement with the Barbary pirates. The last vessel ever to be captured by the Corsairs was in fact the barque *Helsingfors* taken in July 1829, shortly before the fall of Algiers to the French marked the end of this kind of sea robbery. The old trades in pine tar and pitch continued and Britain, especially Newcastle and Liverpool, became the focus of this trade because return cargoes of coal and salt were readily available. Indeed, for a time Cheshire salt partly replaced the Mediterranean product as the agent of food preservation for the long frozen winters on the Finnish farms.

In 1829 the Black Sea ports were opened to international trade and Finnish vessels began carrying grain, chiefly from Odessa, to Britain. This trade grew rapidly and grain replaced flax, hemp, tallow and tar as Russia's chief exports. No less than two thirds of the grain imported into Britain in 1850 came from Russia. Finnish vessels set sail from their home ports in the autumn with pine tar for Britain where they loaded coal for the Mediterranean or Odessa. In Odessa they loaded grain for Britain or western Europe. Sometimes they would be away for several years before their return home with a salt cargo. After refitting they set out again on a further two or three years of trading. As world trade developed with the industrialisation of Britain, and in due course the rest of western Europe, vessels from the Grand Duchy of Finland participated increasingly in the general carrying trade, sailing all the year round. Though they were seen less and less in their home ports the freight money they earned was remitted there as, on the whole, were of the salaries of the master and mates and the pay of their crews.

There were many signs of growth. Between 1845 and 1847 the barque *Hercules* of Pietarsaari (Jakobstad) circumnavigated the globe with a series of cargoes, five years before any Norwegian merchant ship achieved this feat, a whaling company was established at Turku (Åbo) which opened up trade via Cape Horn with the northern Pacific and Alaska and by 1850 the Finnish towns between them owned 526 ships with a total capacity of over 100,000 tons.

The rural shipping and the merchant fleet of the Grand Duchy totalled some 1500 vessels, large and small, able to carry between them about 150,000 tons. This was a respectably-sized fleet for a country at Finland's stage of economic development, although totally dwarfed by Britain, then the world's greatest shipping nation, which owned about three and a half million registered tons of sailing vessels.

The Crimean War interrupted this era of prosperity, for both town and rural shipping. Both the Baltic and the Black Sea were blockaded. The Finnish merchant fleet was roughly halved, fortunately not solely as a result of war casualties, but because wise shipowners proceeded to sell their vessels, sometimes, because of the wartime shipping boom, at good prices. Money was readily invested in shipping when the war was over, so that the merchant fleet, with more modern tonnage, soon prospered more than ever before.

The war was to be of particular significance in the history of Åland shipowning. Between 1842 and 1853 the number of vessels owned in Åland rose gently, but their profitability increased from a net annual total of 10,000 silver roubles a year to one of four times as high. The bigger vessels sailed to Lübeck and Copenhagen in the west and to north Sweden. The smaller vessels sailed to Tallinn, St Petersburg, and Turku (Åbo). The structure of the industry took different forms in different communities. In some, larger Baltic sailing vessels predominated, in others the smaller smacks and *galeaser* of the local trades. The property in the bigger vessels was divided usually into one hundred shares and owned by perhaps four to eight people. The *jakter* and *galeaser* were usually owned by their skippers, with a son, brother, or other family member to make up the crew. There was no navigation school in Åland and the skippers had no formal training or qualifications, though the majority could read, write and calculate. On board the same patriarchal relationships existed between the skipper and crew as between farmer and farmhand in the fields on the islands at home.

The manner in which the crew referred to their vessels in dialect right into the present century gives an insight into their attitudes to them. As Dr David Papp, who has studied Åland rural shipping for the Åland Maritime Museum, has pointed out,

Normally the vessel would be referred to as, for instance, *Svan* [Swan]. Sometimes she would be referred to as *Svanen* [The Swan], or *Svanan* [The Female Swan]. This would be done to stress the special relationship of the speaker with the vessel. The use of this kind of terminology indicates that the vessel was thought of, at least subconsciously, as animate, perhaps almost human.

The size of vessels was increasing because bigger ships made more money. By 1832 there were thirty schooners owned in the islands. Nevertheless, compared with the ports of the mainland, Åland's tonnage was almost negligible. In the middle 1840s Åland's tonnage was less than half of that of the town of Pori (Björneborg) and constituted only about sixteen per cent of Finland's rural shipping and an even smaller percentage of Finland's total shipping. But the islands had begun the long slow process of developing into a major shipowning area. Half a century later Åland owned more shipping than all the towns of the Bothnia coast put together, and, as today, about a quarter of all Finland's merchant shipping.

Indeed, although conditions varied in detail from community to community, in general the economic

and social life of Åland was becoming increasingly dependent on sea trade. For the small farms in the skerries the regular market for produce provided by shipping to the Stockholm market became more and more important as a source of cash revenue. For the bigger farms, where the farmer was a shareholder and possibly the skipper of a *galeas*, the annual summer sailing in the Baltic became essential to the maintenance of a standard of living which had risen above that of the subsistence farmer. It became the accepted norm for the men to be away from the farms for the summer and autumn and the women to do all the work on the land – for by the time the men returned, shortly before Christmas, and the vessels

The barque Appelonia, *built in Finström Community by master builder Johann August Henriksson in 1878 and shown here in Cumberland Basin in Bristol, was a typical product of the boom years of Åland shipbuilding in the 1870s.*
Bristol Museum and Art Gallery

were laid up until the spring and the melting of the ice in April, or May, all the work on the land for the year was over.

The war with Russia reduced the Åland fleet by about a quarter, nearly half of this was due not to enemy action but to the sale of vessels, some of them in Swedish or German ports. Many vessels were saved from destruction by the British Navy by the simple process of hiding them in suitably inaccessible places in the labyrinth of the archipelago. Bamböle Vik in the heart of the Finström Community provided deep sheltered water and is very difficult to find from the sea without charts or local knowledge; many ships were concealed here. Some farmers ran the blockade to Sweden and mainland Finland, usually with small *jakter*, and found it a highly profitable business to carry coal and salt from Stockholm to Turku (Åbo). As soon as the war was over sunken vessels were raised, vessels brought out of hiding in the inner *viks*, half-built vessels were completed and others repaired. There was an atmosphere of hope and optimism in the local shipping community – events were to prove it to be well justified.

Immediately after the war, due to the losses and sales mentioned above there was a shortage of tonnage owned by the towns. This was met to a degree by a series of decrees from the Russian authorities extending the right of rural shipowners to sail further afield than the Baltic. As soon as the war was over Emperor Alexander II commissioned the Russian senate to draft proposals for a series of reforms which involved the relaxation of controls on various forms of economic activity. Free competition began to replace guild rights, trading privileges and shipping monopolies. The rural population of Finland was to benefit greatly from these reforms and they affected specially the shipowners and seafarers of Åland. On 22 May 1856 an order was issued which made it legal for farmers' vessels to pass through the Sound, the deepwater channel between south Sweden and the Danish island of Sjaeland. This meant that the North Sea trade to Britain and western Europe was open to Ålanders. At more or less the same time, under long-standing American pressure the Danes abolished the Sound Dues, the tax on all vessels sailing out of the Baltic. Although there were Russian regulations setting the requirements for the qualifications of masters of vessels sailing outside the Baltic which few Åland skippers could meet for some twenty years, it remained relatively easy for experienced farmer–skippers to obtain exemption from the demands for an examination at a school of navigation – which Åland did not possess. The requirements for formal qualifications for masters and mates were gradually tightened up over the years by regulations introduced by the Russian authorities in 1863, 1866, 1868 and 1875.

Ålanders took a couple of years after the end of the Crimean War to exploit their new opportunities, partly because in the immediate post-war boom there was plenty of money to be made by sailing in the Baltic, and partly because the small, often clinker built and even undecked vessels they had were simply not up to crossing the North Sea. Fresh investment was necessary to take advantage of the changed situation. The first new vessels appear to have been the brig *Olga* built in Eckerö in 1856, the schooner *Lemland* built in the same year, the barque *Klaes*, Åland's biggest vessel to date, launched in Hammarland in 1857 and the schooner *Sandelina*, launched on the same day in the same community. In the same year the barque *Maria* was launched in Finström. The pioneer voyages to the wider seas were made in 1858, when five Åland vessels rounded the Skaw and entered the North Sea. These historic vessels were the barques *Klaes* and *Maria*, and the schooners *Edla*, *Karolina* and *Josephina*. The *Josephina* was lost with all hands. The *Klaes* made a handsome profit on a passage from north Sweden to London with timber and back to Stockholm with coal – the first of thousands of such passages made by Åland sailing vessels until the Second World War. The others covered their costs, though the *Maria* sailed without net profit.

But the way was open, and with a recovery in the freight market in 1859 the fifteen passages across the North Sea made by Åland vessels in that year were much more profitable. New, bigger, vessels were built: barques, brigs, barquentines and schooners. In 1860 there were thirty North Sea passages. It was to be the beginning of a golden era for Åland shipping which lasted until the middle of the 1870s. This was still farmer based shipowning and seafaring by men who were self-taught in both business and sailing – but it boomed. In 1860 Åland farmers owned 68 large vessels, 5 years later they had 98, in 1870 123, and in 1875 no less than 172. During the most rapid period of growth, from 1870 to 1875, (which followed the complete freeing of maritime trade by the Russians in 1868), eleven barques, one brig, thirteen big schooners, four smaller schooners and a *galeas* were built in Åland and seven barques, one brig, ten barquentines and big schooners and twelve smaller

Åland skippers photographed in Grimsby in the 1870s.
C W Von Dix, Grimsby

schooners and *galeaser* were built on the Finnish coast of the Gulf of Bothnia for Åland owners.

In 1872 about 150 timber cargoes were carried to England from ports on both sides of the Gulf of Bothnia and five big Åland vessels loaded timber in the White Sea for England. Another Åland vessel sailed to the Mediterranean and the barque *Preciosa* made the first crossing of the Atlantic on passage to the West Indies. The ports of discharge in Britain were various, predominantly Hull, where Åland skippers soon built up close connections which were to persist for two generations, Grimsby and London, but Exmouth and Wisbech were also visited. By the late 1870s Mediterranean passages and the crossing of the Atlantic were becoming commonplace.

In the years the fortress of Bomarsund was being built Åland acquired her first village settlement of

some size – the beginning perhaps, of a small town. This was Skarpans, which grew from a few houses into the village which complemented the fort. Had it not been for the Crimean War it is likely that this area, in the very heart of Åland, would have developed into the centre of administration and business activities. As it was, for ten years following the destruction of the fort and village, Åland had no town. But in 1861, Mariehamn was founded in Jomala Community, on a point of rocky land between two natural harbours, one, the Western Harbour, had deep water and became the harbour for the big sailing ships. Today it is the terminus of huge ferries and the laying up ground for unemployed vessels. The other, much shallower, became the harbour for the *galeaser*, *jakter* and small schooners and is today a centre for local and visiting yachts. Mariehamn had its custom house and

37

Mathias Lundqvist senior with two of his sons, Joel and Michael.
Hilding Lundqvist

shortly its navigation school, which is still an important institution in the town, and the Åland Mutual Insurance Company to provide a service essential to the growth of a shipping industry. It soon had a savings bank, which had difficulties in its early stages since those with savings were inclined to invest in vessel property, rather than in banks.

At the time of Mariehamn's founding there were three general stores in Åland. One was at Kastelholm, the medieval castle which had been the centre of Åland's administration until the Russians took over in 1809. The second was at Ämnäs, almost in the centre of the archipelago, which was run by Nicolai Sitkoff, of whom more will be written later. The third store was at Vargata in Wårdö Community and was owned by Mathias Mattsson. It is natural in a community developing at the rate Åland was in the

1860s and 1870s that men of action should emerge – entrepreneurial risk takers, who rode high on the tide of expansion and took a leading part in influencing events, becoming in the process very rich men by the standards of their contemporaries. Mattsson of Wårdö was one of these men, as was his great contemporary, Mathias Lundqvist of Flaka in Lemland Community.

The origins of Mattsson's fortune, the necessary initial capital, have been the subject of considerable speculation and many legends about him are still current in Åland. In fact, again, as is often the case, the real story is quite simple. He was the son of the innkeeper who lived amongst the little group of farms and houses called Vargata. The inn was important because it was more or less half way along the Åland part of the post route from Stockholm to

Mathias Mattsson in old age.
Hilding Lundqvist

St Petersburg and the innkeeper had responsibilities associated with providing the post carriers with beds, beer, food and fresh horses. The site of Bomarsund is almost in sight of Vargata. The commercial opportunities provided for local men of enterprise by this vast public works schemes were obvious. Mattsson was just at the right age, twenty–thirty, to make the maximum benefit from the opportunities offered by lively trade and cargo handling activities of all kinds. He worked at first as a clerk in a trading concern at Skarpans. He learned Russian, accounting and the ways of business, and soon was an independent storekeeper, supplying the large international community which grew up around the construction work, and involving himself in ship chandlery, broking, shipbuilding and shipowning.

When Bomarsund fell, his business was already strong enough to survive the blow and to pioneer in benefiting from the expansion of Åland shipping which rapidly followed. His affairs prospered and he became a considerable influence in Åland. His community of Wårdö and the little settlement of Vargata became phenomenally prosperous and Åland's second largest shipowning area. His energetic and positive approach to business brought the criticisms of the less successful and the punning nickname 'Varg Matte', which could be read as Matti of Vargata or, alternatively as Wolf Matte, depending on the inclination of the hearer.

Matts (Mathias) Mattsson married Serafia Matts-dotter (Serafia the daughter of Mathias). The Ålanders used patronymics well into the twentieth century and the name Mathias was much favoured. Serafia was a girl from Lemland, just across the great

39

inland sea called the Lumparfjärd. Perhaps it was this connection that gave him links with Lemland and with men of comparable dynamism. Mathias Lundqvist of Flaka was also busy building up a fortune but on a different basis. It was founded on the old established shipping activities of his community, which, situated right on the ancient trade route from western Europe via the Gulf of Finland and the Russian rivers to the east, had been involved with seafaring from earliest times and played the largest role of all Åland communities in the days of the farmer–shipowners. With the freeing of trade after the Crimean War Lemland shipping, now with new, bigger, vessels, developed rapidly. By 1860 Lemland had the largest fleet of any community, with Wårdö and Hammarland together in second place. Wårdö, however, held the record for the number of tons of shipping and acres of agricultural land per inhabitant.

Matts Mattsson had one son, Robert, and two daughters. One daughter married August Troberg, master of Mattsson's barge *Olga* one of Åland's historic vessels (she was built on Prästö, opposite

The Mattsson family outside the old house at Vargata. Matts Mattsson is seated, left, Serafia Mattsson on the right. Robert Mattson and August Troberg stand behind Matts Mattsson.

Hilding Lundqvist

Matts Mattsson's house and chandlery built in the 'Imperial Russian style' in the 1860s as it stands today in the grounds of Västergård at Vargata.

Basil Greenhill

The barque Olga *at Bristol.*
Ålands Sjöfartsmuseum; photo by John York

Bomarsund, in 1874, and sailed from Wårdö until 1920) – the other married Mathias Lundqvist's son Mathias junior. All three of these men were to become major shipowners on a scale larger than anything envisaged in Åland in the 1870s.

Though the Mattsson (later they dropped the second 's' to become Mattson) and Lundqvist families were the biggest owners of shipping in the great days of farmer–shipowners in the 1870s, there were many other families which prospered in varying degrees. In Vargata itself, in sight of Matts Mattsson's fine wooden house in the Imperial Russian style (which still stands and is used as a summer house by some of the Lundqvist family and their friends) lie the big houses of two other dynasties of successful farmer–shipowners, the Olofssons and the Johanssons.

A couple of miles away is the smaller family home of the Wennströms, its upper floor built like the poop cabin of a wooden barque. In Lemland lived the Erikssons of Granboda, in Hammarland the Sitkoffs, in Geta the Malmqvists, and there were many farmer–shipowners on a smaller scale. Their big houses and great barns, built to a size that could never be supported by the relatively small farms around them, were financed by the ships. These fine buildings, their rooms spacious and delightfully decorated were often filled with souvenirs of wide-ranging sailing vessels. They are a splendid legacy of the days of wooden sailing ships. Many of these houses, and those of the next generation, still stand today.

According to Georg Kåhre, one of the leading historians of this period, Åland's tonnage rose to some 42,000, manned by at least 1600 men, a significant proportion of the active male population.

Detail of painting by K E Jansson showing Åland sailors of the 1870s playing cards in a house ashore.
Art Museum of the Ateneum, Helsinki

Captains' houses in Wårdö.
Basil Greenhill

To meet the rigours of winter on the sixtieth parallel the families of prosperous skipper–farmers slept in bunks in the main room of the house which also contained the stove and ovens. This is Seffers in Lövö, Wårdö.
Basil Greenhill

In Vargata in Wårdö, for instance, John Hackman*
has shown that as late as 1891, 69.8 per cent of the
population of the community comprised ship
masters, mates and seamen. In the early years of
seafaring each man bought his own food at the
beginning of the season's sailing. When larger ships
were built for participation in the carrying trade the
shareholders became responsible for provisioning the
vessel at the beginning of the sailing season in April or
May. Originally the shareholders were responsible
individually for paying crew members, one
shareholder paid one man, a relic of the days when a
farm sent a hand to help in the vessel. Each
shareholder was also responsible for a contribution to
the 'keel' money, ready cash from which expenses
were to be paid until the first freight money was
collected. As far as possible provisions and
equipment were brought from local stores and

*Seamen and fishermen lived more humbly than the
captains. This cottage is preserved at Dånö in Geta.*
Basil Greenhill

*'Shipowner, Estates and Vessels', Rural Community
Navigation in Wårdö, 1868/1918, a Licentiate Thesis in
Scandinavian Ethnology, presented at the Åbo Akademi in
1981.

chandlers, thus these people, who often had shares in the vessels themselves, benefited doubly from their financial involvement.

In the early days of the 1850s and 1860s when the bulk of the crew were recruited locally from the Åland community owning the vessel life on board was very democratic and there was virtually no crew trouble. Vessels in the Baltic trade and the trades to England continued to use this system right to the very end of the Åland sailing ship era, just before the Second World War. But during the period of bigger ships which sailed further afield, in the 1890s and the first two decades of the twentieth century, crews became more and more international and inevitably from time to time, troubles developed on board. Later, in the 1920s and 1930s, in the years of the Grain Races, when the Åland vessels were almost the only sailing ships left in the world competing in general ocean

Above: to heave the vessels down for careening, very large blocks were attached to the upper part of the lower masts. One of these can be clearly seen in the bottom right hand corner of this photograph. Several of these big blocks are preserved in the Ålands Sjöfartsmuseum. Note the studdingsail booms.
Ålands Sjöfartsmuseum

Right: the barque Altai *of Wårdö careened in Mariehamn so that her crew can work on the lower parts of the hull on the port side during the spring fitting out.*
Folkkultursarkivet, Helsinki

trade, the crews again consisted of Ålanders, mainland Finns, Germans and Swedes. All were intent on meeting their country's legal requirement to serve in sail as part of the experience necessary to qualify for a mate's and in due course a master's certificate of competence. Throughout the sailing years the masters and mates were almost always Ålanders, as is the case with Åland vessels today.

In the autumn and early winter the ships returned to the Baltic, to the *viks* and *fjärds* of their island communities, to be laid up and partly stripped of running rigging, and to be visited by their shareholders, while the ice and the frigid gales closed the sea to navigation. Twenty or thirty vessels might lie at any one time in the *viks* of Lemland and Wårdö. While they rested there in the long, cold, dark, sub-arctic nights a shareholders' feast took place in the *salen*, the big drawing room, in the farm of one of the

*'Sails were sewn by men who had acquired the skill at sea'
– sail repair work on board a wooden barque.*
Ålands Sjöfartsmuseum

biggest shareholders. Here in the early days the *huvudredare*, the head shipowner, or managing owner, who did the business for the shareholding group, would distribute the profits of the season's voyaging, but as long range sailing became more common more and more responsibility for the vessels' business passed to the master and it was he who distributed the dividends and chaired the meeting. This business meeting was followed by much drinking of schnapps and a great feast, prepared by the women of the shareholding families. In return for his increasing responsibilities, such as fixing cargoes in distant ports, the master received an additional benefit, over and above his salary and the income from his shares in the vessel. This was the *kaplake*, usually five per cent and sometimes as much as ten per cent of the gross freight money. It was this *kaplake*, often representing the greater part of his income, which, ploughed back into other vessels, founded family fortunes, built the big farmhouses, the *skeppargårdar*, and encouraged the vigorous pursuit of profitable cargoes and their quick delivery.

In the spring, in April, before the ice broke up, the fitting out for the next season's sailing began. Vessels were often careened and recaulked, had rotten planks and defective masts and spars replaced, standing rigging renewed as necessary, running rigging rove off, ironwork renewed if necessary, and painted. When the ice finally melted and the ships floated in open water they were provisioned and stored for the season's sailing. All this work was done, not by professional shipwrights and riggers, but by the vessels' seamen–farmer masters and crews, men who, led by one of Ålands master builders, had helped at the building of new ships.

The majority of Åland vessels in the golden age of shipping in the 1860s and 1870s were built in the islands by local men who might only once or twice in their lifetime be involved in shipbuilding. Suitable shipbuilding sites lay everywhere and there are no less than 111 recorded building places. Wherever a seashore sloped at a suitable angle into sheltered deep water, with suitable forests nearby, vessels could be built. George Kåhre has shown that between 1856 and 1922, the following vessels of over 100 registered tons were launched in Åland: eighteen *galeaser*, sixty-seven schooners of various kinds, sixteen brigs and thirty-three barques. Most of these were between roughly 200 and about 450 registered tons. In addition at least a hundred *jakter* and *galeaser* from 25–50 tons were built over the same period. These little vessels continued to be used in the local trade among the islands, to Stockholm with firewood and to Åbo (Turku), sailing as their ancestors had done from before the Crimean War until the Second World War. Indeed the last *galeas* to be built for this kind of work, the *Merit*, was built in 1947.

A recent list prepared by the Åland Maritime Museum shows by name, building place and master builder, 291 vessels constructed in Åland between 1838 and 1965. In seems that at least some of the original shipbuilding skills came from Swedish-speaking shipwrights from Finnish Bothnia who came to Åland to supervise the building of vessels.

Shipbuilding in Prince Edward Island. The tern schooner Empress, *built at Montague in 1901, lying in Montague Harbour a year later. Two other schooners are under construction.*
Public Archives of Prince Edward Island

Some of these men settled in Åland and their descendants became Ålanders. Be that as it may, it was soon unnecessary to import men from the mainland and enough islanders became skilled master builders to sustain the industry. There were ten great master builders of whom four, Lars Holmstrom, Johann August Henriksson, Eric Söderström and Karl August Lindman, were responsible for some of Åland's most famous locally built vessels. Together they built nearly 13,000 tons of shipping. The peak building years were 1874 and 1875 when twenty-five vessels totalling over 6000 tons were launched. The timber for these vessels was locally felled. The rope for rigging was bought from Åbo (Turku) where it was manufactured in the open streets which were closed from time to time and became temporary rope walks. In earlier days rope had been made in the fields of Åland with simple wooden machinery, an example of which is preserved in the Åland Maritime Museum. The iron for fastenings and fittings was often bought secondhand in Stockholm and fabricated to fit by local blacksmiths on the building site. The sails were sewn by men who had acquired the skill at sea. The canvas was bought in mainland Finland.

It would be as well to draw parallels with developments in merchant shipping elsewhere in the world over the same years. In 1875, which might be regarded as the peak year for the old combination of farmer–shipowner–shipbuilder–seaman or domestic industry shipping, Åland, according to Georg Kåhre, had some 42,000 tons of shipping of over 40 net registered tons, all sailing vessels built of wood. This was only a fraction of the tonnage of similar vessels owned in the old ports on the Finnish coasts of the Gulf of Bothnia. The small scale of the operation under discussion can be further emphasised. The port of Yarmouth, Nova Scotia, usually associated with Canadian maritime enterprise par excellence in the years of wooden sailing ships, the world of 'wooden ships and iron men', had a graph of development not unlike Åland's, peaking in 1879, but, in this case, shipping prosperity slowly faded away as other investment opportunities offered on land to replace the dying wooden sailing ship. Shipowners invested ashore rather than venturing into the unfamiliar technology of steel and steam, already dominated by Europeans who could do it all more cheaply. Yarmouth at the height of its prosperity in 1879, owned 170 vessels totalling 163,000 tons registered – roughly 32 tons of shipping per head of the population, ten times the figure for Åland. In Prince Edward Island, centre of Canada's building of vessels equal in size to those launched in Åland, a population roughly the same as that of Åland in the 1860s launched ninety new ships a year, mostly for sale to Britain. One family, the Yeos, alone built at least 350 vessels between 1833 and 1893. In 1860, Britain, at that time the most advanced industrial nation in the world, possessed some four and a quarter million registered tons of wooden sailing vessels – the Åland fleet was one per cent of this.

In 1865 the compound steam engine was successfully applied to marine propulsion and the small wooden sailing vessel rapidly became obsolete as an ocean carrier. With this development and the general expansion of industry and trade, the competitive sailing vessel became an iron, and in the 1880s a steel, barque or ship. In due course there were four-masted barques, not of 500 tons carrying perhaps 800 tons of cargo, but of 2000, and soon 3000 tons, carrying up to 5000 tons of cargo. Wooden sailing vessels which continued to be built in North America for employment in a limited number of ocean trades were also very much bigger than their precedessors. The classic small wooden barque, the typical ocean carrier for two centuries or more, was at last on its way out. The economies of scale were becoming all important. In the mid 1870s the Åland fleet was able to exploit the tail end of the ancient and traditional ways of merchant seafaring because of low costs and business connections built up over the years. But this situation could not, and did not last.

A world recession in the late 1870s dealt the Ålanders a serious blow and in the early 1880s the world shipping business was changed, fundamentally, by the very successful rapid development of the triple expansion engine for steam vessels. By the middle 1880s the steamer was already as economical as the sailing vessel, bearing in mind that she could make three passages, and thus carry three tons of cargo, to the latter's one. By the beginning of the 1890s the bulk cargo carriers which competed for freight with the new big iron and steel sailing vessels could operate at nine miles per hour on a fuel consumption of half an ounce of coal per mile steamed. Wooden sailing ships of any but the smallest classes were almost completely abandoned by major shipping nations and the ships, which had little scrap value, were sold off at very low prices.

For about twelve years, until the late 1890s and into the first years of the present century, big steel four-masted barques continued to be built in Britain and elsewhere in western Europe. They were remarkable pieces of engineering. Often over 300 feet long, with long square sections and full ends making up a burdensome but very strong and powerful hull, capable of being sailed at consistently high average speeds if well handled, they represented for a few years a class of sailing tonnage which could, in some long range trades, still give a reasonable return on capital, at a time of increasingly competitive freight rates and rising real costs of bunker coal. They carried guano (sea bird droppings used as fertiliser) from the west coast of South America to Europe, salmon from Alaska, timber from British Columbia, coal from Britain to almost anywhere, grain from San Francisco to Liverpool, jute from Calcutta to Dundee, coal from Newcastle, New South Wales, to the west coast of South America, and timber from Sweden to South Africa and Australia returning with wheat to Britain. Their wage bills were lower than those of steamers and the investment in them, and consequently both interest charges and depreciation were smaller. It was possible to operate them with reasonable but steadily declining profit in trades on which the return could not meet steamer freight rates. Such trades were those which involved extremely long delays in loading bulky low value cargoes which often changed hands on the speculative commodity market in the long months the vessels carrying them were at sea.

In fact, these vessels operated on the margins of the maritime economy and only made profits until a small change in trading conditions took place. In 1897 this happened. The outbreak of the Spanish-American War and the Boer War were accompanied by the usual upsurge in business activity. The freight markets for steam vessels recovered and permanently shifted the balance in favour of steam. Also in 1897, a large and general increase in insurance costs in London for sail tonnage further weakened the position of sailing vessel owners. The building of big merchant sailing ships virtually ceased. Within a few years the steel sailing ships of the 1890s were on the market for less than half what they had cost to build. Early in the present century they were offering at less than a quarter of their construction value.

'Long-range deepwater sailing really began with the voyage in 1878–79 of the barque Per Brahe *from Kronstadt to Vladivostock'.* Per Brahe *was built in Finland in 1877.*
Ålands Sjöfartsmuseum

The Ålanders had to stay in shipping. Academic discussion of profitability and alternative investment (of the sort recently focused on Canada) in relation to the history of Åland's wooden sailing ships is irrelevant. There were no possible alternative investments for the Ålanders – there were no other industries. Finland itself was not industrialised and would not be for another fifty years. The Ålanders could either stay in shipping or revert to subsistence farming and fishing. Farming, forestry and fishing would by no means support the economy at the level to which it had developed. This tiny society of 15,000 people had not generated the capital necessary for the purchase and operation of steamers, nor was the necessary professional knowledge available. Neither was there enough capital to order new big sailing vessels to be built in western Europe. But there was a way out of the situation. In the 1880s, with the exception of some ports of New England and eastern Canada, the shipping world was rapidly disposing of its wooden sailing vessels at very low prices. This sort of tonnage with its requirement for highly skilled crews and endless maintenance, its limited life and relatively high casualty rates, its restrictive size and cargo capacity, even though the initial investment cost was very low, no longer attracted the major shipping nations.

To survive, the Ålanders bought about two hundred wooden vessels between 1880 and 1914, to a total of about 90,000 net registered tons. According to Georg Kåhre most of them came from the Finnish mainland ports of the Gulf of Bothnia, the rest from Scandinavia, Germany and England, and some thirty from Nova Scotia. Purchases of the latter were made when the Canadian maritime provinces began to move out of investment in shipping when the coasts began to be linked by railroad and opportunities developed inland. These vessels were bought very cheaply indeed, at a sixth to a quarter of the cost per ton of building smaller vessels in Åland.

Using these older but larger vessels the Baltic timber trade to Britain was maintained, with

This diorama in the Ålands Sjöfartsmuseum shows the building in 1920 of the barque Fred *(Peace) at Bamböle Vik by master shipbuilder Johann August Henriksson, then seventy-eight years of age. The hull of the barque* Per Brahe *is moored off shore alongside the wreck of the galeas* Onni, *her masts, spars and much of her rigging and fittings were used to equip* Fred, *which sailed until 1933 when she was lost off Mariehamn. The wreck of the* Onni *was still lying in the same position in the vik in 1984.*
Basil Greenhill

vicissitudes, as was the trade within the Baltic to Germany and Denmark. But much more important in the long run was a new development: long range sailing all the year round. Now, instead of laying up in the winter months new, bigger, Canadian and British built barques were available to carry cargoes anywhere at any time. Long range deepwater sailing had really begun with the voyage in 1878–79 of the barque *Per Brahe* from Kronstadt to Vladivostock. In 1882 the barque *Mariehamn*, ex *Lieutenant*, built in Dundee in 1866, was the first Åland vessel to round the Horn. Soon a great trade developed loading pitch pine in the Gulf of Mexico for British and west European ports. The vessels sailed out in ballast, or

with a coal cargo from Britain to the West Indies, or with a timber cargo to South Africa from the Baltic and then in ballast to the Gulf. There they loaded at Pensacola, Mobile, Appalachicola, for Britain, frequently for Portishead on the Somerset coast, a creek of the port of Bristol. They frequently loaded softwoods in ports on the St Lawrence for western Europe.

As late as 1900, sixty-two wooden barques and ten brigs were still owned in Åland. This was a completely obsolete class of shipping, more appropriate to the first half of the nineteenth century than to the twentieth, and the acquisition of this kind of tonnage was to continue even after the First World War. It was possible for the Ålanders to run these obsolete vessels profitably for several reasons. They had efficient and highly personalised management, virtually no overhead costs, highly skilled local crews, they had to make no allowances for depreciation, interest charges on the small amount of capital invested were very low, and there was cheap local insurance. In addition the Ålanders had an excellent business reputation and good connections in the trades in which they sailed. Already some brokers in

London, the centre of the world's freight markets, had developed specialist departments for handling the business of these ships in a world which had changed around them.

The long voyages took the vessels far away from the home environment of the Åland Islands. The vessels engaged in these trades did not come back for the winter to lay up in the local *viks*. To make a profit they had to be continually employed all the year round. Farming and seafaring in one form or another had gone together for centuries and their coexistence reached its peak in the 1870s. Now, although the link was only very slowly to die away (and was to survive until the 1920s and even in one community, Wårdö, as long as there were merchant sailing ships still owned in Åland), with the advent of professionalism in management and the different challenges imposed by the new ships the emphasis in shipowning began to change. A generation later the bulk of tonnage was in the hands of men of money, still Ålanders, who lived in Mariehamn and made shipping a full time job, a profession. The process of capital generation continued, now more rapidly than before – Åland had entered a new era.

As well as their houses, there are still monuments to the old farmer–shipowner–shipbuilders to be found in Åland. These are the remains of their old wooden ships: *Per Brahe* lies in Bamböle Vik; *Leo*, *Furstelea* and *Southern Belle* in the Lumparsund or nearby; *Kristina*, almost intact in Wårdö's Östervik with the first *Altai*, built just after the Crimean War, beneath her, visible and mysterious through the clear Baltic water where she has lain since 1876; the second *Altai* in Sandösund, and many more. In the harbour of Turku (Åbo) the barque *Sigyn* of Wårdö lies restored and open to visitors.

Before considering the history of the new stage in Åland's evolution as a modern shipowning society it is important to look in more detail at the way the farmer–shipowners ran their ships and built up their fortunes. In the next two chapters an examination is made of the business of a particular family who lived and farmed at Hansas Farm in the township of Hellestorp in Lemland community – the family from which Gustaf Erikson was to descend. They were relatively prosperous farmers and shipowners and the story revealed by the documentary evidence does not quite match the rags to riches legend current in Gustaf Erikson's lifetime.

The deckhouse forecastle and foredeck of the barque
Kristina *of Wårdö in 1984.*
Basil Greenhill

Gustaf Adolf Eriksson, father of Gustaf Erikson.
Edgar Erikson

Amalia Fredrika, née Förbom, wife of Gustaf Adolf Eriksson and Gustaf Erikson's mother.
Edgar Erikson

Chapter 3

THE ERIKSON FAMILY'S SHIPOWNING HISTORY

Lemland is the most southerly of the mainland Åland communities. It is mostly situated in Åland's inner archipelago. It has both homogeneous areas suitable for agriculture and areas that are either cut apart by *vikar* or consist of small islands where the inhabitants were forced to make their living from the sea. If we look at Åland as a whole and think of the inner archipelago area as a circular belt around its centre we find that besides the main part of Lemland also the main parts of Eckerö, Geta, Wårdö and Lumparland, as well as parts of Jomala, fall within that belt. They were all communities with a fairly strong seafaring tradition; those of Åland's inner mainland never had the same kind of maritime interests and were more involved with agriculture.

The total land area of Lemland is 38 square miles. In 1929 cultivated land totalled 1630 acres and the natural meadows made up 617 acres. The population gradually increased during the nineteenth century, totalling about 1500 people in 1875, 2000 in 1895 and reaching close to 2100 in the year 1900. After that it diminished quickly due to migration both abroad (to America) and within Åland (to Mariehamn); it was about 1600 in the year 1905 and only about 1500 in 1935.

On the part of Lemland that is connected to the mainland by a bridge over the Lemströms Kanal there are thirteen villages including Söderby with the church and the centre of the community, Norrby, Knutsboda, Lemböte, Bengtsböle, Rörstorp, Bistorp, Granboda, Hellestorp, Västeränga, Flaka, Vessingsboda and Haddnäs. In the archipelago lie Järsö, Nåtö and Stackskär.

Lemland lies close to the old sea routes, some of which were known in the Middle Ages, for example the route south of the headland Herröskatan, which was the main link between Sweden and Finland for a long time. This route is described in the so called Danish Itinerary, it went from Sweden via Lemböte on Lemland and on eastward. At Lemböte there is still the ruin of a seafarer's chapel dedicated to St Olof, the protector of seafarers. Today the huge ferries pass between the small island of Båkenskär, Beacon Island and the Herröskatan, leaving only a few yards between the hull and the island rocks. North west, and fairly close to the Herröskatan lie the small islands of Gloskär, Långö and Ljungskär forming the anchorage better known as Rödhamn where for centuries a chapel, sailors' inn and tavern provided comfort, food and shelter for mariners and passengers travelling between Finland and Sweden. The sailors' inn at Rödhamn was a link in a chain of such establishments, dating back to the seventeenth century, joining the eastern and western parts of the Swedish kingdom together. The next inn to the east in the chain was at Korpoström, forty-five nautical miles away.

Lemland has few good natural harbours. The interior of the land was marsh; it is nowadays mostly drained for agricultural purposes, but was still unsuitable for farming in the late nineteenth and early twentieth centuries. Lemland, like Åland as a whole, has worse farmland than the rest of Finland. Agriculture played a different role in various parts of the community, villages where farming was of most importance were Granboda, Knutstorp, Rörstorp and Söderby, all situated in the northern part of the community. The size of the farms varied, the average area of cultivated land being about twenty-six acres. Rye was the chief corn crop until the beginning of the twentieth century, when it was replaced by wheat. In the other villages the landowning farmers were largely occupied with shipping in the early and middle part of the nineteenth century. Being a skipper–part-owner was financially so rewarding that it was reason enough for the farmer to be absent from running the farm during the summer. A good example can be found in the records concerning the re-organisation of land-holding in the village of Hellestorp. These records show that on 10 June 1839 when the surveyor called the farmers in the village to a meeting, Pehr Ericsson, owner of one half of farm No 4, called Hansas, was represented by his wife, because he was on a voyage to Stockholm; in 1841 this occurred again.

In Lemland rural shipowning took the form of joint shipping companies. Such companies were characterized by the fact a particular vessel was divided up between several owners, each of whom had a number of shares in the vessel. The joint company was set up when the vessel was built or bought. The participants in the company then had to pay their share in cash if the vessel was purchased, if the vessel was being built, then the part-owners' cash contribution could be partly substituted by labour, or building timber, or other items required for the new vessel. The joint, or partner company was regarded an an ordinary limited company with decisions made at meetings of the part-owners and executed by the *huvudredare*, (the head shipowner), who was the managing owner. If a meeting of the owners so decided, then the partners had to contribute more capital for the running of the company. The capital might be replaced by contributions in kind, for instance provisions, timber for repairs, or labour. This way of contributing to the running of the company was very necessary and in effect the only way in which the coastal communities of Åland, which were comparatively short of capital, could pursue such a capital-intensive business as shipowning.

The distribution of the shares in a ship and the size of the shares varied, depending on the size of the vessel and the part-owners' wealth. In the early nineteenth century it was common to have vessels owned by two or three partners, but with the gradual increase in the size of vessels the shares became smaller, first eighths, then sixteenths, then thirty-seconds, then sixty-fourths (as in Britain) and finally one hundredths or even two hundredths.

The managing owner in a joint shipping company was very much a central figure, and as much of this book is about the individuals who were occupied in this role at one time or another, the paragraphs which follow will take a closer look at their duties. His first task was to take care of the correspondence dealing with the cargoes each sailing season, or to travel, for instance to Ostrobotnia in Finland, to arrange cargoes. In some cases the general meeting of the joint company might agree that the master of the vessel should also take part in the negotiations over cargoes, or that they should decide together how matters should be arranged. The first cargo contract for the season was usually concluded by the managing owner, in accordance with Russian maritime law which stipulated that the master of a vessel could sign no other contracts in the vessel's home port than the engaging of the crew. During the latter part of the winter the managing owners undertook journeys to the ports where the vessels were registered to pay the annual sailing fees and to obtain certificates for the vessels from the appropriate authorities. Russian maritime law gave the shipping company responsibility to determine the managing owner's powers when it came to employing the master of the vessel. The managing owner did not play a large part in hiring the crew for the vessel, that was the captain's business, but now and again he might take a hand in recruiting a mate, always in the vessel's home port.

The spring was the time for provisioning the vessel. If she had spent the winter in a bay in the community in which she was owned, the provisioning was carried out there. The managing owner then helped to supply the ship according to the number of shares he held and he also checked the provisioning list. If the vessel called at its home port in the course of the season, or some nearby port, then it might be necessary to top up the stores, in which case this was the managing owner's responsibility. When the payment of the freight money for the first cargo of the season was received it was the managing owner's responsibility to pay all outstanding debts for provisions and other necessities.

Russian maritime law stipulated that the managing owner was responsible for distributing to the shareholders all the money not needed for the running of the vessel. Such funds included, for example, the keel money, which the managing owner raised from the part-owners in the spring of each year. This had to be repaid before any other funds were distributed. Revenue was remitted to the managing owner by the master in the form of the

Hansas farm in Hellestorp, Lemland, where Gustaf Erikson grew up. The building on the left still survives as a summer house of the modern farm. Note the windmill, typical of Åland.
National Museum of Finland

freight money. This was often in foreign currencies and the managing owner had to travel to Mariehamn to change these into roubles, or into Finnish marks when these became Åland's currency in the later nineteenth century. Any profit that was left after all the remaining costs had been paid was then distributed amongst the shareholders.

During the sailing season correspondence with the captain of the vessel was an important part of the managing owner's duties. The master usually sent the managing owner an arrival and a departure letter from each port. All these letters had to be answered, and the master informed of the shareholders' views and in some cases receive the managing owner's advice – there are plenty of examples of the latter in Gustaf Erikson's correspondence, as we shall see. Often managing owners were older seafarers who had retired from active duty, but were willing to continue working in shipping, thus sharing their wisdom and experience.

Having looked at the organization of rural shipping in general, Lemland and the village of Hellestorp will be examined in particular. Hellestorp lies in the middle of Lemland, the village centre being about half a mile away from the sea. During the late nineteenth and early twentieth centuries, there were eight farms which were named respectively Erkas, Österby, Ollas, Hansas, Jakos, Vesterby, Joans and

Klemets. Their average size was 298 acres of which 33 acres was cultivated land; the rest was woodland, marsh and rock.

In the year 1872 when Gustaf Erikson, the principal Åland shipowner in the years of the Grain Races, was born, his father, Gustaf Adolf Eriksson (or Melander) was the owner of the farm called Österby (the East Farm) in Hellestorp. Gustaf Adolf Eriksson was born in 1845 in the village of Granboda in eastern Lemland, quite near the Lumparsund which divides Lemland from Lumparland. Axel Erik Melander (Gustaf Adolf's father and Gustaf Erikson's grandfather), owned a fairly big farm in Granboda called Nybondas. The farmhouse no longer exists but the Melanders are still remembered in local tradition as active people and there are meadows in the village that still carry their name.

Axel Erik Melander had eight children of whom Gustaf Adolf was the youngest. The eldest son, Carl Abraham, later took over the farm, the second son Eric Herman moved abroad while the two youngest sons, Axel Arvid and Gustaf Adolf, moved to other parts of the community to earn their living from shipping and farming. Axel Melander already had interests in shipping. He was part-owner and managing owner of the *galeaser Delphin*, *Neptunus*, *Storfursten* and *Constantin*; his shipping can be traced in records up to the Crimean War. His vessels were employed in trade between Gulf of Bothnia ports and Stockholm, mainly with firewood; the *Constantin* made a round voyage to Germany in 1845.

After the Crimean War, Axel Erik Melander's eldest son, the farmer Carl Abraham, entered the shipping business, at first on a small scale with only one vessel, the schooner *Hengist*, bought in 1862. In 1864 she made two voyages to England from Sweden carrying timber, returning to Åbo (Turku) with case-goods. The profit for the season was 6000 marks, which is good in comparison with other ships' incomes given in the official records. Gradually Carl Abraham Melander's shipping interests grew. In 1869 he was managing two ships, the *Hengist*, rebuilt in 1868 and the barquentine *Aimo* built in 1868. At his peak as a managing owner in 1877–78 he had four vessels to look after.

Axel Erik Melander's youngest son, Gustaf Adolf took the surname Eriksson. He went to sea in his elder brother's ships and became master of the schooner *Hengist*. From 1868 to 1870 he was master of the new barquentine *Aimo*. In 1868 he made two voyages to England with timber, and in January 1869 he took the *Aimo* to Bilbao in Spain with coal from Swansea and also from Swansea to Hanko (Hangö) in Finland with coal, and then with timber from Pori (Björneborg) to Hamburg and with salt from Hamburg to Riga. The ship made a profit of only 200 marks in her first year (1868) which was very common for newly built ships with outstanding debts. The next year when he took the *Aimo* with a cargo of timber from Archangel and subsequently Porvoo (Borgå) in Finland to Hull the profit was a good 4500 marks. The *Aimo* was wrecked in 1873.

Lemland shipowners insured their ships at least partly. The *Aimo*, for instance, was insured from the beginning of her career in 1868 to a value of 18,000 marks which should have provided three-quarters cover. The insurance was placed with an Åbo-based insurance company. Lemland ships were often insured with the Åbo company, but from 1874 onwards there was an insurance company in Åland and most of the Lemland ships' insurances were changed over to it.

In 1872 Carl Abraham Melander and his fellow shareholders built a new ship in Sippy (Sideby) in

Ostrobotnia in mainland Finland. During the year Gustaf Adolf Eriksson, who was to be master, of the new barque, *Amalia*, spent much of his time supervising her building. That same year he married Amalia Fredrika Förbom, the daughter of the owner of the farm called Ollas in Hellestorp. In October 1872 their first son, the future Gustaf Erikson, was born and given the names Gustaf Adolf Mauritz Gustafsson in the parish records. By now Gustaf Adolf had bought Österby, and it was here that Gustaf Erikson was born in a house which no longer exists. Gustaf Adolf did not keep Österby for very long, in March 1875 he sold the property and bought another farm in Hellestorp, Hansas, of 363 acres of which 32 were cultivated. In 1875 a daughter, Emilia Alie, was born and in 1876 another son, Axel Theodor.

The house at Hansas was a typical Åland farmhouse, of which a photograph, (see page 55), luckily survives. The length of the building ran north to south, and it faced west. At an angle of ninety degrees to it was the outbuilding, still standing today, and the cow shed. There were usually two hired hands on the farm. While Gustaf Adolf Eriksson was at sea his wife had to take care of the farming, with the help of the hired hands and the children if they were at home. This situation was typical of Åland farms at that time.

Today when you come to Hellestorp's village centre the first new building on the right hand side of the road (west) is where the farm called Ollas, Gustaf Erikson's mother's home, used to stand. If you look to the left there lies a short distance away across a field a beautiful red farmhouse, the Österby house built in 1875, the same year Gustaf Erikson's father sold the farm. Then, a few hundred yards further to the left from the main road stands Hansas with a new farmhouse, and an outbuilding which was there in the early 1870s.

The new barque *Amalia*, named after Gustaf Erikson's mother, was insured in Åbo for 39,600 marks, covering 60 per cent of the ship's total cost. In 1873 Gustaf Adolf Eriksson took her from Gävle in Sweden to London with timber, making no profit in the first year. In December 1874, she was wrecked and became a total loss. He gave the following account of the *Amalia*'s last passage at the subsequent court hearing at Visby in Gotland, Sweden:

> After having taken a full cargo of coal in the ship that was not overloaded and was strong and in good shape and fully seaworthy in all respects and fully manned, we sailed from Hull 20th of November [1874] with a pilot

The Canadian-built full-rigged ship Albania, *of which Gustaf Erikson took command in 1905, seen here in Bristol floating harbour. The entrance to the drydock where* The Great Britain *now lies is on the left.*

Bristol Museum and Art Gallery

on board, for Grimsby where we anchored the following day at 9.30 a.m. From Grimsby we put out to sea, the wind was north-westerly. We sailed with varying winds without anything remarkable until 27th November 8 a.m. when the main topsail yard broke and the main topsail was lost. The sea was heavy and the wind south-easterly with snow. We set course for Norway to put in for repairs. We came to Korshamn where the damage was repaired. We sailed from there 5th of December at 9.30 a.m. and continued the journey without anything to remark through the Drogden in stormy weather with snow. It was 13th of December at 0.30 a.m. when we sighted the Landsort lighthouse tower, at NNE distance 15. The wind was E to NE. We sailed on the wind to SSE. The weather was cloudy with snow and full storm.

At about midnight the air cleared somewhat but after a while it was filled with snow again. At 01.45 a.m. the rudder was put to starboard for turning when the ship ran hard aground and the heavy seas threw her more and more to landward. The ship's boats were made ready to save the crew, but the weather was too bad to put any people ashore. The ship was immediately filled with water. At daybreak we discovered that we were aground at Sneipklint near Stenkyrkohuk in Gotland. One of the boats was put out but it turned over immediately and the able seaman S. Sandell was killed. His life was impossible to save. At 4 p.m. we came ashore. All precautions were made to save the ship's inventory and cargo. I went to Visby to make a protest and to get assistance. 15th of December the salvage steamer *Poseidon* came, but could not do anything because of the heavy seas and so returned to Visby. 16th of December we took ashore the sails and running rigging in local boats. 17th December there was a severe storm and the ship was completely demolished and masts and the rigging went overboard ... Visby 19th of December 1874.

Apparently an auction of the salved goods was held since Axel Eriksson was mentioned as the owner of half of the property. The document was signed by the master and his crew in June 1875. Axel Eriksson was at sea and Gustaf Adolf Eriksson did the accounts with his wife (it is especially written in the document 'the accounts made up with the wife at home'). This is a very real example of how important women were for the successful operation of rural shipping.

During the next year Gustaf Adolf Eriksson was employed as *konstapel*** in the schooner *Mathilda*, another of his brother Carl Abraham's ships. This may have been a demotion, but it may also have been that in the official records (the register of Mariehamn's *sjömanshus*) he had to be signed on as a *konstapel* because he had no master's certificate of competence which had, in 1875, become compulsory. In fact he made only one voyage in the *Mathilda* because he was involved in the building of the new barquentine, *Ax*, in Sideby.

In the records of the Åland Insurance Company the *Ax* was registered as being both managed and commanded by Gustaf Adolf Eriksson in the year 1875. From 1876 onwards she was registered as managed by Carl Abraham Melander. The insurance placed in Åland covered ⁹/₁₆ths of the ship at 25,875 marks. Her first voyage was to London from Kristiinankaupunki (Kristinestad) on the mainland and then from Archangel to Britian. The net profit was 2150 marks which was good for the first season. Gustaf Adolf Eriksson continued to command the *Ax* until the end of the 1879 sailing season. During these years the ship sailed to England several times with timber cargoes and her total net profit was 4000 marks.

What Gustaf Adolf Eriksson did from 1879 to 1882 is not precisely known. In 1882 he was the master of the barque *Ljuba*, one of the ships in the Nicolai Sitkoff fleet. In 1885 he commanded the barquentine *Adele*, managed by his brother Axel Arvid Eriksson, and his son Gustaf Adolf Mauritz, the future Gustaf

Gustaf Erikson in the master's cabin in Albania. *Note the fiddle on the table, the desk, the mirror and the lace curtains. Albania had a very high standard of accommodation aft.*
Ålands Sjöfartsmuseum

Erikson, went with him as nominal cook in his father's vessel.

In order to give a complete picture of Gustaf Adolf Eriksson's shipping interest it is necessary to list his shares in different ships and also his managing ownerships. Presuming that he had shares in the vessels he commanded, which was usual, the list is as follows: *Hengist, Aimo, Amalia, Mathilda, Ax, Ljuba, Adele, Två Bröder, Toivo, Fennia, Heimo, Ansgar, Leo, Ceres, Irene, Elida, Neptun, Mathilda, Satama, Gessner* and *Southern Belle*. He was managing owner of the galeas *Två Bröder* in 1869–70, the barquentine *Ax* in 1875, the barquentine *Fennia* in 1875–88 and finally the barque *Southern Belle* in 1889. He died before he had time to take part in the business of the latter vessel in December 1889.

In the foregoing some aspects of kinship and its importance for rural shipping in Åland have been touched upon. If a family tree is made starting with Axel Erik Melander from Granboda and his sons and daughters, and including their shares in ships, it will

---

*The term *konstapel* has no exact English translation and his role on board had no real parallel in British and American vessels. The *konstapel* was a mature and experienced seaman (without a certificate of competence) who acted as second mate, even in the Baltic trade as the only mate. He was also responsible for organizing provisions and issuing them to the cook. In addition he took the lead in practical work on board and acted as the master's right hand in port. This situation was somewhat similar in British merchant schooners, which sometimes went to sea with no mate but a man signed on as a boatswain who performed the mate's duties. The schooner *Thomas Edwin*, partly owned in Boetheric where this note was written, cleared for Canada from Plymouth in 1867 so manned.

show how the shipping interests of one family were linked together, passing by inheritance from father to son and from husband to wife. For instance, Amalia Eriksson inherited shares from her husband and took advantage of the development of Åland shipping by buying more shares in ships after his death. From her husband she inherited shares in the *Ansgar*, *Heimo*, *Adele* and *Ceres*. Later she bought shares in the *Alma*, the *Suomalainen*, the *Europa*, the full-rigged ship *Vanadis*, the *Augusta*, the *Endymion*, the full-rigged ship *Mermerus*, the *Ida*, the *Hermes* and the full-rigged ship *Albania*, a total of fourteen ships.

We can also see how family traditions and relationships influenced the younger generations to continue investing in shipping and how they finally culminated in the successful business of Gustaf Erikson himself. This is clearly shown when the ownership of the vessels in which Gustaf Erikson served is examined. He started as a cabin boy in the barque *Neptun* in 1883, a vessel in which his father owned $1/32$nd. Gustaf Erikson then went to sea in the barquentine *Adele*, serving as cook under his father's

The barque Lochee. *Gustaf Erikson commanded her from 1909 to 1913.*
Ålands Sjöfartsmuseum

Gustaf Erikson photographed in 1946 at the age of seventy-four.

Ålands Sjöfartsmuseum

command, first in 1885, and again in 1886 under Captain J W Karlsson. His father owned $^3/_{16}$ths of this vessel and his uncle, Axel Arvid Eriksson was her managing owner and had $^8/_{32}$ shares. Gustaf Erikson himself acquired $^3/_{32}$ shares in *Adele* in the year 1893. In 1888 he again served in the *Adele* under Captain J W Karlsson and in 1889 he was *konstapel* in the barque *Ansgar*. His father had a $^1/_{10}$th share in the *Ansgar* and both his uncles had shares in her. In 1890 he was *konstapel* in the barquentine *Fennia*, a vessel that his father used to manage, now managed by his Uncle Axel, who also had $^{21}/_{96}$ in the ship. Later in the year 1890 he was *konstapel* in the barque *Southern Belle* bought to Lemland under the managing ownership of his father who also, as mentioned before, had a $^1/_{10}$th share in her. Gustaf Erikson passed his quartermaster's examination at the navigation school in Mariehamn on 13 April 1892. The same year he was employed for five months and twenty-nine days as mate on the barquentine *Adele*.

In 1893–94 he got his first command, again on the *Adele*, though, since he had not yet got his master's certificate, officially he was employed as second mate;

his Uncle Axel was managing owner. In 1895 he served as first mate in the barque *Mathilda* for four months, a ship his Uncle Axel had a $^1/_8$th share in and he himself had inherited a $^1/_8$th share from his father. After that he was employed in Robert Mattson's ships, the barques *Finland* and *Mariehamn*, as first mate.

On 25 April 1895 he passed his mate's examination and also the *kofferdiskeppar* (merchant skipper) examination, at the navigation school in Oulu (Uleaborg) and finally in 1899 he passed his master's examination, also valid for steamers, at the navigation school in Vaasa (Wasa). In 1899, according to the registry at the Mariehamn *sjömanshus* he took command of the *Southern Belle*, the last of the real rural ships in his career. He served in the *Southern Belle* until 1905, then in the full rigged ship *Albania* of Mariehamn from 1905 to 1908. He served finally in the barque *Lochee* of Nystad in mainland Finland, from 1910 until 1919. In the *Albania* Gustaf Erikson had from $^3/_{100}$ to $^{10}/_{100}$ shares during the years 1903–08.

Gustaf Erikson gave his own account of his early years at sea when applying for a place in the navigation school in Mariehamn, as follows:

1883 May 14	Sailed as cabin boy with the skipper K. Eriksson in the barque *Neptun* from Åland to Kotka, Dunkirk and Hernösand for 4 months and 3 days.
1885 April 14	Ditto as cook with the skipper G A Eriksson in the barquentine *Adele* from Åland to Husum, Courselles and Åland for 3 months and 15 days.
1886 July 23	Ditto with the skipper J W Karlsson in the last named ship *Adele* from Åland to Sundsvall, Caen, Skeppsvik, Shoreham and Åland for 4 months and 16 days.
1888 May 13	Ditto as steward with the last named skipper in the same ship from Åland to Sundsvall, Newhaven, Söderhamn, Newhaven and Åland for 5 months and 22 days.
1889 June 23	Ditto as *konstapel* with Captain E K Eriksson in the barque *Ansgar* from Åland to Räfsö, Goole and Hernösand for 4 months and 6 days.
1890 March 2	Ditto with skipper E P Lemquist in the barquentine *Fennia* from Åland to Hernösand, Sandviken and Åland for 2 months and 14 days.
1890 Sept 29	Ditto with Captain M R Widlund from Cardif to Dakar, Haiti and Riga for 8 months.

Mariehamn October 15 1891
Gustaf Adolf Mauritz Eriksson
[here he still spells his name with two Ss]

Chapter 4

THE SOUTHERN BELLE

The barque *Southern Belle* was bought by Lemland owners on 26 April 1889. She can be considered an Erikson family ship because as we have seen Gustaf Adolf Eriksson (Gustaf Erikson's father) was her first intended managing owner, but as he was taken ill and eventually died before he could take up his duties, his brother Axel seems to have taken the first necessary business steps, preparing the official papers for the ship as she was still on her passage towards Åland. From the first list of shareholders, filed by Axel Eriksson with the registrar of shipping in Mariehamn as part of the process of obtaining her certificate of registration, it is apparent that Gustaf Adolf Eriksson

The Southern Belle.
Åbo Akademi

had $^8/_{80}$ths in the ship, as had his brothers Carl Abraham Melander and Axel Eriksson himself. The complete list is as follows:

Skipper Axel Eriksson	Lemland	$^8/_{80}$	
Captain Matts Robert Widlund	Lemland	$^4/_{80}$	
Skipper Gustaf Adolf Eriksson	Lemland	$^8/_{80}$	
Farmer Carl Abraham Melander	Lemland	$^8/_{80}$	$^{37}/_{80}$
Skipper Johan Karlsson	Lemland	$^4/_{80}$	
Captain Erik Emil Sjölund	Lemland	$^2/_{80}$	
Skipper Manne Eriksson	Lemland	$^2/_{80}$	
Skipper Johan Erik Gustafsson	Lemland	$^1/_{80}$	
Mrs Eva Wikman	Pargas	$^2/_{80}$	$^2/_{80}$
Crofter Karl Johan Ekholm	Föglö	$^4/_{80}$	
Senior Pilot Daniel Sjölund	Föglö		$^8/_{80}$
Farmer Emil Eriksson	Föglö	$^2/_{80}$	
Farmer Erik Eriksson	Föglö	$^2/_{80}$	
Shopkeeper Isak Rosten	Mariehamn	$^1/_{80}$	
Mrs Sofia Nyström	Mariehamn	$^2/_{80}$	
Mrs Helena Sittkoff	Mariehamn	$^8/_{80}$	
Mrs Beda Sittkoff	Mariehamn	$^1/_{80}$	
Miss Hilma Fraser	Mariehamn	$^1/_{80}$	
Baker Erik Wilh. Borenius	Mariehamn	$^3/_{80}$	$^{26}/_{80}$
Houseowner Johan Erik Sjöström	Mariehamn	$^2/_{80}$	
Mrs Amalia Isaksson	Mariehamn	$^4/_{80}$	
Viceconsul Hugo Tamelander	Mariehamn	$^4/_{80}$	
Farmer Johan Hansson	Jomala	$^2/_{80}$	
Skipper Karl August Karlsson	Jomala	$^1/_{80}$	$^7/_{80}$
Farmer Olof Eriksson	Jomala	$^2/_{80}$	
Farmer Johan Fredriksson	Jomala	$^2/_{80}$	

The main body of the shares, $^{37}/_{80}$ths, were held in Lemland, followed by Mariehamn with $^{26}/_{80}$ths, Föglö with $^8/_{80}$ths, Jomala with $^7/_{80}$ths and finally there is the odd share of $^2/_{80}$ths in Parainen (Pargas) in south western Finland. The *Southern Belle* was clearly a Lemland ship with Gustaf Adolf Eriksson and his brothers controlling $^{24}/_{80}$ths of the capital invested in her, the main part of which must have comprised her purchase price of £2050.

The *Southern Belle* was bought from Nova Scotia through a shipbroker in Cardiff. Her Canadian register in the public archives of Canada, Ottawa,

records her date of purchase as June 1899 but according to the sources in Åland's county archives in Mariehamn it was 26 April. It is possible the later Canadian date is when the sale was registered in Canada. She was built in 1871 at Church Point, Digby, Nova Scotia, a predominantly French speaking area, by J Mulcaha, whose name perhaps suggests an Irish family origin. The first registration of the vessel in Canada gives the following particulars:

Stern – 'Oval', Head, 'Figure',
146 × 31.4 × 18.8 feet

Tonnage under tonnage deck	519.35
Poop	51.78
Trunk or poop	16.56
Gross tonnage (being register tonnage if a sailing ship)	587.69

The first owners were:

Shipowner Abel C Robbins, Yarmouth, Nova Scotia	$^{24}/_{64}$
Shipowner Samuel B Robbins, Yarmouth, Nova Scotia	$^{16}/_{64}$
Shipowner Daniel W Clark, Saint John, New Brunswick	$^{24}/_{64}$

Abel C Robbins was one of the leading group of shipowners in Yarmouth during the great period of shipping expansion from 1860 to 1879. He had a grocer's store as well as shares in vessels.

From the Canadian records it is evident that she was offered for sale in 1873, a fact that may indicate that she was built on speculation, though this practice does not seem to have been usual in Yarmouth. The exact employment of the *Southern Belle* during her Canadian years is not known but she was probably in the North and South Atlantic trades as were most of the other Yarmouth vessels. She was certainly at Pensacola, Florida, in the mid 1880s. Her first Finnish master was Matts Robert Widlund who bought her in England and her first passage under the Russian flag was from Cardiff to La Plata with coal. In 1890 Captain Widlund took her across the Atlantic again, with Gustaf Erikson on board as *konstapel* sailing from Cardiff to Dakar, Haiti and back to Riga, arriving in early May 1891. From Riga she was fixed to Bordeaux but entered Mariehamn for the first time on the way in order to be measured and registered and to get provisions and complete the crew.

The *Southern Belle* was in Mariehamn again late in the summer of 1891. In August a meeting was held on board. Captain Widlund was again elected master of the vessel and J E Sjöström of Mariehamn was confirmed as managing owner.

The Finnish ship historian, Lars Grönstrand, in an article in the *Åland Shipping Journal* gives details of the voyages of the *Southern Belle* in the 1890s:

The *Southern Belle* flying the Imperial Russian flag. This photograph was probably taken on one of her visits to Canada to load timber.
Ålands Sjöfartsmuseum

The *Southern Belle* was probably employed in the Baltic timber trade in the latter part of 1891. On 7th November she passed Copenhagen on her way from Kotka to Cherbourg. In the North Sea she collided with the German steamer *Ida* and came to Cherbourg with her bowsprit broken and other minor damages. After that Captain Widlund took her over the Atlantic once more for a cargo, presumably of pitch pine, from Pensacola to Dublin. After that passage she sailed for home. On 27th June she anchored in the western harbour of Mariehamn. Captain Widlund left her for a job as lighthouse keeper. The new captain was K A Karlsson who took her to Söderhamn where a load of timber was waiting. From Soderhamn the *Southern Belle* sailed to Newhaven, where she arrived on 7th August. After that she took timber from Lappvik near Hanko (Hangö) in Finland to Cartagena arriving on 1st November. Then she crossed the Atlantic again. On the 6th July 1893 she lay in Apalachicola loading pitch pine for Glasson Dock

in England. On 8th April she left from Apalachicola and after discharging she was back in Mariehamn on 23 July. Repairs to the deck were carried out and on 1st October she was ready, provisions were taken on board and she set sail for Hamina (Fredrikshamn) in the eastern part of the Gulf of Finland to load timber for Barcelona. After a difficult passage she arrived in Barcelona on 9th February 1894. After that she was employed in carrying timber from Scandinavia to the Continent with occasional trips over the Atlantic. In 1898 when she was in Liverpool the owners decided to have her surveyed. She went through a special survey and got back her old Class A.1 $^{1}/_{2}$ for five years.

In 1898 Gustaf Erikson, now twenty-six years old, began a campaign of acquiring shares in the *Southern Belle*, in which his father and two uncles already

It took fourteen women and two boys ten days to load the
Southern Belle *when she was in Stugsund. Women*
stevedores, splitvedjäntor, *which can be translated*
'lathwood lassies', were frequently employed loading timber
cargoes on both the Finnish and Swedish shores of the Gulf
of Bothnia. Here women are loading the barque Warma *in*
1935.
Lars Grönstrand

owned $^{24}/_{80}$ths. In 1898 he acquired $^{7}/_{80}$ths from
shareholders other than his own family, $^{8}/_{80}$ths were in
the name of his deceased father's estate and in 1900 he
bought another $^{12}/_{80}$ths. He thus had control of $^{27}/_{80}$ths
of the vessel and became the biggest shareholder. He
soon acquired more shares, paying from $47^{1}/_{2}$ marks
to 175 marks per share. Evidently the *Southern Belle*
was then considered a good investment. Not
surprisingly in the following year, 1899, Gustaf
Erikson appears in the records of the *sjomanshus* in
Mariehamn as the master of the vessel, taking over as
soon as he had passed for his master's certificate of
competence at Vaasa (Wasa) and perhaps providing
the incentive for taking the qualification at this
particular time.

Gustaf Erikson now had command of a barque and
was also her principal owner. The *Southern Belle* may
therefore be regarded as the first of the Erikson fleet.
The vessel was destined for Kemi in Finland at the
head of the Gulf of Bothnia. She arrived there on 16
September, loaded timber and sailed for London.

The *Southern Belle* was still run in the old
fashioned way as regards provisioning, that was
practised in the countryside when the ships used to lie
over the winter in their home bays. The only
difference was that the paper slip that the managing
owner used to send to the part-owners with the
provisioning figures was now substituted by an
advertisement in the local newspaper. On 27 April
1901 such an advertisement appeared in the
newspaper *Åland*: the *Southern Belle* was to be
provisioned by 3 May. The part-owners were to
deliver for each $^{1}/_{40}$ths share in the ship the following
amounts of provisions: 53lb of bread, 12lb of butter,
35lb of beef, 12lb of pork and half a barrel of potatoes.

Because of the survival of an account book it is
possible to give a detailed account of the operations of
the *Southern Belle* and her principal owner and
master in 1902. As early as February Gustaf Erikson
attended an auction of equipment from the barque
Hilda which had been wrecked in the Björkör

archipelago in Föglö, Åland. Gustaf Erikson had a $^1/_{16}$th share in *Hilda* so he must have been well informed of what was worth buying for use on the *Southern Belle*. In March he bought some sails at another auction and from the barquentine *Jenny* a sail and a compass. He also advertised in the local newspaper, for the benefit of the shareholders, that timber was needed for repairs to the *Southern Belle*. In March Gustaf Erikson travelled around the Åland Islands to recruit a crew for his ship. On 13 May he went by steamer with his crew of seven men to Stockholm, and on to Stugsund by train. The money for the train journey was advanced by the managing owner (100 marks) and by Gustaf Erikson's mother Amalia Eriksson (also 100 marks).

In Stugsund the ship was loaded by fourteen women and two boys in the course of ten days. The provisions were topped up by some beef and herrings and five litres of spirits. Two men from Stockholm were signed on as additional crew. The timber cargo was destined for London and the *Southern Belle* sailed from Söderhamn via Mariehamn where the ship was provisioned. Gustaf Erikson even accounted for some spirits to be offered to the shareholders. After this stay in Mariehamn the *Southern Belle* sailed for London where she arrived on 27 June. The ship's outlays in London where she remained until 11 July totalled £235 15s 7d. The disbursements are given in full below because they can be considered typical for a vessel of *Southern Belle*'s kind, and because they give a good picture of the activities of one of the last of the old farmer-owned vessels during a season and the way in which she was run.

Shipbroker's bill	£56	11s	6d
Ship's chandler's bill	19	0	6
Paint shop	6	13	0
Butcher's	2	1	6
Ironmonger		11	8
Water	1	2	6
Pilot (outgoing)	2	3	6
Steam tug (outgoing)	11	10	0
A clock and a teapot for the ship		12	6
For extra pumping of the ship		15	0
Travels ashore and food		10	0
To first mate for finding a leak		17	0
Sent to the managing owner	100	0	0
To the crew	20	0	0
Balance to the charge of the master	13	6	1
Total	£235	15s	7d

On the credit side Gustaf Erikson has put the following:

The entire freight for 228 cubic units of firewood at 28s.		£319	4s 0d
Minus advance at Nyhamn	80 0 0		
Minus insurance	15 3		
Minus discount on half freight	2 13 2	83	8 5
Total		£235	15s 7d

Note the amount given to the mate for finding the leak; this was customary in the days of wooden vessels. Gustaf Erikson followed the old practice when as late as 1918, he promised an extra amount to the watchman on the *Southern Belle* if he found a leak.

From London the *Southern Belle* sailed for Oulu (Uleåborg). She had no return cargo and sailed in ballast. On 11 August she was ready to start loading her second cargo for the year. The disbursements for the stay in Uleåborg amounted to 3010 marks. They were as follows:

Pilot (incoming)	Fmk	59	26
Customs office bill		575	51
Harbourmaster		244	13
Sjömanshus bill		11	70
Repair of the pumpshaft		40	00
Ship's chandler's bill		154	90
Stevedore bill and unloading the ballast		570	15
1 barrel of tar		24	00
Advertise for a lost ship's boat		4	50
Ironmonger's bill		14	35
Butcher's bill		28	60
Three bags of potatoes		20	00
Spirits in Öresund		17	15
Arrival and departure telegrams		2	50
Expenses for the found ship's boat		10	00
Freight for the pumpshaft to and from the shop		2	80
Dock labourers 11 days@1 fmk		11	00
Dock labourers 10 days@2 fmk		20	00
Travels from the ship to Uleåborg and back		18	00
Pharmacy bill		3 00	1771
Paid for the travelling money to Amalia Eriksson			100
To the crew			666
Balance to the charge of the master			473
Total Fmk			3010

On the credit side was

Advance on the freight £120 (£ = fmk 25)		3000
Balance to the shareholders from earlier accounts		10
Total Fmk		3010

The *Southern Belle* left Oulu on 28 August but sprang a leak in the Gulf of Bothnia and went into Mariehamn on 6 September. The survey involved discharging the cargo which was sent to London in another vessel. The immediate disbursements in Mariehamn were as follows:

Sjömanshus bill	Fmk	58	85	
Customs office bill		11	00	
Coppersmith's bill		14	50	
Hilda – auction		35	00	
Pharmacy bill		5	00	
To the steward for guarding effects		12	00	
Two litres of spirits		3	20	
One barrel of potatoes		5	00	
Fresh beef 5 kg at 60 pennies		3	00	
Balance from the provisioning and repair timber bill		98	23	245 78
To the crew				795 07
Balance to the charge of the master				1384 00
Total Fmk				2425 85

On the credit side there was

The rest of the first freight (Stugsund–London) from the managing owner	Fmk	2206	00
Interest on above		2	60
Sold to *Europa* 160 kilo of beef at 45p		72	00
Sold to *Europa* 44.3 kilo of pork at 1.15		50	95
Sold to Borenius 38 kilo of butter at 1.60		60	80
Lent the crew to *Rock City*		32	50
Total Fmk		2425	85

The master's own account with the shareholders was as follows:

5% of the total freight Nyhamn–London £319 1s 5d Fmk	399	00	
5% of the freight advance 2nd journey £120	150	00	
Wages for 4 months 7 days at 50 mk	211	66	
Commission for getting the freight 2nd journey	30	00	
Balance from earlier accounts	227	46	
Balance from earlier accounts	133	70	
Balance from earlier accounts	110	48	
			1262 30
Balance			1135 00
			2397 30

The sum of 2397.30 marks was balanced on the credit side with the same amount which came from adding up the balances in former accounts. Of particular interest in these accounts is the sale of the provisions left over to the barque *Europa*, a vessel in which Gustaf Erikson also had shares and the sale of

the surplus butter to a Mr Borenius, baker, from Mariehamn who was also one of the shareholders in the *Southern Belle*. Noteworthy also is the fact that the crew is lent to another ship, the *Rock City*, apparently to help with repairs. The *Rock City* was a former Canadian barque in which Axel Eriksson, Gustaf's uncle, had shares. Thus the business was kept among the owners of *Southern Belle* to their mutual advantage. For instance, baker Borenius in effect got his butter at a discount.

The *Southern Belle* was repaired in Mariehamn. Apparently some of the side planking was renewed, perhaps also some of the deck planking. The ship was most likely hove down in the Western Harbour, above which the Nautical Club stands today. Some timber for repairs was supplied by the shareholders, the rest was bought from five different suppliers. Two women were employed spinning the oakum for caulking, altogether twenty-four and a half bales of it. Two women in Mariehamn were also busy carding and combing animal hair, also used for caulking purposes, there was even a basket bought for keeping the animal hair. Gustaf Erikson was busy travelling around Åland obtaining the timber for the work. The repairs took two months altogether, during which time the master received his normal wages of 50 marks a month. The repair crew was paid a total sum of 1898 marks, the number of men employed is not recorded. The payment for labour and all the other expenses in Mariehamn totalled 5162 marks. It was paid by the shareholders after Gustaf Eriksson and his mother had first advanced to the ship over 5000 marks. The shareholders paid 62½ marks per ⅛₀th to which sum was added or taken away the value of delivered provisions or timber.

On 17 February 1903, the annual shareholders' meeting took place in Hellestorp. The accounts for the year 1902 were audited by J E Gustafsson, a shareholder who was elected auditor.

In 1903 the *Southern Belle* was ready for sea. On 5 May she sailed for Hudiksvall in Sweden where she loaded timber for Southampton. She arrived at Newport, Monmouthshire, on 22 June where she was taken to the Alexandra dry dock, and again re-caulked – she was becoming rather an old lady. After the repairs were completed she was freighted with coal from Swansea to Gävle in Sweden and from there back to Londonderry with timber. The season of 1903 ended in the Western Harbour of Mariehamn on 8 November.

In 1904 the ship was twice freighted with timber from Sweden to England with return cargoes of coal

Rock City *hove down in Mariehamn's Western Harbour.*
This photograph may well have been taken on the occasion
in 1902 when the crew of the Southern Belle, *which may*
be one of the two barques lying careened in front of her,
was lent to help with the work on her.
Ålands Sjöfartsmuseum

and coke. During the last homeward passage of the season the *Southern Belle* was damaged in bad weather in the North Sea but in spite of this the passage from Hull to Stockholm took only six days – a fast voyage which was even noticed by the newspapers. The season of 1905, which was to be Gustaf Erikson's last as master of the *Southern Belle*, began, according to his accounts, with a passage to Stockholm in the *jakt Freja*. The *Southern Belle* had been laid up in Stockholm during the winter. The damage of the previous season was repaired in Stockholm, partly with materials brought from Lemland to Stockholm in the *Freja* which also brought provisions for the next season's sailing.

In 1906 Gustaf Erikson was appointed master of the wooden full-rigged ship *Albania*, the property of another Åland shareholding group centred in Mariehamn and in which he held shares. At a meeting of the shareholders in the *Southern Belle* on 6 March 1906, Gustaf Erikson's brother Axel was appointed master for the next season. The managing owner, Emil Sjölund, made his accounts ready for another meeting of the shareholders on 29 December. From

the records of this it is apparent that the shareholders received altogether 5500 marks during the season. To that amount the sum of 1084 marks paid for the provisioning should be added, giving a sum of 82.3 marks per eightieth in the ship. Gustaf Erikson with $^{20}/_{80}$ths got 1646 marks for his shares and provisions during the season of 1905. Axel Eriksson, born in 1876, was to remain master of the *Southern Belle* for eight years.

The *Southern Belle* was employed for the next few years carrying timber and pit-props to Britain from the Gulf of Bothnia ports, returning to the Baltic with coal. Shares changed hands and the vessel was formally sold by auction in 1910, but the new shareholding group contained familiar names. Gustaf Erikson, his mother and his brother Axel continued to own more than half the vessel between them. In his

Southern Belle *in a Swedish timber port.*
Åbo Akademi

absence at sea in command of the *Albania* and in due course the *Lochee*, Gustaf Erikson's wife Hilda acted for him in business affairs. Her authority was given in powers of attorney, which again emphasises the importance of Åland women in the life and economic development of the islands. Thus on 9 November 1909, Gustaf Erikson wrote:

> I herewith authorise my wife Hilda Ottlia Eriksson during my absence in foreign places to sign for the dividend from the ships I own shares in, take out money from the bank, both my own money and the money I am authorised to handle . . . receive the final payment for the selling of forest belonging to our farm Hansas as well as receive the annual lease for the leased land on our farm, crofters leases, days works etc . . .

Besides the $^1/_{10}$th of the *Southern Belle* which he then owned, Gustaf Erikson at that time had shares in the barquentines *Deo Gloria* and *Ceres* and the barques *Ocean, Montrosa, Duguay, Wolfe, Christiane, Augusta* and *Isabel Browne*.

The *Southern Belle* continued to sail mostly to

England with timber and pit-props. After the sailing season of 1913 Gustaf Erikson, who had now left the *Lochee* and retired to the farm, was elected managing owner. In 1914 she made only one voyage, from Härnösand in Sweden to London with timber. From London she sailed to Lovisa in the eastern part of the Gulf of Finland and was laid up there because of the uncertain international situation. Valkom harbour near Lovisa was the shelter for the *Southern Belle* during the whole of the First World War. Here she lay, first under the care of a customs employee, K E Söderlund in 1917 and then in 1918 watched over by one Albert Andersson. These were disturbed times in Finland. The Civil War between the Reds, who wanted union with Soviet Russia, and the Whites, who were determined on Finland's independence, was raging. Ship-keepers were certainly necessary. As early as 1917 Captain A Öfverström from Mariehamn went to Valkom to supervise repairs. Gustaf Erikson wrote to him before he left.

> The sides of the ship are to be painted at least once with oil paint, preferably with the same green colour as before. The decks must be well tarred. The cabin roof, skylight and the poopdeck must be painted. The masts

and the yards are to be oiled, at least the most necessary parts of them. Some of the seams are to be caulked and tarred as before. The sails must be inspected and aired . . . the ballast must be shifted amidships if it is found to be stowed too much in the ends of the ship. If the above mentioned works should be too costly I leave it to you to decide if they are necessary, as well as for you to decide if something else has to be done to the ship . . . If it is difficult to get labour in Valkom it should be possible to get men from home [Åland] for 10 marks a day plus travelling expenses.

Captain Öfverström was very dissatisfied with the ship. She was, as he put it, 'a disgrace for the owners'. In 1918 when Gustaf Erikson sensed the coming demand for tonnage after the war he began intensive work to get the *Southern Belle* back in business. From the very minute matters he dealt with in his frequent letters to the ship-keepers and other people we learn the story of what proved to be a desperate and ultimately unsuccessful venture. Let us follow it in Gustaf Erikson's own words:

To Albert Andersson, Valkom.
July 24th 1918:

Now when it is summer and warm I would like the decks to be tarred, since there should be some tar left on board since last year. On such spots where the tar dries fast, do it once more and preferably on a hot day so the tar really goes into the wood. The cabin roof and poop deck shall be painted if necessary . . .
  There will probably be no sailing any more this summer, a passage in the autumn is perhaps possible. Hoping that you take good care of the ship.
Cordially, G.E.
Managing Owner

P.S. If it is necessary, tar the deck twice.

Albert Andersson did not answer this letter for a while so Gustaf Erikson wrote again on 16 September:

let me know immediately in what condition the ship is, if she is well pumped at all times . . . Now when the autumn rains have started it is important to see that no rainwater leaks on the sails or the ropes . . .

On 25 September Andersson answered Gustaf Erikson's letters. The ship, he said, had been adrift and that had resulted in more extra outlays for towing and anchor lifting. Gustaf Erikson answered on 18 October:

It was sad that the ship has been adrift. The towing and lifting of the anchor I estimate to be about 500 fmk, but Askolin [the owner of the tugboats] asks 6000. I refuse to pay that much. How much chain was out and what was the reason for the coming adrift with the wind coming from land and the ship thus lying leeward of the land?

On 29 November Gustaf Erikson wrote again to A Andersson:

It was good that the anchor held and that you were on board when *Forsby I* [the tugboat] came to move the ship without orders from you or me. I have refused to pay the 6000 marks they ask calling it 'salvage money'. If they had been reasonable asking a few hundred marks for moving the ship I would probably have paid, but now I refuse and make them all responsible according to the law when they entered the ship without permission . . . Have the sails on the windmill pump repaired and pump with it as much as you can since pumping with hired hands is expensive . . .

In the same letter Gustaf Erikson sent an inventory list made up by Captain Öfverström in July 1917 and asks Andersson to check that everything is still there and to take away for the winter some of the smaller items on board, such as running lights, compasses etc. He continued:

The ship has to be caulked all around before loading and Andersson can ask if there are any skilled carpenters around who know how to caulk a ship. If Andersson can find the leak and stop it from the inside I will pay some extra for it. One day when it is absolutely calm without any noise from the sea you have to go around in the hold and listen with the ear against the inside bilge planks where the water comes in and stop the leak from the inside. I have myself found and stopped such leaks. It is mainly through holes in the planking made by worms that the water leaks in.

On 10 December Andersson answered to say that he had found the leak. Gustaf Erikson replied to him on 17 December:

I am glad to hear that nothing has been stolen from the ship. . . . I did guess that the leak could be found in the front of the ship. Captain Gustafsson who rigged the ship down [1914] said that the leak was probably forward. . . . I have heard that the ship lies listed over to one side. If so, then shift some stones in the hold on the opposite side so that she lies on an even keel or else she may be strained.

He ends the letter by wishing Andersson a peaceful Christmas.

On 19 January in a letter to a Swedish firm which apparently tried to get the charter business for Gustaf Erikson's ships, he wrote '. . . the firm H. Clarkson in London has for several years chartered all of my 6 ships and that is why it is difficult to turn to another unknown firm without any reason'. Then follows a short account of the situation of the ships *Grace Harwar* (spelt by Gustaf Erikson as *Graceharwor*), *Professor Koch* (*Professorkock*), *Lawhill*, *Tjerimai*, *Ingrid* and finally the *Southern Belle* of which he writes:

Southern Belle of about 250 standard cut loads lies in Lovisa, Valkom unchartered so far. I am trying to get a cargo from here to Copenhagen or the eastern coast of England at 150–250 Skr per standard. The Gulf of Finland and the Baltic are mined and all traffic has to be under tow along the Finnish and Swedish coasts with an obligatory pilot on board. It is obvious that one cannot accept a lower freight than that mentioned above.

Eventually the *Southern Belle* was chartered for Aalborg in Denmark to load in Strömfors quite near Valkom, just a few miles east. The master was to be Axmar Eriksson from Åland. He went to Valkom at the beginning of April and there received written instructions from Gustaf Erikson as to what he should do to get the ship in sailing order. To cite from the instructions, dated 29 March 1919:

Start immediately to put in a new main piece in the windlass. . . . If the lining is in order and can be used again it has to be broken loose etc. Until the weather gets warmer you can overhaul the sails. . . . Go through them all to see what has to be done on them and at the same time dry and air them on deck. . . . Since there are two mainsails but one is half rotten the other half can be suitable for mending purposes. . . . The ship lost the port anchor on the passage from London to Lovisa in 1914 outside Copenhagen. Instead there is now used a reserve main anchor, but if a suitable anchor can be obtained in Lovisa or nearby and at a reasonable price about 1000 fmk then you can buy it on condition that it is freighted on board for the same amount. . . . If it is too cold to live on board then you have to live ashore, preferably on full pension in a larger room that can be used as a sail-loft at the same time and then you can take ashore one sail after another and have them repaired. Pay off the present ship-keeper the day that you yourself can take over the guarding on board. As soon as the ship is clear of the ice you can have her trimmed bows up and stop the leak if it is not possible to stop the leak from the inside. Examine at the same time the seams in the waterline to find out if the ice has pulled out any oakum. . . . Examine the seams on the outside of the ship to find out if they need to be re-caulked, if so use red-lead putty in the seams over the waterline where she is already caulked in this way. It is as cheap as ordinary pitch, half of which usually gets spilled while one doesn't spill red-lead putty which is applied by a small brush into the seams.

A few years before the war the ship's bottom was caulked on the outside in the yard on Gävle by skilful caulkers, so the outside should be in fairly good condition. . . . If it has started to break loose from the old planking, examine the sheathing carefully, it is $2^1/_2$ inches thick. It was fastened with bolts.* Examine the upper main topgallant yard [*Duguay*'s mainyard of pitch

pine] if it is sound and can be changed to be a lower main topsail yard and the new yard to be put as upper main topgallant yard. . . . If the ship can sail directly through the Gulf of Finland or from Hangö she must put into Mariehamn in ballast on the next journey to take the yards on board. . . . If so, the provisions that have been acquired like meat, pork, peas, potatoes, some butter etc. have to be transported to Valkom or Hangö. . . . The ship is chartered by the shipbrokers Ljungqvist and Gjörding in Lovisa who can give more specific details about the cargo in Strömfors where it is to be loaded. . . . Find out about the loading, if the sawmill will take care of it, or if it is cheaper using the crew.

Gustaf Erikson ended this eight-page letter of instructions: 'In haste, Gustaf Erikson'.

A few days later after having written this long letter of instruction he sent another letter to the new master of the *Southern Belle*. He had made a mistake concerning the windlass; it had not got a single mainpiece but one made up of four different parts. This Gustaf Erikson had found out while talking to his brother Axel. Early in April the master and part of his crew arrived in Valkom and Axmar Eriksson wrote giving his first impressions of the *Southern Belle*:

Valkom Lovisa, April 6 1919

Your letter of April 1st received and the content of it noted. We arrived here last Wednesday afternoon and came on board in the evening. On deck there was about two feet of snow and ice. The snow has now been shovelled overboard and also some of the ice that could be gotten loose from the deck. . . . She is badly hogged . . . the whole ballast is one heap of ice so I do not know how we shall be able to shift it. The hull and the rigging has otherwise kept itself in a fairly good condition. I have not detached any deck leaks . . . We live ashore with a Captain Johansson. Full boarding is impossible to get here. There is such a shortage of food and here in Valkom they [the inhabitants] have even more difficulties because they are so Red. Do you know that the deck-beams are broken in two places by the hatch?

In the years after the Civil War in Finland the people who had been on the Red side (which had been defeated) faced many difficulties. This was particularly so in places where there were many working class people, as in harbour communities like Valkom. In his instructions Gustaf Erikson had mentioned a carpenter, Tallgren, and his partner who had been working before on the *Southern Belle*, but when Axmar Eriksson found him he discovered that Tallgren had just been released from jail and his partner was still there. He wrote about this to Gustaf Erikson, who in his next letter asked if they had had any connections with the Reds. Besides the

---

*It is evident that the *Southern Belle* had at some stage, probably before she was brought to Åland, been 'sheathed', that is replanked over her original planking. This was often done with old wooden ships when the frames had begun to rot and the vessel had been weakened by service with heavy cargoes over many years.

carpenters, Gustaf Erikson also discussed the leak and other matters in a further letter, of 12 April: 'Have you found the leak? Can it be heard in the hold? What about the deck-beams, they have been broken in recent years. Put up firm supports under the place where they are broken'.

On 10 April the master wrote his next letter, telling the managing owner that they were caulking the ship. He also asked for some more members of the crew – the cook and the *konstapel*. The leak had been found, but there was so much ice on the inside of the planking at the bilge that it was impossible to get at it.

Gustaf Erikson answered on 15 April:

If the leak cannot be fixed from the outside you have to try from the inside if it is of such importance that it cannot wait until docking at Aalborg. Look at the rudder-iron bolts above the water to find out if they are still there since the lowest pair of rudder-irons under water are completely away and will have to be renewed at Aalborg. During the difficult passage to Boulogne in 1913 on the last voyage under Axel Eriksson's command

when everybody thought the ship was lost, the rudder broke loose but a pair of rudder-irons were fastened by a diver who said that the lowest pair was missing. But since the ship has made several voyages after that and the rudder is new it will probably hold for one more voyage, but one has to be careful. . . . On Easter Day, 20th, the cook, leading seaman Svibergsson and the carpenter Hugo Lindblad, the brother of the mate, will leave from here. Then there will be an ordinary seaman and an A.B. The rest of the crew will be deckboys. . . . Ask for towing, preferably with a pilot for both the tugboat and the ship included, since the cost for piloting only can mount to one or two thousand marks depending on if it is to Hangö or Mariehamn.

The badly hogged Southern Belle *in her last days. This photograph illustrates a phenomenon which often occurred in the smaller square-rigged vessels. When the yards were braced sharply round, as here on the mainmast, because the lower topsail yard had no lifts, the lee brace pulled down its yardarm and consequently lifted the other, the 'windward' one, until it touched, or nearly touched, the upper topsail yardarm.*
Ålands Sjöfartsmuseum

The repairs to the vessel were carried out in Valkom. The men caulked standing on the ice as long as it was strong enough to bear their weight. When the ice melted two more leaks appeared in the vessel. Gustaf Erikson signed on the crew in Mariehamn and he took a personal interest in them. He arranged matters so that the mother of the two brothers Lang was paid their wages over and above 50 marks each per month. Of Nils Mattsson he wrote that he seemed a good enough boy, and that he had him in mind for the future if he 'intends to learn navigation'.

On 11 May the ship finally reached Strömfors after a six hour tow from Valkom, and began loading. On 18 May Gustaf Erikson wrote to the captain 'It is good to hear that the loading goes so fast that the ship will be able to make two more passages on the Baltic this season'.

The same day he wrote to H J Johansson in Åbo (Turku), a man from Åland who had a tugboat and had promised to take the *Southern Belle* from Strömfors to Mariehamn for 1000 fmk, the pilotage fee included. Gustaf Erikson had previously asked the captain of the *Southern Belle* to inquire about the prices for towage, but the offers were much higher than H J Johansson's. Now he appealed to him as one Ålander to another:

> I have not asked for the prices from others because I can not at all, being an Ålander, do business with the Finns from the mainland, and that is why I now turn to you . . . If we come to this first agreement it is easier for us to come to other ones. I will then point out the *Wellamo* [the tugboat] to other Åland ships in which I have interests and are in need of towage.

On 30 May the skipper wrote to Gustaf Erikson to tell him that the *Southern Belle* had been ready to sail for many days but no tugboat had been heard from. The skipper had had enough, he wanted to leave.

> And I am not well. I have had troubles with my stomach for a week so I'm beginning to feel weak in the legs . . . I think it is better that you try to get another skipper. I think I will not stand it in the long run, it is too tough . . . I herewith resign . . .

On 31 May the tugboat finally arrived, not the *Wellamo* as planned because she had run aground, but another tug commissioned by the same H J Johansson. The journey from Strömfors to Mariehamn took about four days. At Sottunga in the eastern Åland archipelago they ran aground and pieces of the keel were seen floating up. Gustaf Erikson protested at the court in Mariehamn and refused to pay the full amount for the towage until the matter was cleared up. Gustaf Erikson did manage to

get the skipper to stay on, in a letter to Aalborg dated 26 June he wrote that he was willing to raise the monthly wages by 100 marks from 900 to 1000 'for much work during the repairs etc'. He promised even more if there was to be one more voyage that season across the North Sea. Axmar Eriksson did not want to sail with the *Southern Belle* across the North Sea but Gustaf Erikson wanted him to try to arrange a load of cement or some other cargo to take from Aalborg to northern Finland or Sweden and then one more load of timber to Denmark.

But it had for long been more than evident that the *Southern Belle*'s sailing days were over and on 1 July Gustaf Erikson wrote to shipbroker Otto Hellsten in Stockholm and offered her for sale for 75,000 to 80,000 Skr.

The same day he also wrote to a lawyer in Helsingfors asking him to get an export permit for the vessel which as he put it '. . . is almost unusable although I put 35,000 fmk in her repairs, she leaks so much that one pump has to be going day and night, she is expected to Aalborg in Denmark where I want to sell the wreck.'

Meanwhile the *Southern Belle* had reached Helsingör on 27 June after having experienced some rough weather off Bornholm where the leak increased. On 1 July the ship finally reached her destination and started to discharge. After this was complete the skipper tried to get the *Southern Belle*

The Lumparsund in 1984. Here the Southern Belle *was dismantled and the* Carmen *built on the opposite shore. Part of the* Southern Belle's *last ballast, of flint, can still be found among the granite rocks in the foreground.*
Basil Greenhill

The barque Carmen *building at Granboda, Lemland in 1921. Of much the same size as the* Southern Belle, *the latter's masts, spars, rigging and many fittings were used in her construction. Built to be converted to a motor ship as soon as she had earned enough money, in fact the engine was never fitted and she remained a sailing vessel until her loss in 1934.*
Ålands Sjöfartsmuseum

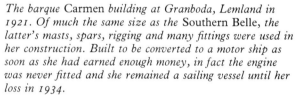

docked, but because of the very bad hogging (no less than 41 inches) the yard at Råå refused to take up the ship.

After several attempts to dispose of the vessel abroad Gustaf Erikson finally managed to sell her to the owners of the shipyard in Granboda, in Lemland. The price was quite high, 56,000 marks. *Southern Belle* began her last passage, from Helsingborg on 12 August. Even on this last passage there was trouble, one of the rudder-irons mentioned before had broken loose, part of the rudder was missing and the ship would not steer. The mate and the *konstapel* were lowered over the side and managed somehow to fix the rudder. On 19 August she anchored at Föglö and the following day she was towed to Granboda. There the barque *Carmen* had been under construction since the spring of 1917. *Carmen* was designed by shipbuilder Georg Grönfors and he had drafted her to the dimensions of the *Southern Belle*. The yard used the equipment from the latter vessel in finishing, rigging and fitting out *Carmen*.

When the *Southern Belle* was sold she had only four shareholders and they divided the sum as follows:

Ivar Eriksson	$^3/_{40}$	4,200
Eligius Sommarström	$^2/_{40}$	2,800
Erik Nylund	$^4/_{40}$	5,600
Gustaf Erikson	$^{31}/_{40}$	43,400
		56,000

If Gustaf Erikson's quoted sum of 35,000 marks for the outlay on repairs is correct then he probably made a profit from her in the end. In 1929, ten years after her last sailing season, the final dividend to the part-owners of the *Southern Belle* was paid out, a sum of 10,241.15 marks of which Gustaf Erikson received 7936.31 marks.

Carmen.
Åbo Akademi

Chapter 5

ÅLAND IN TRANSITION

Åland's seafaring history would have been very different had it paralleled the pattern of development evident in a number of other seaboard communities. If this had been the case, after the turn of the century no more vessels would have been acquired. The old wooden barques would have been slowly worn out, first in ocean trade and then, as they became more and more leaky and delapidated, in the timber trade from the Gulf of Bothnia ports to Britain. Finally they would have been employed only inside the Baltic in the short summer months, taking timber to Denmark and North Germany. As in some other areas dependent on wooden sailing vessels and without outlets for investment ashore, it is possible that Åland might have reverted to a sleepy rural area of marginal farming and fishing, with a few *jakter* and *galeaser* employed in local trade. In due course tourism might have developed and unusually enterprising farmer–shipowners who had managed to acquire sufficient capital might have invested it in mainland Finland. This decline of a seafaring society took place in Prince Edward Island in Canada, a community of comparable size, which once launched a hundred ships a year, and much the same happened in the small ports of south west Britain, like Bideford, and in the Welsh villages, like Porthmadog. The pattern was repeated in a slightly more complicated fashion, with an intermediate period of investment locally ashore, in Yarmouth and other Nova Scotian ports which were once the homes of greater fleets of wooden deep sea sailing ships than Åland ever mustered.

Åland's micro-economy took a different course. The old barques wore out, and they went in various ways through the stages described above. Fowey, Plymouth, Teignmouth, Exmouth, Bridport, Newhaven, Dover, Ramsgate, the discharging places on London's river, Ipswich, Yarmouth, Grimsby, Hull, Shields and the Tyne, were a few of the places which saw Åland vessels in the decades around the turn of the century. The very last of them, the venerable *Sverre* of Wårdö, (aged sixty-nine but rebuilt in 1920 and the last barque-rigged sailing vessel working at sea in the Western world) was lost as late as December 1941 near Lågskär Lighthouse south of Mariehamn. But as the old ships gradually became less and less profitable, the men who had been most successful in the operation of old wooden vessels did not transfer their money to Helsinki or Turku, instead they invested in the relatively new iron and steel sailing vessels. By the 1890s such vessels were beginning to come on to the world tonnage market at lower and lower prices. By 1900 besides the sixty-two wooden barques with their total tonnage of 38,000 tons there were eight iron and steel vessels owned in Åland, much larger vessels than their wooden predecessors, totalling between them 11,000 tons.

The principal, if not sole, occupation of the new generation of professional shipowners who began to emerge in the 1870s, was the management of new bigger wooden ships. These sailed the oceans all the year round and rarely came home to Åland. Their owners no longer farmed but set themselves up in business in the new town of Mariehamn. Here international communications were much easier than in the country districts and banking and insurance services had developed. The enterprise to acquire the new big iron and steel vessels was initially that of the families of the great pioneers, Mathias Lundqvist

75

The barque Sverre *of Wårdö, built in 1872 and lost in December 1941, was the last barque-rigged sailing vessel working at sea in the Western world. She is seen here lying in Turku (Åbo) in 1927*

Lars Grönstrand

senior of Lemland and the almost legendary Mathias Mattsson 'Varg Matte' of Vargata in Wårdo.

The first of Åland's great professional shipowners was Nicolai Sitkoff. He was the storekeeper of Ämnäs in Finström and his name indicates a Russian origin, of a family which had been brought to Åland by the public works at Bomarsund. He began his career in the boom years of wooden ships at the beginning of the 1870s and was concerned only with

wooden vessels. When he died in 1887 he had become the foremost person involved with shipping in Åland. In all he managed twenty-two vessels of which the largest, tiny by comparison with later vessels, was the 800 ton barque *Svea*. Among his vessels was the barque *Mariehamn*, built at Dundee in 1866 by the Tay Ship Company as the *Lieutenant*. In 1882 after carrying a cargo of timber from Stockholm to Capetown under Captain August Lauren of Mariehamn, she sailed for Melbourne, and she was the first Åland vessel to visit Australia. In Melbourne she received orders to load guano at Malden Island, east of Samoa, for Kastrup in Denmark. On this passage on 30 July 1882, she became the first Åland vessel to round Cape Horn and when she arrived at Kastrup after a passage of 136 days she became the first Åland vessel to have circumnavigated the world.

Nicolai Sitkoff died in 1887 at the early age of fifty-nine. Robert Mattson, son of Mathias Mattsson, succeeded him as Åland's greatest shipowner. He had been a sailor in his father's vessels and had commanded the family barque *Olga*. Although Åland's first iron vessel, the full-rigged ship *Theodorus*, was owned in Lemland partly by Gustaf Erikson's brother Axel (lost on her maiden voyage as an Åland vessel in 1884), it was Robert Mattson who began the large scale acquisition of iron and steel sailing vessels. The shares were still relatively widely distributed, but the ships were run (in conjunction with a shipchandlery) from a small office in a Mariehamn house as a full-time business and the sums of money involved in their operation were considerably larger than any handled a decade before.

Robert Mattson was to be the principal owner of thirty-one vessels, including eleven large iron and steel barques. These vessels were sailed profitably by the Ålanders at the beginning of this century, at a time when the shipowners of western Europe and Britain were disposing of them at less than half, perhaps a quarter, of the amount they cost to build a few years before. The Ålander's were able to do this because economic necessity, social custom and a strong seafaring tradition, coupled with the rigours of life ashore, had produced a very strong and virile people, and ensured first class masters, mates and crews at low cost. Management was highly personal and overheads were reduced to an absolute minimum. When the Dumbarton-built iron full-rigged ship *Thomasina MacLelland* was bought in 1905 her name was shortened to simple *Thomasina*, to save cable charges, so it was said.

A man of the same calibre as Robert Mattson was

Above: Thomasina, *ex* Thomasina MacLellan, *owned by August Troberg from 1905 to 1915.*

Åbo Akademi

Below: August, *ex* Tropic, *owned by August Troberg from 1911 to 1917.*

Ålands Sjöfartsmuseum

another former master of the *Olga*, Matts Mattsson's son-in-law August Troberg. His family came from Lemland and began shipowning in 1897, the year in which the final disposal of big sailing ships by British owners began, and continued for exactly twenty years until 1917, during the First World War when the value of tonnage reached astronomic heights. At one period August Troberg owned nine large iron and steel barques, including some of the finest vessels ever to sail from Åland, *August, Borrowdale, Garnet Hill* (in which the father of the present president of Finland, Mr Koivisto, served as carpenter) *Lawhill, Margareta*, and the long-lived barque *Prompt*.

From a house and farm at Västergård in Vargata in Wårdö came the third of Åland's great shipowners of the period of transition from wooden barques to great iron and steel sailing ships. This was Mathias

Mathias Lundqvist junior in the big dining room of the house he built at Västergård, Vargata. Note the great stove in the background.
Hilding Lundqvist

Garnet Hill *owned by August Troberg from 1912 to 1917.*
Åbo Akademi

Mathias Lundqvist junior's Frieda, *ex* County of Edinburgh, *the only four-masted full-rigged ship to have been owned in Åland.*
Ålands Sjöfartsmuseum

Lundqvist junior, son of the pioneer capital generator of the years after the fall of Bomarsund, Mathias Lundqvist of Lemland. Mathias junior married another daughter of 'Varg Matte', but while his brothers-in-law moved to Mariehamn and operated as full time professional shipowners, Mathias Lundqvist junior stayed on the old Mattsson estate at Västergård and, though he operated a fleet of iron and steel sailing vessels second to none, he and his son Arthur continued the old life as farmer–shipowners, in the style of the flourishing days of the 1860s and 1870s. Among his big vessels were the four-masted full-rigged ship *Frieda*, the magnificent full-rigged ships, *Parchim* and *Pera* and, after August Troberg had disposed of her, the barque *Prompt*.

Today Vargata is a quiet little group of houses on the high ground above a valley of fertile fields flowing up from Båthusviken, the western harbour of Wårdö. Only a few centuries ago this valley was itself a *vik* and before the land rose out of the sea small vessels moored where the road from Båthusviken sweeps round to the church and the junction with the north–south road which runs the length of the island. This is one of the most historic places in Åland. A staging post on the post route, roughly halfway across

the Åland archipelago, it has known travellers for centuries. There is an account from 1799 by Edward Clarke portraying the conditions in which people stayed when they stopped off on the long winter nights on their journey from Stockholm towards St Petersburg. He describes how the naked company slept in bunks, one above the other, and breakfast began, even for the babies, with a dram of firewater.

Matts Mattsson's house of the 1860s stands quietly on the edge of the garden of a much bigger house, built higher up the hill by Mathias Lundqvist junior at about the turn of the century. Great barns stand around the contour of the hill to the west. The Lundqvist house is full of the evidence of the prosperity of the dynasty which built it; family portraits, contemporary paintings of great ships, relics of seafaring. After Mathias Lundqvist died in 1926 his son Arthur, master and principal owner of the full-rigged ship *Parchim*, lived here. He farmed and was a shareholder in a number of the wooden vessels, which survived in this rural community of Wårdö to the very end of the sailing ship era. Today the estate of Västergård is farmed by his son Hilding and the relics of the last old ships are still to be found as pieces of garden sculpture – a spiderband from the barque *Altai* around a conical pillar of the local pink granite, anchors and chains, and a signal gun. In an outhouse on the north side of the garden is the old bakehouse where the bread was made which lasted the Baltic and North Sea traders for the whole summer and autumn sailing. All sorts of odds and ends of equipment lie around.

Matts Mattsson's house, 'the yellow house', once half home, half general and ship chandlers store, is now the summer home for some members of the family and of close friends. The big room which was once the shop is a delightful, light, airy living room. The only shop on the island today, the Samgång, is a few hundred yards up the sandy road. This functions as a little supermarket, post office and bank and people come to it from all over the island and from the other inhabited islands nearby. Once teeming with activity, now well farmed and maintained, Västergård and the neighbouring properties of the Olofssons and the Johanssons and the other big, red painted, wooden houses clustered round the little hills, are the historic centre of the most intensive rural shipowning in Åland.

Today there is a very tangible relic of Vargata's past to be seen in Turku (Åbo). The barque *Sigyn* of Wårdö, is magnificently restored and preserved in the harbour. For years owned in this community, she sailed from here in the traditional way, until the end of the 1930s, lying each winter in Båthusviken and fitting out in the spring for the summer sailing. She is the world's last wooden three-masted square-rigged cargo-carrying merchant sailing ship – the very last example of a vehicle which, from its development in the fifteenth century to its demise in the late nineteenth century, played a fundamental part in European history, in the exploration and colonisation which shaped the modern world, in the development of world trade and industrialisation, and in the migrations of people which populated the north American continent and Australia. It is possible to go on board her and see how her people lived in the hut-like forecastle on deck, and the tiny poop cabins, with the thick tree-like mizzen mast coming down through the little saloon and right through the table where the master and mates ate together. One can see the galley where the food was prepared and the massive windlass which the crew laboured, with the pumping

Mathias Lundqvist's house at Västergård shortly after it was built in the early years of this century. The old Matts Mattsson house (page 40) can be seen in the background to the right.
Hilding Lundqvist

action characteristic of these devices to bring up the anchors. She was saved from slow decay in one of Åland's *viks* by the farsighted and continuous enterprise of a group of men associated with the Swedish Language University, the Åbo Akademi, to which she belongs. She is a monument of world importance and on her transom in raised gold-painted lettering are the words *Sigyn*–Wårdö.

The development of Åland's fleet of iron and steel sailing vessels was very rapid after the turn of the century. In 1900, besides sixty-two wooden barques and sixty-one other large wooden sailing vessels, Ålander's owned eight iron and steel sailing ships. In 1914 at the outbreak of the First World War the Åland-owned tonnage comprised nineteen wooden barques, twenty-seven other large wooden sailing vessels, and no less than twenty-six large iron and steel sailing ships, fifteen of which had been acquired in the three years since 1911. Of these some $^4/_5$ths were owned by the triumvirate: Robert Mattson and August Troberg of Mariehamn and Mathias Lundqvist junior of Wårdö. The wooden vessels were still mostly owned and managed in the old way by farmer–shareholders distributed widely in the archipelago, though principally living in traditional shipowning communities.

The initial purchases of iron and steel sailing vessels showed great courage and business foresight. It was this investment in relatively modern, if obsolescent, tonnage at the crucial point when Åland might simply have reverted to rural slumber as the old wooden ships were disposed of, that set her on the road to modern prosperity. Mattson, Troberg and Lundqvist were perhaps the most important figures in Åland's modern history.

During the First World War, Åland shipowners were in a peculiar position. Until 1917 and the collapse of the Czarist regime, the Ålanders, as Russian nationals, were formally on the side of the Western Allies. The Baltic was closed to the Western Allies by the German navy and the Åland vessels which were in that sea at the outbreak of war in August 1914 remained there. The unlucky ones were caught in, or on their way to, German ports and fifteen of these were taken as prizes of war by the German government. Other Baltic traders, caught either loading in Finland or discharging in Danish ports, were laid up, a number of them to be sold in

A Russian officer visits young people at Västergård during the First World War.
Hilding Lundqvist

Above: Sigyn *outward bound for Pernambuco from* Göteborg *on 25 May 1899.*

Lars Grönstrand

Below: the simple saloon in the typical wooden barque Sigyn *can be compared with the splendid accommodation for the master of the* Herzogin Cecilie *(see page 108).*

Basil Greenhill

Sigyn *as she lies in Åbo today*.
Basil Greenhill

due course to Danish or (after 1917) to German owners. For some months following the outbreak of war the world freight market was more or less paralysed while industry and shipowners waited to see what the initial effects of hostilities would be. Not until the late autumn did prospects improve, panic abate, and freights begin slowly to rise. By 1915 the situation began to look very satisfactory from the shipowners' point of view. Many of the Åland vessels which had been outside the Baltic when war broke out had been laid up in the friendly harbours of Western powers.

The old wooden North Sea barques began to make money. No less than ten of them were caught in British ports and as freight rates rose some of these vessels, which had previously been employed only in the North Sea trade, being quite obsolete as tonnage competing in the world freight markets, were able to find employment at increasingly lucrative rates in the long range deep sea trade which they had sailed in their youth. A classic example is provided by the old barque *Fredenborg*, built in Geta Community in 1881, which arrived in Rochester with a cargo of timber from the Gulf of Bothnia on 1 August 1914. She had recently been acquired by an Åland shareholding group whose total investment had been some 17,000 finnmarks. She was sold to mainland Finnish owners in May 1916, for three times her investment cost and at once fixed to load timber in Canada at a freight which represented something like fifteen times the value of the vessel in 1914.

But, of course, it was the big iron and steel sailing vessels which really made money once freight rates began to rise. All of them were outside the Baltic at the outbreak of war. By 1915 it was worthwhile getting men out of Åland to man them and sail them, despite the appalling difficulties of communication.

83

The barque Slamat, *owned by August Troberg from 1896 until 1913 when she was wrecked in a snowstorm on the Swedish coast. She is seen here lying in Bristol, the building behind her is now the Arnolfini Art Gallery.*
Bristol Museum and Art Gallery

The crews travelled by devious routes, for instance from Åbo by steamer, by train to the Swedish frontier to the north, by train across Sweden and Norway and steamer from a Norwegian port to Britain. Freights by 1917 were astronomically high. In the trade from Pensacola to Britain with pitch pine they multiplied about fivefold between 1914 and early 1917. In addition freights were now prepaid, that is, instead of having to raise money to outfit for the voyage and pay interest on the loan, shipowners found shippers competing to pay them in advance, so that far from having to pay interest, they could invest the surplus money at once in additional tonnage and earn yet more big prepaid freights.

Freights were paid to the Ålanders in sterling or US dollars, and in general were kept in British banks, which meant that they represented a first class asset when ruinous inflation of Finnish currency developed after the Civil War. Thus the Åland shipowners were able to survive the awful losses which followed the intensification of the German U-boat blockade of Britain and France in 1917. During

the first half of that year, nine of Åland's finest deep sea sailing vessels were sunk in the western approaches to Britain: six barques and three full-rigged ships. Robert Mattson and August Troberg both sold out their shipping interests during the boom years of tonnage values and transferred their business operations to Helsinki. August Troberg donated some of his money to build Mariehamn's modern church and presented the town where he had made his fortune with his house, which was later used as an old peoples' home, the *Trobergshemmet*. Robert Mattson's house in Mariehamn, pulled down in recent years, disgorged his business papers which are now owned by the Ålands Sjöfartsmuseum. Robert Mattson continued his successful business career on the mainland and remained a shipowner. In 1930 he

Robert and Adele Lundqvist setting out to visit relatives in Lemland by travelling on sleighs across the ice of the frozen Lumparfjärd in the winter of 1919.

Hilding Lundqvist

was the owner of three of Finland's largest steamers of the time.

By the end of the war the Åland fleet had been reduced by wartime losses, capture and sales, to some twenty-five vessels with a total tonnage of 23,500. Locally constructed tonnage, twenty-two wooden barques, barquentines and schooners, was mostly completed too late to earn its building costs, much less make fortunes in the shipping boom which collapsed so soon after the end of the war. But during the war a new big shipowner emerged in Åland, Gustaf Erikson, who had begun his career as principal shareholder and managing owner with the *Southern Belle*. His story has been told many times, most fully and authoritatively in Georg Kåhre's *The Last Tall Ships*.* He was to become internationally famous as the last shipowner in the world to operate a fleet of big square-rigged merchant sailing ships in general ocean trade. It was Gustaf Erikson's vessels

which dominated the Grain Races which made Åland famous in the 1930s. It can be argued that perhaps more important in the long run was Gustaf Erikson's persistence and business acumen which enabled Åland to survive the recession in shipping after the First World War and to continue as a shipowning society for a further period of capital accumulation, which made possible the eventual transition from sailing to powered vessels. The actual initiative for this great transition, so important to the continuity of Åland's history and the development of her present day prosperity, was taken by Hugo Lundqvist, eldest son of Mathias of Wårdö.

To summarise Gustaf Erikson's story, as it has emerged from recent research (some of it involving documents not available when George Kåhre wrote his account): Gustaf Erikson came from a relatively prosperous Lemland farming and shipowning family and by the early years of this century had acquired shares in ten or more vessels. Though his holdings were small, he was very different to sea captains who lacked the capital and opportunity of acquiring any more money, like many of his British contemporaries. His background was by no means that of the barefoot boy. He was maintaining a family tradition of farming, shipowning and seafaring which went back

The Last Tall Ships by Georg Kåhre edited by Basil Greenhill, London, 1978.

to his grandfather before the Crimean War. How wide his horizons actually were in 1913 is a matter of speculation.

When, in 1913, he gave up active seafaring and returned to the family farm, besides his managing ownership of the *Southern Belle* he had shares in six other vessels. In the same year he joined a shareholding group set up to purchase an old Dutch-built composite barque, the *Tjerimai*. Gustaf Erikson took up $^{40}/_{100}$ths and was appointed managing owner. He was then forty-one with twenty-nine years spent largely at sea behind him.

Troberg, Mattson and Lundqvist and one or two others in the three years before the outbreak of the war acquired fifteen big steel barques, magnificent new tonnage by Åland standards, alongside which the

A votive model of Gustaf Erikson's barque Tjerimai *hangs today in the great church built by shipowner August Troberg in Mariehamn.*
Basil Greenhill

The 'Lucky' Lawhill, *owned by Gustaf Erikson from 1917 to 1942.*
Åbo Akademi

little old *Tjerimai* looked rather a small enterprise. She was put into the Baltic timber trade to western Europe with a cargo from a Finnish mainland port to London at a freight of £1080. On her first two passages her shareholders were paid £650, and Erikson himself must have received £260, more than a third of his investment, back in six months. This was the way Åland shipping worked in the era of secondhand tonnage in the good years.

But not every year was a good year. The freights offered in the Baltic timber trade in the summer of 1914 were down more than a quarter on 1913 and Gustaf Erikson, despite the age and condition of *Tjerimai* (her copper sheathing is said to have been in rags and tatters which made her unsuitable for trade in southern waters) succeeded in getting a good fixture for her to load lumber at Matane on the Gulf of St Lawrence for Liverpool. When the First World War broke out *Tjerimai* was not in the Baltic but in mid Atlantic, and it can be argued that the survival of the big merchant sailing ship in European waters until the middle of the twentieth century resulted from that one accidental circumstance alone. In the next few years the *Tjerimai* made a series of voyages with timber across the Atlantic at very high rates. She received (at 1985 values) £17.50 per standard from Matane to Portishead in October 1916 and £23.80 from Pensecola to Liverpool in 1917, freights which before the war would have been nearer £2.12. As a result, dividends paid out to shareholders in 1916 amounted to 550 per cent of the old vessel's purchase price. These profits were ploughed back into newly acquired sailing tonnage and a fleet was built up.

By 1919 Gustaf Erikson had purchased in total seven big iron or steel square-rigged sailing ships, a wooden barque and the big three-masted schooner *Ingrid*, (though some of these vessels had been sold again, one had been wrecked and two others sunk by U-boats). He had acquired shares in a number of other vessels of which he was not the principal owner. Perhaps the most important and successful of his fleet at this stage was the steel four-masted barque *Lawhill*, which was Finland's largest merchant ship. She was dubbed in the Erikson family the 'Lucky *Lawhill*' because of the important role she was to play in saving the fortunes of the fleet during the shipping depression of the early 1920s. At the other end of the scale in size was the Geta-built schooner *Ingrid* which was later sold to become a British rum runner during the American prohibition period. She is believed to have been the only Åland-built vessel ever to have been sold to and owned in Britain.

Had it not been for the luck of the *Tjerimai*'s availability to earn big freight on deep water during the First World War, Gustaf Erikson could never have acquired the capital to operate on the scale which was open to him after the war. He was a man of driving restless energy and enormous business flair and he found fulfilling and perhaps quite unexpected use for these assets in a second career as a big shipowner.

At the end of the First World War Gustaf Erikson and other Åland shipowners found themselves faced with a difficult choice – to remain in sailing-shipowning or to give up shipowning altogether. Åland was now a significant shipowning area of Finland. During the war considerable fortunes had

Paul Kåhre, master of Mozart, *who used the long hours at sea under sail to translate Byron and Shelley into Swedish.*
Karl Kåhre

Mozart *in the Southern Ocean. She is running in wild weather under her square sails only. The gaff sails, as so often in* Mozart *under such conditions, are on deck under repair.*
Karl Kåhre

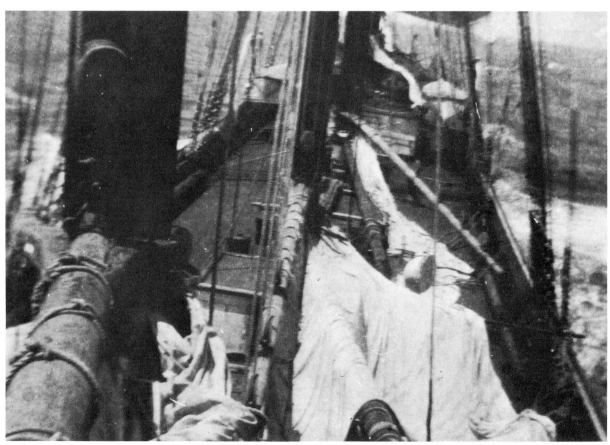

been made by running appalling financial risks in what retrospectively seems to have been an almost impossible situation of vessel management. Money was now available for further investment, but not enough, under the old patterns of shares ownership and management of the vessel by the ship's husband,

Herzogin Cecilie *photographed on 22 March 1922, shortly after she had been bought by Gustaf Erikson.*
Rederi ab Gustaf Erikson

to acquire and operate secondhand steam tonnage. Much else was in their favour. Åland had a first class seafaring and ship management tradition and a corps of highly competent shipmasters and mates with a high educational standard. To give just one example, Paul Kåhre, master of the four-masted barquentine *Mozart*, used to while away the long hours on the annual voyage to Australia in the 1920s by translating Byron and Shelley into Swedish. There could have been few shipmasters in the world at the time who

Gustaf Erikson aged fifty in 1922, the year in which he bought Herzogin Cecilie.

Edgar Erikson

combined the cultural skills necessary to do this with the seamanship skills required of the commander of the *Mozart*, which was not an easy vessel to sail.

Some big owners like Mattson and Troberg and a few smaller owners had, of course, left the business in Åland at the end of the war while the going was good and tonnage commanded very high prices. The Lundqvists remained sailing ship owners, operating from their farm in Wårdö and expanding their fleet with both long range and Baltic trading vessels. Many small shipowners also continued their operations. Like the Lundqvists, but with more vessels, Gustaf Erikson, the newest big shipowner, went on buying ships as the rest of the Western world disposed of the very last of its sailing fleet. His vessels attracted more and more attention as merchant sailing ships became rarer and rarer and their names, *Herzogin Cecilie*, *Olivebank*, *Killoran*, *Viking*, *Eläköön*, *Carmen*,

Hougomont, *owned by Gustaf Erikson from 1925 to her dismasting in 1932. Her handsome cast iron forecastle bell mounting is now in the Ålands Sjöfartsmuseum and is being copied for the mounting of* The Great Britain's *forecastle bell.*

Åbo Akademi

Valborg, Baltic, Hougomont, Penang and many more became almost legendary in Europe and North America.

So, in the later 1920s, the shipowning and farming community in the Åland Islands presented an extraordinary phenomenon. More than forty years after the development of the triple expansion engined steamship had rendered the large square-rigged sailing ship obsolete, exactly thirty years after 1897, when the building of such vessels in any number ceased in Britain, and nearly twenty years after the continuous building of big wooden schooners in North America had ceased, in a Western world in which long range sea transport was almost totally conducted in powered vessels, the Åland shipowning community was living entirely off the operation of sailing tonnage. But as no new sailing vessels were being built, and because the cost of building them would be so high they would be unable to earn their keep, this situation could not last.

On 5 February 1927, the newspaper *Åland* published an article by Captain Hugo Lundqvist, son of Mathias Lundqvist junior of Wårdö. Hugo Lundqvist was the managing owner of a fleet of sailing vessels including the *Mozart, Ponape, Plus, Prompt, Thekla, Zaritza* and *Hildur* which he operated from a single room in his house in Mariehamn. In his article he said:

> With good reason, Åland's maritime traffic may be called its second principal industry. In order, however, to maintain it in a lively condition, it is necessary for it to undergo a development which will bring it into line with the conditions of our day . . . The transition from old to new always entails some hesitation and the same prudence was to be observed when Ålanders ceased to buy old wooden merchant vessels from America and made their transition to the then modern steel and iron vessels built mostly between the years 1885 and 1895 . . . That problem was, however, relatively easy to solve as compared with the present one, namely the transition from sail to power driven tonnage . . . Åland is not sufficiently strong in capital for the purchase of newly built steamship tonnage, rather it is reduced for a start to the buying of secondhand vessels of this kind.

Hugo Lundqvist believed that it was time for history to repeat itself if Åland was to survive as a prosperous shipowning community, and that the way to enable this to happen was to abandon the system of ownership of vessel property in one hundredth shares and adopt the limited liability joint stock company. He also strongly urged changes in the local tax laws to allow depreciation to be offset against tax.

A few days earlier he had written a letter to Gustaf Erikson which can be freely translated as follows:

Hugo Lundqvist's Thekla *in Cumberland Basin, Bristol.*
Bristol Museum and Art Gallery

I imagine that as usual you are interested in what is going on. For this reason I will get straight down to business. Our mutual interests dictate it as my duty to offer you before anyone else the opportunity to join in the steamship company I plan, and which is now almost certain to come into being. When I was in Helsinki I succeeded in persuading my cousin Curt Matsson [a son of Robert] to take shares in the venture and I think he will put in half a million marks . . . I dare to hope that you will participate in the reorganisation of Åland shipping to the extent of a few hundred thousand.

Gustaf Erikson replied at once,

I will join your steamship company with great interest. It is very clear that we have to start sooner or later with steamers since there are no more sailing vessels for sale. I will decide the size of my investment after I know if *Olivebank* reaches Port Lincoln before her charter is cancelled.

On 12 March 1927, the *Åland* carried an invitation to subscribe to shares for the Alfa Steamship Company Limited, with Hugo Lundqvist as executive director. He put half a million finnmarks into the new company; Gustaf Erikson invested a hundred thousand finnmarks and others invested similar sums. The new company bought the twenty-two-year-old German-built, 3000 tons deadweight, tramp steamer *Thornbury* for £13,000 and they were to run her profitably for thirty years.

After 1927 other steamship companies were formed in Åland. Although Gustaf Erikson invested in shares in steamship companies and purchased steamers, he continued to invest in sail until he bought his last large sailing vessel, the four-masted barque *Moshulu*, in 1935. In 1942 he bought his last sailing vessel of any kind, the three-masted *galeas Sirius*. The acquisition of steam vessels by the Erikson company began in 1937, though two wooden motor ships, the *Sweden* and the *Vera*, had been bought for the timber trade in 1933, and as early as 1947, the year of Gustaf Erikson's death, sixteen steamers and eight motor ships were owned and operated under the G E Flag. But the last deepwater sailing passages with cargo were made by the four-masted barques, *Passat* and *Pamir* under the management of Edgar Erikson as late as 1949. These voyages were not profitable.

Hugo Lundqvist (1878–1936), the pioneer of Åland steamships.
Ålands Sjöfartsmuseum

Thornbury, *built in 1905 and bought by the Alfa Steamship Company of Mariehamn in 1927. She was run profitably for thirty years.*
Lundqvist Rederiana

Penang's *foremast. She is being sailed too close to the wind. The royals are doing nothing and the upper topgallants little more.*
C S Cooper-Essex

Chapter 6

THE GRAIN RACES

How were Åland's last big sailing ships employed and how was the capital generated which made possible the prosperous Åland of today? In Åland some thirty gross registered tons of modern shipping are owned per capita – six times as much tonnage owned per head of the nearest northern rival, Norway.

For a short time after the end of the First World War there was a shipping boom. The war risks were gone but there was a continuation of the high pre-paid freights which had prevailed from 1916 onwards. For four years the whole world had in one way or another been preoccupied with Europe's civil war and there were shortages of everything everywhere, particularly of food in Europe. The shipping boom did not last long because the rapid building of steam-propelled bulk carriers, mainly in British yards, soon brought about a surplus of tonnage and a drop in freight rates, which was catastrophic for those who had speculated too late in new vessels. But while it lasted there was money to be made with sailing ships. Gustaf Erikson, as George Kåhre clearly shows in *The Last Tall Ships*, now had relatively large sums of money at his disposal with which he purchased new tonnage. In 1921 some sixty-two sailing vessels were fixed to carry nitrate from Chile to Europe. In the same year no less than sixty-eight sailing vessels were fixed to carry grain from Australia to European ports. But the next year only seven vessels were employed in this trade.

Nevertheless in the early 1920s because of Åland's unique local conditions, described in the previous chapter, Åland sailing vessels could continue to be sailed profitably. In the disastrous year of 1922 Gustaf Erikson had, besides the venerable money spinner *Tjerimai*, the full-rigged ship *Grace Harwar*,

the barques *Woodburn*, *Professor Koch* and *Loch Linnhe* and the four-masted barques *Lawhill*, *Herzogin Cecilie* and *Pommern*. Mathias Lundqvist and his sons managed from their farm in Wårdö, the full-rigged ship *Parchim* and the barque *Altai*, and from Mariehamn the barques *Prompt*, *Plus*, and *Zaritza*, and the four-masted barquentine *Mozart*. The employment of these vessels was still very varied. Between 1922 and 1932 *Grace Harwar*, although she is remembered principally as a Grain Racer, took timber from the Baltic to Australia, saltpetre to Bristol, timber from the Gulf of St Lawrence to Buenos Aires, timber from Canada to Australia (twice), coal from Swansea to South Africa, guano from Peru to North Carolina, fertiliser from England to Mauritius, and only four wheat cargoes from Australia to England. But in the last three years of her life from 1932 until she was broken up in 1935 she did nothing else. In the early 1920s *Lawhill* was similarly employed with coal, timber and nitrate, but after 1927 until the Second World War she carried nothing but Australian wheat. From time to time she took timber cargoes on the outward voyage and in 1933, during a Russian embargo on the export of timber which led to great prosperity in the Finnish and Swedish timber trade, an historic cargo of timber from Finland to London at a high freight. This was one of the largest timber cargoes ever carrried by a sailing vessel to London; other big cargoes were transported by *Mozart* and *Parma* in the same year.

The Grain Race was, in fact, a phenomenon of ten years, the period from 1928 to 1939. By then, though there were large numbers of sailing vessels of various sizes and varieties at work throughout the world, virtually the only big square-rigged steel and iron

Grace Harwar, *owned by Gustaf Erikson from 1916 to
1935, lying in Mariehamn's Western Harbour. She was
the Western world's last merchant full-rigged ship.*
Åbo Akademi

sailing vessels offering for cargoes in the general
carrying trade were owned in Åland, and, when the
Lundqvists turned to steam in the late 1920s, they
were almost entirely vessels owned by Gustaf
Erikson. After 1928 it became increasingly difficult to
find any but the rarest cargoes, other than bagged
wheat from Australia, at freights which made for
reasonable net return on the capital invested in the
venture. Meanwhile the Baltic timber trade and the
trade from the Bothnia ports to Britain also continued
to provide paying employment for sailing vessels in
good years.

In the 1920s grain from Australia comprised only
twenty-three per cent of the total of cargoes carried in
Åland sailing vessels. Timber, guano, nitrates, coal
and other cargoes made up the remaining three-
quarters of the total. But in the 1930s grain
completely dominated. Outward freights to Australia
were few and far between. The most common was
timber to South Africa – sixteen cargoes of timber

Penang *in Falmouth, June 1936.*
C S Cooper-Essex

Below: **Viking, Penang** *(right) coming up to join* **Killoran** *and* **Herzogin Cecilie** *(left) in the Western Harbour, Mariehamn.*
Ålands Sjöfartsmuseum

Virgo.
Ålands Sjöfartsmuseum

Oaklands, *owned by Arthur Andersson.*
Åbo Akademi

were carried in the decade. Eight cargoes of guano were taken to New Zealand from the Seychelles Islands and four cargoes of artificial fertiliser from Britain to Mauritius.

It was in 1928 that the Grain Races really began, and at the same time became an almost exclusively Åland phenomenon. It would be as well to look at the composition of the Åland fleet of sailing vessels in that year. It comprised twenty-one iron or steel square-rigged sailing vessels totalling 33,200 tons. Of these Gustaf Erikson was principal shareholder and managing owner of thirteen: *Grace Harwar, Lawhill, Herzogin Cecilie, Loch Linnhe, Pommern, Penang, Olivebank, Killoran, Archibald Russell, Hougomont, Lingard, Winterhude* and *Lalla Rookh.* Of the remaining eight, one, the barque *Montrosa* was owned by a group of shareholders in Lemland and was the last of the many deep sea sailing vessels to be owned in that community; *Mozart, Plus, Prompt, Thekla* and *Ponape* were owned by Hugo Lundqvist, now deeply involved in the management of Åland's only steamship, the *Thornbury;* the barque *Virgo* was managed by Captain Erik Nylund in Mariehamn who had $^{36}/_{100}$, Gustaf Erikson holding $^{5}/_{100}$, and the barque *Oaklands* by Captain Arthur Andersson of Mariehamn.

Above: Atlas, *built at Bath, Maine, in 1908 as the* Bertha L. Downs *and longest lived of all the great New England schooners, shown when sailing under Estonian ownership.*

National Maritime Museum of Sweden

Below: the crew of the Atlas *when she was owned in Åland in the 1920s. Captain Karl Karlsson is seated third from left with his wife and son. Chief mate Elis Mattsson is seated second from the right.*

Karl Karlsson

Frideborg, ex Cleta, *built for the China trade at Sunderland as a barque in 1866 was destined to be the last tea clipper at sea. She is seen here in her old age in the 1930s in Mariehamn.*
Lars Grönstrand

There were three wooden barques and one composite barque. These were *Carmen*, owned by Gustaf Erikson, *Fred*, owned by a group largely in Finström community, *Altai* and *Sverre* owned in Wårdö and managed by Arthur Lundqvist. There were thirty-three big wooden schooners and barquentines, including the magnificent four-masted schooner *Atlas* built at Bath, Maine, in 1908 as the *Bertha L. Downs*, and the longest lived of all the great four-masted schooners of New England, owned by Arthur Andersson and others; the Canadian built four-masted *Gunn* and *Valborg*; the old British tea clipper *Frideborg*, built at Sunderland in 1866 and lost as late as 1937, and the old Swedish barques, now rigged as barquentines, *Kristina* and *Sigyn*, both owned in Wårdö. Of these thirty-three vessels one was owned by Gustaf Erikson and no less than twelve were owned by shareholding groups centred in Wårdö. Arthur Lundqvist, brother of Hugo, who had now taken over the family property at Vargata, was a shareholder in a number of them and managing owner of several others.

Eleven of these wooden vessels, including two four-masted barquentines, had been built in Åland during, or immediately after the First World War. There were also eleven motor schooners, almost all owned in Mariehamn, and a large number of *galeaser* and *jakter*. Of these vessels the smaller ones could be profitable in the Baltic and North Sea trades, but only Gustaf Erikson's largest iron and steel vessels and Hugo Lundqvist's four largest vessels could be operated profitably in ocean trade. In fact *Plus* and *Prompt* were already too small to be economical with Australian wheat cargoes, though *Plus* was employed in the guano trade.

The Grain Race in its first years was between the Erikson vessels, the two largest Lundqvist ships, and two subsidised Swedish training ships, the four-masted barques *Beatrice* and *C. B. Pederson*. Soon, with the development of steam interests, Hugo Lundqvist sold the *Ponape* to Gustaf Erikson (see Chapter 7), keeping only the economical *Mozart* until the necessity for expensive repairs made her no longer profitable, the *Beatrice* was broken up and another Swedish training vessel, the *Abraham Rydberg* began to take up grain cargoes. From time to time three German four-masted barques, *Padua*, *Priwall* and *Magdalene Vinnen*, normally employed in the trade with nitrates from the west coast of South America to Hamburg, were fixed with Australian grain cargoes and, consequently, involved in the Race. These German vessels were, to some degree, subsidised

Above: Kristina *of Wårdö in Åbo in the winter of 1927.*
She was built in Göteborg in 1874 for the coffee trade from
Brazil.

Lars Grönstrand

Below: L'Avenir *in Mariehamn.*

Åbo Akademi

because their crews, largely composed of trainees for naval and merchant shipping, were two or three times larger than the crews which worked the purely commercial barques of Åland.

Gustaf Erikson, operating his vessels largely in the Australian trade and the Baltic and North Sea timber trades, did so with such success that he was able to expand his interests, acquiring new vessels of which he was the sole or principal owner and also shares in other vessels and companies. His sailing fleet was at its greatest in 1935 when it comprised fifteen big steel barques and four-masted barques, the full-rigged ship *Grace Harwar*, and eight smaller vessels and six motor schooners employed in the timber trade. The big vessels acquired after 1928 were the four-masted barques *Ponape*, bought from Hugo Lundqvist, *Moshulu*, bought from American owners (she had been laid up for years), *Passat* and *Pamir* bought from the Hamburg fleet of German nitrate traders referred to above, and *L'Avenir*, a former Belgian training ship. The *Hougomont* and *Loch Linnhe* had been sold, the former after dismasting in 1932. After 1935 there were no more big steel or iron sailing ships left to acquire which were in good enough condition to be likely to produce a reasonable return on invested capital.

Freights took a marked upward turn in the late 1930s and the fleet became very profitable in the years just before the Second World War. In 1937–38 the Australian traders earned around £150,000 in freights as opposed to £68,000 in 1935–36. I remember the interest with which one watched the rise in rates offering for sailing ships in the fixtures reports in Lloyds in that year and wondering what effect this would have on the future of the Erikson fleet and of Åland generally.

Gustaf Erikson and his elder son Edgar, who joined the company in 1935, ploughed back the new capital into small motor ships and old steamers. The first of these was the *Kirsta*, bought in 1937, to be followed in the same year by the *Gottfried*, the *Argo* (in which Gustaf Erikson's younger son, Gustaf Adolph, was to be lost when she was torpedoed by the Russians) and soon after by the *Olivia*, the *Bonden* and the *Avenir*. As late as 1942 they bought their last sailing vessel, the three-masted motor schooner (locally called a three-masted *galeas*) *Sirius*, for the wartime trade on the Norwegian coast. After the war newer and newer vessels were acquired and from 1947 onwards the Rederi Ab Gustaf Erikson began to order the construction of new tonnage for its own specialised trades all over the world. The first of these was the

Kungsö of that year.

At the same time Ålanders were investing the hard-won accumulated capital of these good years and of past generations; capital ground out by the endless hard labour of working small wooden vessels. By 1939 Arthur Andersson, who had owned the *Atlas* and the *Oaklands* was managing five big steamers; Algot Johansson, founder of the Sally Company, had five including the original *Sally*; Arthur Karlsson had seven; Erik Nylund three and there were a number of other owners. In that year Åland's fleet numbered eleven big iron or steel sailing vessels, the wooden barque *Eläköön* and the composite barque *Sverre*, two big schooners, eleven motor schooners, and thirty-three old steamers employed principally in the Baltic and North Sea trades.

The structure of the Australian grain trade has been described before in detail in a number of books, most fully in W L A Derby's *The Tall Ships Pass*, in Georg Kåhre's *The Last Tall Ships*, in Alan Villier's *Falmouth for Orders*, *Voyage of the Parma*, *The Way of a Ship* and other books, and in Elis Karlsson's *Mother Sea* and *Pulley Haul*.

Bill Derby was a Lloyds underwriter who sailed as a passenger in *Herzogin Cecilie* and who was fascinated by the business processes involved. Georg Kåhre was the official historian of the Erikson fleet, his brother Hilding worked for many years in the small office from which the whole enterprise was run. Alan Villiers was an Australian by birth; during his teens, in the period immediately after the First World War, he was a professional sailing ship seaman. One passage he made as a boy of seventeen was in *Lawhill* in 1921, from Bordeaux to Port Adelaide for orders under Captain J E Gustafsson. Although rated as an able seaman he was signed on at 430 finnmarks per month, while experienced Åland seamen were signed on in Bordeaux at 900 finnmarks. For four months' and one day's work he drew 1815 finnmarks (less than £18). The documentation of this passage contains the note, 'This man Alan Willer was sent by Clarkson and Co. in London to serve on a Finnish salary and to leave the ship in Australia.' Though the account of these events he gave in his autobiography, *The Set of the Sails* was more romantic, it appears that he was working his passage home and at this stage the employment of an Australian or British seaman in an Åland ship was something unusual. Thus Alan Villiers began a connection which was later to be of

One of the smaller steel barques in Gustaf Erikson's fleet in the 1930s was the Kylemore, *here shown entering the floating harbour at Bristol.*
Åbo Akademi

some importance to Åland. He was subsequently able to give much publicity to the ships, which was of considerable importance to the survival of interest in these vessels, and in sailing vessels generally, right up to the present day.

Realising that there was little or no future in merchant shipping at the time of the post-war depression, Alan Villiers became a journalist and writer. He sailed again in the *Herzogin Cecilie* in 1928 as an able seaman under Captain Reuben de Cloux, on this occasion for the express purpose of writing *Falmouth for Orders* (which was, in fact, largely written on board). Later he developed his Åland connections to the extent that he owned one-fifth of the *Parma*, in which he sailed in the early 1930s (see Chapter 8). Villiers grew up in an underprivileged environment in Australia and at sea in his middle teens and he found nothing unusual in the hardships of Grain Race sailing as a foremast hand. Later he had a highly successful career as a travel writer, lecturer

and publicist of sailing ships. He was deeply dedicated to the idea of training through sail. Almost inevitably he romanticised, and his books present Åland seafaring as high adventure, rather than as normal work – albeit of a community fifty years behind the times. Elis Karlsson was an Ålander, a professional seaman from a Wårdö family of gifted linguists, deeply involved with sailing and shipowning who wrote of his early life spent partly in Erikson vessels. All these men in their various ways knew the business and experienced the Grain Races at first hand and their books are strongly recommended to those who wish to learn in detail about the sailing of the last big merchant sailing vessels.

I will very briefly outline the conditions under which the sailing ships operated in the later 1920s and 1930s. Each voyage in the Australian grain trade involved a circuit of the earth. For a sailing ship to reach Australia from Europe she must follow the known wind systems of the world eastabout, that is, from south of Africa to Australia, for in the southern latitudes the winds blow predominantly and very strongly from west to east. To go the other way round the world is a different story. Sailing down into the South Atlantic should present no problems, but to enter the Pacific from the Atlantic round the southernmost tip of South America, Cape Horn, is very difficult indeed, because the vessel must generally speaking round the Horn against the wind system, the constant westerly gales. Captain Ivar Hägerstrand, one of Gustaf Erikson's most experienced masters, used to describe this passage between the southern limit of the land and the northern limit of the drifting Antarctic ice as the 'bottleneck' or 'funnel'. The world's first circumnavigations were made in this direction, and in 1769 Captain James Cook entered the Pacific in search of the southern continent by this route.

It cannot be easy for people today to imagine what it must have been like to round Cape Horn in a westerly direction in a small wooden square-rigged sailing vessel. To live in the sort of conditions which were experienced required a high degree of psychological and physical immunity to the effects of continuous extreme cold and wet, exhaustion and a poor diet – an immunity which can only be acquired by people brought up in conditions which scarcely exist at all in north Europe and North America now. Yet the westabout route was the shortest way to the west coast of the Americas and, until the continent was crossed by railroad in 1869, the shortest way into the Pacific. It was the way the gold rush traders sailed in 1840s and the way American wooden sailing ships went to load grain in San Francisco for Europe in the 1870s and 1880s. The little wooden barques of a few hundred tons from Swansea sailed this passage year after year to load copper ore, as did the sailing vessels which loaded Chilean nitrates for European ports.

The Grain Racers did not sail west about Cape Horn. Quite apart from the difficulty of getting into the Pacific Ocean at all, which was less for them than for their wooden predecessors, to get to Australia from the vicinity of Cape Horn in a westerly direction means a long passage north in search of the east wind systems across the South Pacific and then a long sweep down to the Australian coast. The grain ships went east about the world. They sailed down both the Atlantics and picked up the westerly wind system well to the south of the Cape of Good Hope (perhaps having discharged a timber cargo in a South African port on the way) because the further south the stronger and more constant the wind. With strong winds aft or on the quarters, and in high seas, they ran for Australia, for the wheat ports that lay on the south coast.

Spencer's Gulf is a long inlet running nearly two hundred miles north into the State of South Australia. It was the natural outlet for the south Australian wheat belt, but in the 1920s and 1930s it had no modern port and very poor communications with the rest of the country. The vessels often cleared from their European port as sailing towards 'Adelaide for Orders'. Adelaide lies on the east shore of the Gulf of St Vincent and it is the nearest big town to the Spencer's Gulf area. Remember that none of these big Åland sailing vessels were equipped with two-way radio, so they could not be told at sea where to proceed to load their grain. While at sea they were offered on the London freight market, the Baltic Exchange. With luck, as the three months voyage went by they were 'fixed'. This meant arrangements had been reached between Gustaf Erikson and a shipper (in fact between his agents in London, H Clarkson & Co and the shipper's agent, but with Gustaf Erikson's explicit approval in detail) under which they would load bagged wheat at one of the Spencer's Gulf outports and take it to Falmouth or Queenstown, where they would again receive orders to proceed to the port of discharge in Britain or northern Europe. It was only on arrival, not usually at Adelaide to which they had formally cleared, but at Port Lincoln or Port Victoria at the mouth of Spencer's Gulf, that the vessel's masters learned where they were to load their cargo – perhaps not even then if they had not been fixed before their arrival. Very occasionally they were never fixed at all and had to sail home in ballast, or lay up in an Australian port until the next wheat season.

The grain came down to the little outports: Port Lincoln, the only one on the west side of the Gulf, Port Augusta at the very head of the Gulf, and Port Germain, Port Pirie, Port Broughton, Wallaroo, and Port Victoria on the Gulf's eastern shore. It was to these primitive little places that the vessels were ordered and here they slowly loaded thousands of tons of wheat in jute bags. They lay either at the end of long jetties down which the bagged wheat came in trucks, or (sometimes several miles) offshore, where they were loaded from locally owned ketches which carried out a hundred tons or so of wheat at a time. It was a very slow process which meant that sailing vessels could operate profitably. They could afford to accept lower freight rates than steamers (and there were plenty of steamers in the business), because their overheads in the slow weeks of loading were, in comparison, very low. Thus, in 1935, the year in which the Erikson sailing fleet was at its greatest, the

The Grain Racers often lay at the end of long jetties for loading. Penang, L'Avenir *and* Pommern *at Port Lincoln.*
Ålands Sjöfartsmuseum

average freight for a sailing vessel was 25s 6d (£25 at 1985 values). In the same year streamers were paid about 27s 6d per ton. Freights were a good deal lower then than they were in the late 1920s at the beginning of the Grain Race era when sailing vessels were getting as much as 47s per ton.

In the slump year of 1930 freights were disastrously down, at 20s or even 16s 6d, and some vessels were not fixed at all. Ships were actually making net operating losses but conditions greatly improved the next year. Some of the difficulties of this period are described by Gustaf Erikson in his business correspondence in connection with the *Ponape*, quoted in the next chapter. In the late 1930s freights rose to highly satisfactory levels which

enabled extensive investment in steam tonnage to take place.

The freight figures do not have much significance unless they are considered alongside the outgoings involved in operating the vessels. Bill Derby in *The Tall Ships Pass* analysed the economics of the Erikson fleet in the early 1930s in great detail. From his figures it appears that the total operating cost, very roughly, of a four-masted barque in the grain trade was in the region of £5000 per year. A vessel of 4500 tons capacity therefore required, very generally speaking, a freight of 25s to break even. This is confirmed by the

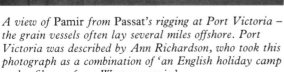

A view of Pamir *from* Passat's *rigging at Port Victoria – the grain vessels often lay several miles offshore. Port Victoria was described by Ann Richardson, who took this photograph as a combination of 'an English holiday camp and a film set for a Western movie.'*
Ann Richardson

Five four-masted barques and Mozart *lying off Port Victoria. The cluster of ketches, three-masted schooners and small steamers in the foreground took the wheat in bags out to the waiting sailing ships.*
Åbo Akademi

comment in one of Gustaf Erikson's letters (see page 140) that 'it is very difficult on a freight of twenty five shillings to cover the costs of the smaller vessels' which loaded less but cost almost as much to run as the big four-masters.

Of course the picture was by no means as straightforward as this. In the bad years costs could be and were cut to a minumum (see Gustaf Erikson's correspondence, quoted in the next chapter). Nothing was ever wasted. W J Slade, whose family owned the last considerable fleet of wooden schooners and ketches to sail out of a British port, recalled that he had never known a block be bought new – everything came from older vessels. On a larger scale Gustaf Erikson's office pursued the same enconomies. When the *Hougomont* was dismasted all possible equipment was brought back to Åland and used in other vessels. When a vessel was sold for breaking-up, gear that could be used in other vessels was often not included in the contract of sale. When the *Herzogin Cecilie* was wrecked on the Devon coast in 1936 everything that could be saved, even deckhouses, was taken off her for use elsewhere.

In the long run this habit of saving gear immensely enriched the Åland Maritime Museum, which is a veritable treasure house of sailing vessel equipment. The complete saloon of the *Herzogin Cecilie* was dismantled and packed into crates which were landed by motor boat at Kingsbridge in Devon. Here they were loaded, with 30 tons of other gear, into the trading smack (the equivalent of an Åland *jakt*) *Triumph*, out of Calstock, and taken to Exmouth

where they were transhipped to the Erikson motor ship *Vera* which was discharging timber. Taken to Mariehamn, the saloon was eventually rebuilt in the Maritime Museum and today you can walk into it and see the master's cabin, the stewards' pantry, and sit at the great saloon table.

In 1933 Gustaf Erikson bought the Nystads Slip och Mekaniska Verkstad on the mainland coast to be a repair base for his fleet (incidentally he also bought the wooden barques *Eläköön* and *Warma* as part of the deal). The yard was very busy, working on thirty-four vessels in its first year of Åland ownership and continuing at this level of activity until the Second World War.

There were several factors operating to the shipowners benefit among which the rate of exchange of the Finnish mark against the British and Australian pounds was important. For example, in the early 1930s when freights were at their lowest, the pound was effectively devalued when Britain went off the gold standard, and Finnish holders of sterling, among whom Gustaf Erikson was prominent, found their sterling balances worth a sixth as much again in terms of finnmarks. (Gustaf Erikson referred to this in a letter to Captain Uno Karlsson, quoted on pp 137–38.) In good years the profits were considerable. In the outstanding 1937–38 season the £150,000 earned in freights by the ten Erikson vessels fixed in the grain trade must have represented a net profit of the order of £80,000 to £90,000 even allowing for increased costs – nearly 200 per cent on the outgoings. This represents about £9000 per vessel – a considerable

Young David Gibson comes ashore from the wrecked Herzogin Cecilie.
Father Sir David Gibson

The reconstructed saloon of the Herzogin Cecilie *in the Ålands Sjöfartsmuseum. Captain Karl Kåhre is at the head of the table.*
Basil Greenhill

improvement on the £800, which Gustaf Erikson is said to have calculated as the average annual profit of each vessel in the early 1930s.

To the total net profit of the units of the fleet employed in the grain trade would have been added the earnings of the fifteen vessels in the Baltic and North Sea trade. These Baltic and North Sea traders were an essential part of the whole operation, complimentary to the larger long voyage vessels, providing alternative employment for crews and a demand for the same shore services. Their operation would merit study in the same detail as has been given to the long voyage vessels. In good years their earnings on two or three voyages to western Europe and Britain could be considerable and the investment in many of the old vessels was very small. Estonian owners were bringing more old sailing vessels into the

The Tamar barge Triumph *of Plymouth, the equivalent of an Åland jakt, lies between the* Industry *and the* P.H.E. *in Falmouth.* Triumph *shipped Herzogin Cecilie's saloon fittings to Exmouth where they were transhipped to the Erikson motor ship* Vera.
H Oliver Hill

trade even in the late 1930s. The last British square-rigged merchant sailing vessel, the barquentine *Waterwitch* of Fowey, was bought by an Estonian share-holding group in 1939 for £400. In her first five months of summer sailing between the Gulf of Bothnia and Denmark she recovered half her investment cost. A net profit of £500 a year was expected and all was going well when the Second World War broke out and Estonia and the *Waterwich* were engulfed by Soviet Russia.

Moreover, because the world price of scrap was rapidly rising in the late 1930s the value of the vessels was going up all the time. When a vessel's maintenance costs rose to the point at which she consistently failed to return a net profit she was sold for breaking up, as was *Grace Harwar* in 1935, and *Ponape* in 1936, but with great reluctance. In 1936 *L'Avenir*, bought for £2820 in 1932, was sold for £17,000 to the Hamburg Amerika Line for use as a cargo carrying cadet ship. Freight rates generally were high and rising and the Åland fleet of steamers and motor ships were also earning, perhaps at even higher rates of profitability. The process of capital accumulation, from the days of the home-built

wooden barques of the 1860s to the huge ferries and sophisticated specialised tonnage of today can be seen, despite all its ups and downs, the latter particularly in 1929–30, and during the Second World War, as, generally speaking, continuous.

When they had completed loading in Australia the grain ships set sail on the long haul to Britain. Once out of Spencer's Gulf they sailed eastwards, sometimes through the Bass Strait between Victoria and Tasmania, sometimes even through the Cook Strait between the North and South islands of New Zealand, more often making course to the south off the Australian coast and heading far to the south of New Zealand. For to make the best of the world's wind system – the almost constant westerlies of the higher latitudes leading to Cape Horn – the barques

The barque Warma, *acquired by Gustaf Erikson with his purchase of the Nystad shipyard. She is laid up in Göteborg in 1932 and her lower yards have been cockbilled to protect them from rot by rain water, which will run off them.*
Ålands Sjöfartsmuseum

had to go right into the high fifties, into Ivar Hägerstrand's funnel between the land of South America and the ice. It was this easterly passage round Cape Horn, which was the subject of so many books written in the 1920s and 1930s by passengers and temporary crew members who were not professional sailing ship seamen. Besides the eight books on this subject by Elis Karlsson and Alan Villiers, who were professionals, I have on my library shelves twelve books in English, each by a different author, describing an eastbound Cape Horn passage in an Erikson vessel. In the opinion of some of the

men who meet to lunch each month at the Nautical Club in Mariehamn, among the best of these is W M Hutton's *Cape Horn Passage*, an account of the passage made in 1933 by the *Viking* under Ivar Hägerstrand, written by a passenger who was a very experienced traveller and who had been in sail before. It is an unromantic, down-to-earth account of a working passage, exaggerating neither the hardships and discomforts nor the splendours – seen in much the same way as the Ålanders saw it.

Life in these ships in the 1920s and 1930s must be seen in the context of the contemporary standard of living on land, and the simple fact is that Finland, which gained her independence from Russia only in 1918, was a very late developer in the European family of nations. One of the happy economic miracles of the second half of the twentieth century has been the emergence of Finland as a nation with an economic growth rate exceeding that of Japan and a

Warma discharging timber in Surrey Commercial Docks in September 1935. The sails have been cut loose from the jackstays and are hanging in the clewlines and buntlines while the yards are painted. A man can be seen painting on the foreyard and another on the mainyard.
Lars Grönstrand

The barquentine Waterwitch *of Fowey, the last working square-rigged merchant sailing vessel to be registered at a home port in the United Kingdom. In 1938 she was sold to Estonian owners and employed in the timber trade to western Europe.*
Amos

A photograph of the foremast of the barque Eläköön *(approximately 'Hooray' in Finnish) taken on 26 June 1937. The royal yard has been sent down and is stowed upright abaft the fore lowermast with the yardarm projecting up through the foretop.*
Lars Grönstrand

higher general standard of living than that of North America. But in the days of the Grain Races Finland was still a poor country, dependent on forestry, on farming and sailing ships. Life on shore during the youth of the Mariehamn Cape Horners was even more rugged than life in the villages of North Wales in the 1890s when Porthmadog schooners sailed to Newfoundland to load salt fish, or than life on the small farms of North Devon in the 1850s, when small locally owned wooden barques beat their way westwards across the Atlantic to load timber in the Gulf of St Lawrence. In many ways, life on board the Grain Racers was less arduous than on the farms or in construction work or forestry in the sixtieth parallel.

Seafaring was one of the better paid occupations in Finland before the Second World War, although an ordinary seaman (still essentially a trainee) received only £2 per month, a fully trained able seaman was paid only twice as much, and the chief mate £10 or £12. The master received £15 to £20. Mariehamn today is a smart, prosperous, leafy, small town, in appearance at first sight rather like a well-to-do small town in New England, but without any shabbiness or poverty. In 1935 it was also delightful, but compared with most of western Europe it was primitive and poor. The streets were unpaved, the buildings almost

Captain Ivar Hägerstrand successively master of Loch Linnhe, Woodburn, Hougomont, Winterhude, Viking, Yxpila *and* Passat *as well as a number of steamers. He was the last man but one ever to command a laden merchant sailing vessel rounding Cape Horn.*
Ålands Sjöfartsmuseum

all of wood, and the cost of living was extremely low.

Recalling the building of his summerhouse on the island of Styrsö Edgar Erikson told me, 'I find it surprising to remember now, that when we built this place after the war, materials for the house were carried by horse and cart to the wharf in Mariehamn and we hired a *galeas* to bring them alongside our wharf at the bottom of the garden here'. Now Styrsö, and islands much more remote, are linked by paved roads and bridges to the mainland of Fasta Åland and you can drive there in twenty minutes from the heart of Mariehamn. Edgar Erikson went on to say that he could not remember a time when there was not a local telephone service in Åland (he was born in 1915) with

Lawhill *photographed off Cape Horn on 26 January 1945, from the Newfoundland rigged steam sealer* Eagle *bound for the Antarctic.*
Scott Polar Research Institute

The summerhouse of Edgar and Solveig Erikson on Little Styrsö stands on the smooth curved granite typical of all Åland.
Basil Greenhill

an operator and calls made with a hand turned magneto. When lines to Helsinki and Stockholm arrived they were in parallel with the inland service with separate instruments. The Erikson office had the first telex – but not until after the Second World War.

In the 1920s and 1930s young men from Åland, and from the rugged interior of mainland Finland, regarded sailing in the Grain Racers as a perfectly normal job. The ambitious saw it as a necessary preliminary to qualify them for the relatively well paid jobs of mate and master. Such was the strength of the sailing ship tradition, even in the mid 1930s, that a Finnish national, seeking to qualify as second mate, had to have three years in sail behind him. Experience in sail was the only door to a respected profession with possibilities of investment and even, eventually, relative wealth.

Against this background the Grain Racers were cheaply manned by able and enthusiastic young men who found, on the whole, no great hardships in life at sea in comparison with what they had been accustomed to ashore. In due course, if they stayed in sail to become masters and mates, they often acquired skills in handling their vessels which today seem almost beyond comprehension. It is possible to get a good idea of the matter of fact way in which Ålander's approached seafaring under sail from Captain Karl Karlsson's account of his life (National Maritime Museum Monograph entitled *Karlsson*). He went to sea under his father's command in a wooden barquentine at the age of thirteen and left deep-sea sail from command of the *Parma*, then the world's largest merchant sailing ship, at the age of thirty-six. Great skills were acquired. It seems almost unbelievable now, in an age in which few yachtsmen will pick up a mooring in a yacht of any size except under power, that the big four-masted barques used to sail right into Mariehamn's Western Harbour, and sail out from the old wharves and in Australia sail up to the loading jetties. In the Baltic timber trade Kalle Karlsson, when he was master of the big four-masted schooner *Atlas*, a vessel nearly 200 feet long, used to beat her amongst the ice floes when going north to load his first cargo at a Gulf of Bothnia port at the beginning of the season.

Throughout the 1930s several European governments required future merchant shipmates and masters to have sail experience but there was a

Archibald Russell *sailing from Mariehamn for Australia via Copenhagen in September 1930,* Viking *is in the background.*
Alands Sjöfartsmuseum

shortage of vessels in which to gain it. This meant that Gustaf Erikson was able to cut his crew costs by the introduction of an apprenticeship system which was used as an entry into seafaring life by many young Germans (until the government forbade sailing in foreign vessels), Swedes, and Danes. In addition to these serious apprentices who intended to make the sea a career there were a number of young adventurers of both sexes from Britain and America who signed on for single passages and whose labour could be put to use on board. But the bulk of the crews were always Ålanders or mainland Finns and almost all the officers were Ålanders.

Examples from the beginning and end of the history of the Eriskon fleet illustrate the change in crews. When Alan Villiers signed aboard the *Lawhill* as a temporary ordinary seaman in Bordeaux in 1921 for the passage to Australia, the vessel's crew list, preserved in the Erikson archives in Mariehamn, shows that every single one of his shipmates was Finnish, the great majority from Åland. When the *Viking* came into Sharpness from Australia in June 1937, twenty-four of her crew of twenty-seven were Ålanders and mainland Finns. The other three comprised one Swedish ordinary seaman, and one American and one English apprentice. The Englishman, Joseph Walter Cooper, was intent on making the sea his career, but he was, tragically, lost overboard on the following passage. A year earlier,

Work on the main lower topsail yard of Archibald Russell.
Karl Kåhre

when the *Herzogin Cecilie* arrived at Falmouth from Australia, her crew comprising twenty-six Finns and only four foreigners. This was on the ill-fated voyage which terminated with her loss, a traumatic affair for all closely concerned with the fleet and in Edgar Erikson's words 'due to gross navigational error in fog', an attribution of cause which appears to be confirmed by the last entries in her log.

The risk of industrial accident on board sailing vessels, more especially square-rigged vessels has always been very high. The Grain Racers overall, excluding disasters in which many men were lost as in the sinking of *Melbourne* and the loss of the *Admiral Karpfanger*, lost perhaps one to two per cent of their crews through fatal accidents every year. The working conditions on board late nineteenth century merchant sailing ships – and by definition on board the Grain Racers – would not be acceptable, or indeed legal, today in any Western country, nor would unions tolerate them for one moment. This one fact alone (and there are many others) makes nonsense of the romantic idea sometimes put forward of reviving traditional sailing vessels for commercial purposes.

At the British end of the voyage, the Grain Racers called at Falmouth or Queenstown, (again, as on arrival in Australia, because of the lack of wireless communication) 'for orders' as to where they were to discharge. This depended on the requirements of the final purchaser of the cargo, which might have changed hands on the commodity market many times while it was being carried to England. Falmouth is a huge sheltered harbour, one of the best in the world, into which vessels could be sailed without a tug and where they could lie free of charge.

It was here the press and radio treated the race as finishing. In fact the Grain Race was a figment of the media's imagination. The grain trade vessels differed widely in size and shape and rig; they were built for different trades in different countries at different periods in the last years of sailing ship building, sailed sometimes by different routes, and there was no system of handicapping. Only once was there a formal race, with a challenge and trophy, and that was between the *Herzogin Cecilie* and the *Beatrice* in 1929 and this was the occasion that provided the inspiration for the writing of Alan Villier's book *Falmouth for Orders* which, more than anything else, began Britain's widespread interest in the Åland sailing ships which has persisted ever since. The Grain Races bore no relation the tea clipper races, when vessels sailed from China on the same tide, and

arrived home within hours of each other the winner being the first to drop anchor.

After getting her orders, the barque set sail again for the place of discharge, usually in Britain. Discharge points on the west coast included Bristol, Sharpness, Barry, Cardiff, Liverpool and Glasgow and on the east coast, Southampton, London, Ipswich and Hull. Here they were unloaded (at the shipowner's expense) which normally took several weeks. Then, in ballast, the barques usually sailed for Mariehamn. This passage was equivalent in length to the return of the old North Sea traders after discharging a cargo of Baltic timber, though four-

The master and mates of the Garthsnaid. *Alexander Turner who took the remarkable photograph alongside is on the left, Captain James Simpson in the middle and Mr McLeod, mate, on the right. Alexander Turner was nineteen years old at the time and already had four years war service at sea behind him. In February 1920 he became acting mate of* Garthsnaid. *He subsequently had a career in business ashore but returned to the sea during the Second World War for distinguished service in the RNR.*
J W Simpson

The kind of industrial conditions found on board square-rigged merchant sailing ships are illustrated in this outstanding photograph taken on board the barque Garthsnaid *(Captain James Simpson) of Montreal. The crew are securing a section of the foresail which had come free from the gaskets in heavy weather on passage from Iquique to Delagoa Bay with nitrate between 24 April and 26 July 1920. The photograph, perhaps the finest ever of work aloft in bad weather, was taken by the acting second mate, Alexander Harper Turner, from the jibboom end with a camera he had bought in Iquique, and was first published in a Bristol newspaper when the* Garthsnaid *discharged a grain cargo from Australia there in December 1921.*
Commander Alexander H Turner, DSC, RNR

masted barques were never meant to sail regularly in
the relatively treacherous waters of the Baltic and
things could go disastrously wrong in sudden adverse
weather conditions. Even regular Baltic traders like
the barques *Loch Linnhe*, *Plus* and *Fred* were lost near
their home port in the Åland archipelago. A tale of
near disaster, skilfully avoided, is told in Georg
Kåhre's *The Last Tall Ships*, of how the *Pamir* was
blown away from the entrance to Mariehamn's
Western Harbour and, lightly ballasted as she was for
the summer passage, was saved from disaster only by
brilliant seamanship.

In the central years of the Grain Races from 1928 to
1939 the vessels nearly always discharged at British
ports and often were drydocked there. Their cargoes
were British property for the greater part of the
passage. They were fixed on the Baltic Exchange in
London and their cargoes were insured on the
London insurance market (though the Erikson
vessels were latterly not insured). All the business of
the Australian trade ships was carried out by a
London shipbroking company, H Clarkson & Co.
They set up a special department to handle Swedish

Viking discharging in Sharpness in 1937.
Basil Greenhill

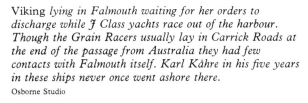

Viking *lying in Falmouth waiting for her orders to discharge while J Class yachts race out of the harbour. Though the Grain Racers usually lay in Carrick Roads at the end of the passage from Australia they had few contacts with Falmouth itself. Karl Kåhre in his five years in these ships never once went ashore there.*
Osborne Studio

Grace Harwar *with lower yards cockbilled to clear the wharfside sheds, discharging in Glasgow.*
G W Munro

Left: Viking's *mizzenyards from the lower topgallant.*
Basil Greenhill

Centre: detail of Viking's *jigger mast.*
Basil Greenhill

Right: making fast the crossjack on Viking *in the Baltic.*
Basil Greenhill

and Finnish tonnage under an Ålander, Matti Ingman, who in 1934 became a director of the company. After his death in 1928 Mr A S Calder, a Scot, who had been with the company since 1896, took over the business of handling the Erikson fleet until his retirement in 1939. In effect, Clarksons carried out all the business of the Erikson fleet, except the running of the ships themselves, right from the

days of the *Southern Belle*, and even with earlier vessels in which Gustaf Erikson had shares.

The company provided business training facilities for the sons and employees of the great Åland shipowners. These and many other Scandinavians came to London to serve as 'Foreign Clerks and Volunteers' for a few months or a year. Matti Ingman himself arrived in London to do this and stayed on. In

1928 Hilding Kåhre served in this capacity. He was the elder brother of Captain Karl Kåhre who presides over the Cape Horners' lunches each month in Mariehamn, of Paul Kåhre, master of the *Mozart* and of Georg Kåhre who recorded the Erikson history in *The Last Tall Ships*. Later he was to spend years in the Erikson office in Mariehamn and play an important part in the development of the business. In

1934, before entering his father's company a year later, Edgar Erikson, then aged nineteen, served in Clarksons, living with a family in Harley Street. He was followed by Frank Lundqvist of Mariehamn and a number of others. There were times, especially in the depression of the early 1920s and the beginning of the 1930s, when the financial accommodation provided by Clarksons must have been vital to the successful operation, indeed the very survival, of the Erikson fleet. To a considerable extent therefore, the operation of the Åland sailing vessels in the 1920s and 1930s was an Anglo-Åland affair.

But there was a further connection. Finnish and Åland law did not permit the holding of shares in Åland vessels by non-Finnish nationals. It is not therefore surprising that a search of the central register of Åland vessels in Mariehamn has revealed little evidence of direct British investment in Åland tonnage, but it has revealed some, and there is further evidence from other sources. Although Clarksons never took up shares in Erikson vessels another firm of London shipbrokers, Applebys, who specialised in handling vessels in the timber trade, did directly invest. The register reveals that the four-masted schooner *Atlas*, (one of the finest and most constantly employed, and certainly the longest lived of all the big New England-built wooden schooners) managed by Arthur Andersson of Mariehamn (who owned $^{52}/_{100}$ths) and registered there, was $^{18}/_{100}$ths owned by Mr Percy Appleby 'Merchant of Nystad.' This device of concealment apparently satisfied the registrar.

From Mr Bo Lindholm, (son of Arthur Andersson's daughter, Managing Director of Rederi Ab Asta, the modern company which developed from the shipowning activities of Arthur Andersson), I learned that Percy Appleby also held shares in the barques *Oaklands* and *Transocean* and that Applebys had a relatively large shareholding in the Asta Company until the end of the 1960s. Correspondence in the shipping records of the Community of Wårdö reveals that Percy Appleby also held shares in *Parma* which, together with Alan Villier's holding in this vessel (though Australian by birth, he had made his home in Britain), made her almost one third British owned (see Chapter 8). Good oral tradition has it that the Applebys also invested in the Lundqvist Company which purchased the steamer *Thornbury* and began continuous investment in Åland in steam tonnage in 1928, and also in other vessels. Apart from the dividends, such shareholding meant, of course, that the agency, shipchandlery and supply work for

these vessels went to Applebys. It would appear that in total, London business houses played no small part in the development of Åland shipping in the crucial years of the 1920s and early 1930s.

There were other even less overt British contributions. The wooden barque *Njaal* was built at Son on the Oslo fjord in Norway in 1881. In 1913 she was bought by Captain Gustaf Lindström of Sund community in Åland who had $^{95}/_{100}$ths and Captain Gustaf Johansson of Wårdö who had $^{5}/_{100}$ths. In July 1914, she discharged a timber cargo in Great Yarmouth and was still in British waters when war was declared at the beginning of August. During the war she was, no doubt very profitably, employed in the timber trade from Norway to Britain until she was sunk by a German submarine off Flekkafjord on 12 April 1918. The records of the Wårdö seamens' house show that even in 1915 mates and other crew members were being got out to her in Britain through Sweden.

Captain Lindström, the managing owner, was, in fact, a permanent resident of West Hartlepool in Britain where he had settled and where a few years ago descendents were still living. *Njaal*, registered in Wårdö, was up to ninety-five per cent owned in Britain. She and *Ruby*, a similarly-employed, Norwegian-built vessel owned by Captain Lindström may well have been the last classic small wooden barques ever to have been owned in this country.

There were other examples of the same kind of ownership of Åland registered vessels by expatriates living in Britain. The wooden full-rigged ship *Elgar* built in Germany as the *Roland* in 1879, was purchased in her old age in December 1914 through Clarksons for £1000 by Captain Oskar Engman of Wårdö. In fact a very important shareholder, possibly the largest, was Frantz Johan Hansen of Hansen & Co, No 1 Elgar Street, Rotherhithe, south east London. She was a good investment. On her first voyage from London to Nova Scotia and back to Bristol with timber, she recovered her investment cost and made a net profit of more than this sum. She made a good profit on her second voyage and was then lost off the Portuguese coast in 1916.

Taking a long view from fifty years later, what was the significance of the Grain Races? They can be seen in three ways. The situation which produced them brought about the conspicuous survival of the big iron and steel square-rigged deep sea merchant sailing ship until the Second World War. If it had not been for the Åland participation in the Australian

Elgar, registered as of Wårdö but owned largely in London, passing under the Clifton Suspension Bridge outward bound from Bristol in August 1915.
Lars Grönstrand; photograph by J Darling

grain trade, vessels of this type would have vanished from the seas about the time of the breaking up of the last British vessel of this kind, the *William Mitchell*, in 1927. They attracted a great deal of public attention and in the late twentieth century there are still living memories of these vessels, strengthened by photographs and cinematic records. The Åland sailing ships were never forgotten, and the fact that they survived until the Second World War played a large part in the development of the widespread interest in youth training through sail and in sailing ships generally. More than that, modern youth training in sailing vessels can trace its origins largely to the inspiration of Alan Villiers' long voyage in the *Joseph Conrad* in 1934–37, essentially a private youth training venture, which was made possible by the capital accumulated from his ownership of $^{1}/_{5}$th of the Åland four-masted barque *Parma*.

The next significance of the Grain Races was less international in its scope, but certainly more important. They made possible the generation of capital for the second stage in the conversion of Åland

shipping to steam, at a time when the community was able to profit significantly from this development. Thus the continuous process of capital accumulation went on, and Åland, having survived the transition from Baltic traders to ocean sailing wooden barques and from these to iron and steel sailing vessels, was now able to continue the transition to secondhand steam driven tonnage and small motor ships. David Papp and Karl Kåhre of the historical section of the Åland Sjöfartsmuseum are currently working on the history of this short, largely unstudied, era of the secondhand steamers. It did not last long, but was profitable while it lasted. After the Second World War Åland shipowners passed through an economic crisis, but with the aid of credits from Dutch banks they survived and were able to place orders in the second half of the 1940s for new tonnage. This was almost the first new tonnage since the great days of

the farmer–shipowners of the 1870s – and the foundations were laid of the efficient modern Åland fleet and of the prosperity of modern Åland.

The other really significant issue is the speed of the Grain Racers. In comparison with fast ships of earlier days, for instance the wool clippers of the 1880s, many of Erikson's ships made excellent passages:

Pommern	Copenhagen to Spencer Gulf	76 days
Herzogin		
Cecilie	Port Lincoln to Falmouth	86 days
Pamir	Copenhagen to Port Victoria	77 days

and a vessel in which Erikson had shares,

Parma	Port Victoria – Falmouth (under Captain de Cloux)	83 days
	Barry Roads – Port Victoria (under Captain Karlsson)	73 days

The best passages in the wool trade were sixty-three days by *Thermopylae* and sixty-seven by *Cutty Sark*, though their average times overall whilst on the Australian run were between seventy and eighty days, and that of the majority of wool clippers was well over a hundred days. It must also be remembered that clipper ships were built for speed, and the majority carried no more than 1500 tons of cargo. In comparison Erikson's 'windjammers' had all been built for carrying capacity, and because of this their tonnage varied from 3000 to 4700 tons. These facts clearly establish that the ships of Erikson's fleet more than held their own and deserve a special place in the history of the merchant sailing ship.

What, then, were the Grain Races? The phenomenon can be summed up very briefly. The Grain Races represent the very successful exploitation of an anachronism – the poor loading facilities in Spencer's Gulf. The Ålanders applied highly personal and skilled management, backed by well run and financed London business houses, to the operation of low-investment obsolete tonnage, which they ran at low cost from an under-developed country

Gustaf Erikson (second from the left) comes on board.
Captain Uno Mörn is on the right.
Edgar Erikson

where professional seafaring skills were still cheaply and readily available.

In the next two chapters John Hackman, drawing on the records of the Rederi Ab Gustaf Erikson and on the shipping records of the community of Wårdö, shows in great detail how this was done in the cases of two vessels, the steel four-masted barques *Ponape* and *Parma*. In Chapter 9 Brigadier Ferguson-Innes gives the life story of another Grain Racer, the steel barque *Killoran* and in Chapter 10 we record the atypical career of another Erikson vessel, contemporary of the Grain Racers, the wooden schooner *Ingrid*.

Ponape.
Abo Akademi

Chapter 7

PONAPE

The steel four-masted barque *Ponape* was built at the yard of Soc Esercitzio Bacini, Genoa, for Pietro Milesi Co of Genoa in 1903. Her dimensions were 283.8 × 42.5 × 23.2ft, her gross tonnage was 2342 and net 1973 (after 1933, 1895 tons) and she was 3500 tons deadweight. She was initially named *Regina Elena*, after the leading lady in one of Mollis' operas, after whom her figurehead was modelled.

The Italians sold the *Regina Elena* to Reederei F Laeisz GmbH in Hamburg in 1911 and she was renamed *Ponape*. At the outbreak of the war in 1914 she was taken by the British, and James Bell of Hull became her new owner. She was renamed *Bellhouse* but sailed under the Norwegian flag and in 1915 she was bought by A Monsen in Tönsberg, who had administered her for the British. On 3 November 1925 Captain Hugo Lundqvist and co-owners in Mariehamn bought her for £4600; she was named *Ponape* again.

The first Åland ownership was as follows:

Captain Hugo Lundqvist	Mariehamn	$^{35}/_{100}$
Captain Erik Nylund	Mariehamn	$^{8}/_{100}$
Captain Axel Melander	Mariehamn	$^{4}/_{100}$
Bank manager B Lundqvist	Mariehamn	$^{3}/_{100}$
Captain E M Eriksson	Mariehamn	$^{2}/_{100}$
Captain Arthur Ekbom	Mariehamn	$^{2}/_{100}$
Captain Oscar Engman	Mariehamn	$^{2}/_{100}$
Captain Ruben de Cloux	Mariehamn	$^{2}/_{100}$
Businessman Karl Eriksson	Mariehamn	$^{2}/_{100}$
Farmer J A Lundberg	Geta	$^{1}/_{100}$
Farmer Erik Karlsson	Geta	$^{1}/_{100}$
Farmer Axel Karlsson	Geta	$^{2}/_{100}$
Mrs Anna Olofsson	Wårdö	$^{2}/_{100}$
Captain Arthur Karlsson	Wårdö	$^{3}/_{100}$
Captain Einar Marander	Wårdö	$^{3}/_{100}$
Captain John Wennström	Wårdö	$^{4}/_{100}$
Captain Arthur Marander	Wårdö	$^{2}/_{100}$
Farmer William Boman	Wårdö	$^{2}/_{100}$
Farmer Emil Friman	Lemland	$^{2}/_{100}$
Captain Elegius Sommarström	Lemland	$^{4}/_{100}$
Mate Martin Karlsson	Lemland	$^{2}/_{100}$
Mate Simon Karlsson	Lemland	$^{1}/_{100}$
Farmer O W Johansson	Saltvik	$^{2}/_{100}$
Farmer K F Blomroos	Saltvik	$^{2}/_{100}$
Estate owner E A Karén	Saltvik	$^{2}/_{100}$
BA Torvald Sundblom	Hangö	$^{3}/_{100}$
Mrs Frida Isaksson	Åbo	$^{2}/_{100}$
		$^{100}/_{100}$

Even as late as 1925 this old-fashioned nineteenth-century type of shareholding was common. Hugo Lundqvist was elected managing owner. The majority of the shares in *Ponape* were owned by sea captains and businessmen in Mariehamn. Sea captains and one farmer in Wårdö had the second biggest body of the shares, followed by the communities of Lemland, Saltvik and Geta. Two of the part-owners were from outside Åland, from the towns of Åbo and Hangö. Notable among the shareholders were Captain Axel Melander, son of Carl Abraham Melander a cousin of Gustaf Erikson; Captain Ruben de Cloux who in 1925 was active as master of Gustaf Erikson's *Herzogin Cecilie*; Mrs Anna Olofsson of the great Olofsson shipping family of Wårdö, who was Hugo Lundqvist's mother-in-law; Captain Arthur Marander, who would later command the *Ponape* and finally Captain Elegius Sommarström who had been one of the last shareholders in the *Southern Belle*.

Captain Erik Nylund, who owned $^{8}/_{100}$ths in *Ponape*, was also one of the last shareholders in the *Southern Belle*. He had widely spread shareholdings and was managing owner of some twenty vessels. He was born in Lemland in 1872, took his master's certificate in 1896 and became master and co-owner of the Nova Scotian-built barque *James L Harvey*, brought to Lemland in 1896 and renamed *Nikolai II*. The *Nikolai* was wrecked at Signilskär near Åland in 1899. After that Erik Nylund took his master's certificate in steam and commanded the steamers *Ilmari* and *Osmo* of Björneborg in Finland. In 1904 he left active sea-life and became an established businessman and banker in Mariehamn where he also had a shipbroker's and ship-chandler's business. He was, however, first and foremost an active shipowner and later managing director of several steamship owning companies.

Hugo Lundqvist was born in Lemland in 1878 and was a son of Mathias Lundqvist junior of Lemland, later of Wårdö. He took his master's certificate at the navigation school in Mariehamn in 1901. He had an active sea-life until he bought the four-masted barquentine *Mozart*, after which he worked ashore and became an important shipowner in Mariehamn. He was at various times the managing owner of the sailing vessels *Prompt*, *Thekla*, *Else*, *Mozart*, *Ponape*, *Valborg*, *Hildur*, *Plus* and *Zaritza*. As was said in Chapter 5 he was also Åland's pioneer in successful steamship operation and manager of the steamship company Alfa, with the steamers *Thornbury*,

Mozart sailing from Mariehamn's Western Harbour
Åbo Akademi

Charterhague, *Hildegaard* and *Dagmar*. He died in 1935.

Ponape's first passage under her Åland owners was from Fredrikstad in Norway with lumber for Melbourne. This passage turned out to be very difficult with several severe storms which forced Captain J A Danielsson to take the ship on courses that resulted in a 34,000 mile trip instead of the normal 13,000. No return cargo was obtained so *Ponape* was laid up in Melbourne until the wheat season in 1927. She left Melbourne for Falmouth on 13 January and made a 117-day passage, discharging in Gdánsk. She then had a fairly slow round-trip to Australia. She took 121 days to sail from Dungeness to Australia, and sailed from Wallaroo for Falmouth,

leaving on 9 March 1928, arriving on 8 July, and discharged in Belfast. The *Ponape* made one more round-trip under Lundqvist management in 1929. On her passage back from Australia she left Geelong on 30 April and arrived at Falmouth on 6 August. She discharged in Cardiff.

In 1929, perhaps not expecting the disastrous fall in freights, which occurred in 1930, Gustaf Erikson had bought several vessels. The first, in March, was the *Gustav*, bought from Herman Engel in Hamburg for £4000 and renamed *Melbourne*. Then he bought

Viking under full sail in the English Channel.
Ålands Sjöfartsmuseum

the four-masted auxiliary wooden schooner *Madare* in May and in July the *Viking* from Denmark for £6500. Finally in August he bought the *Ponape* for £5500, nearly twenty per cent more than Lundqvist had paid for her four years before. The payment for the ship went through Clarksons in London. He had sent Captain Uno Karlsson to Cardiff to act as his agent and to inspect the ship.

With a deadweight tonnage (which is roughly indicative of cargo capacity) of only 3500 tons as against the 4000 tons deadweight of *Viking* and the 4250 of *Melbourne*, but costing much the same to run and with the same size crew, she was never going to be among the more profitable vessels of the fleet and indeed, as the correspondence quoted in this chapter shows, she was not. Nevertheless she was a very handsome vessel with a relatively fine underwater body, a good sheer and very well placed masts.

The *Ponape* was registered in the magistrates' ships register in Mariehamn with the following shareholders:

Shipowner Gustaf Erikson	Mariehamn	$^{96}/_{100}$
Mr Edgar Erikson	Mariehamn	$^{1}/_{100}$
Miss Greta Otilia Erikson	Mariehamn	$^{1}/_{100}$
Mr Gustaf Adolf Erikson	Mariehamn	$^{1}/_{100}$
Miss Eva Viola Erikson	Mariehamn	$^{1}/_{100}$

Gustaf Erikson, by giving each of his four children a share in the vessel had moved away from the old-style extended shareholding group gathered to finance a vessel, towards exclusive family ownership of the capital, a pattern which has been maintained by the Erikson family to the present day. He nevertheless retained minority shareholdings in other vessels and companies. This was the pattern of ownership Gustaf Erikson adopted until the end of 1935 when single ship limited liability companies were formed for each vessel.

On 14 August 1929 the former master of the *Ponape*, Captain Arthur Marander, wrote to Gustaf Erikson: 'To begin with may I congratulate you for buying the *Ponape* and wish you good luck. It is with a certain sadness I depart from here because one has to search for a better vessel'. He also wrote about the original crew, some of whom were willing to stay on, mostly providing they got higher wages, or a better position on board. Captain Uno Karlsson was signed on as master and a contract with him was made up in Mariehamn on 29 August 1929:

I Uno Karlsson herewith take over the Mastership of the 4/m barque *Ponape* from Mariehamn with all the responsibilities and rights the Finnish Sea Law gives against a salary of Fmk 2,750 per month which will be

raised to Fmk 3,000 for the second voyage and later according to the salaries of other masters in the company.

The contract had six articles, mostly dealing with the master's responsibilities to the company over matters of cargo and the economies of the ship's operation.

At the beginning of September the new master sent a telegram from Cardiff to the owner to say that four more of the original crew would stay on. Gustaf Erikson wrote back to say that he was sending six men and that the crew should then be sufficient. The ship had been offered a fixture to load salt for Japan but Gustaf Erikson did not accept. On 16 September the master wrote to say that *Ponape* was ready to sail, though the crew had been too small both for bending sail and bringing the provisions on board. He also discussed the crew and their wages.

It is of great interest, and probably very typical of Gustaf Erikson, that he underlined much of the captain's letter and pencilled remarks and questions on it, probably for his principal assistant, K A Fredriksson, to sort out. For instance:

J Nordenfeldt third mate, wages 1200:- Nordenfeldt said that he has been promised higher wages on the long voyages, but since I have not received any information from the company about it I have not been able to do anything about it.

On the side of the letter Gustaf Erikson wrote 'The wages now for a third mate are $^{11}/_{1200}$. Who has given the said promise?'.

In the same letter the captain wrote about a man who had got blood poisoning whom he had discharged. This worried Gustaf Erikson and in a letter of 15 November to Captain Uno Karlsson sent to Port Lincoln he wrote as follows:

What have you done with Kanervo? One can not irresponsibly and indifferently leave a man in a foreign country like that. When the man has got blood poisoning it is obvious that he has got an injury, that can be because of an accident, of which a report should have been made according to law. These are matters which can have uncounted consequences and may in no case be neglected.

He also wrote about the freight possibilities. He said that the whole market seemed dead (this was the beginning of the Great Depression of 1929–31) and that the only freight that had been discussed was one from South Australia to Callao for 20s, which seemed to be the highest possible rate. Gustaf Erikson continued:

If it should be Callao I want to point out to you that it is useless to try to enter Callao Bay after sunset; it will

Ponape *as* Bellhouse *under the Norwegian flag but British-owned, during the First World War.*
Åbo Akademi

never succeed unless there is a northerly wind, which may happen but rarely. I cannot remember how thorough the instructions I have given to you personally. I now want to remind you that the ship which according to your predecessor is in tip top order and free from rust both inside and out should be kept that way also in the future. . . .

In South American harbours you have to remember that the pilots are more or less unpractical and irresponsible, so you cannot trust them too much and the people in general are apt to postpone for tomorrow (manjana), so you have to push for yourself if you want the things to go on.

This is in short some of my opinion. My main principle is that every ship must be kept in first class shape and the cost of that is less important, but at the same time I expect everybody to do what he has been entrusted to do with interest, consideration and energy, so that nothing will be destroyed or wasted. These long explanations are not to be taken as any vote of distrust against you, but as a guidance in our future co-operation. . . . finally I may wish Captain and everybody on board welcome to port, Merry Christmas and Happy New Year.

Cordially, Gustaf Erikson.

Next is an example of the quite severe tone that Gustaf Erikson could use to some of his captains, and

Uno Karlsson being new in the line and quite young, only thirty-three years of age and, as he once put it himself in a letter, 'inexperienced', got perhaps even harsher treatment at first.

The *Ponape* arrived in Port Lincoln on 12 December after eighty-six days and loaded 2761 tons of wheat. On 20 January she sailed for Callao, arriving there on 10 March, and according to the captain started discharging at about 200 tons a day. His letter of arrival from Callao to Gustaf Erikson is quite short, only a meagre page. In a letter of 1 March Gustaf Erikson had remarked about the captain's inadequate correspondence and complained about the way the captain had done his accounts in the preceding ports. He wrote:

Coming to the accounts, I must say that they are incomplete, since I have absolutely to know what every man in the crew has drawn in every port, before the ship leaves. Thus, an excerpt from the crew-book [folk-bok] has to accompany every account as a verification. If the ship should be wrecked it is impossible for me to clear up the matters with the crew.

This remark goes also for the accounts from Cardiff, even if I did not make any remarks then.

Coming to correspondence I have to demand that you in your answers, with dates, state which letters of mine you have received. I understand from the letter received that you have got mine of Nov 15. You pass with silence though the matter of Kanervo . . .

When a crew-member has run away, is signed off, or otherwise is separated from the ship, copies of the said person's accounts should be sent to the company, and if he has run away a certification, preferably certified by the mate, that the man has run away also stating the time and place. This is because it in many cases is difficult to get out the warrant. In the case of Hagerström everything seems to be clear though, because he has deposited money in cash instead of warranty. I expect excerpts out of the crew-book both for Port Lincoln and Cardiff and after that from every port at the departure of the ship, this without exceptions, and it is easy to do if you can stop all the payments to the crew a few days before departure and thus have time to make up the crew-book.

Nothing is yet decided for the future. The guano freighters are not yet willing to employ sailing vessels and the freights are very bad. That is why I cannot give any information, so you have to wait for orders, that of course comes through Clarkson by telegraph. Hoping that as soon as possible you will send the corrections to the mistakes you have made and wishing you all welcome in port I sign

Cordially,
Gustaf Erikson

A week later Gustaf Erikson notified the *Ponape* that there was a possibility of guano cargoes to Europe from Guanape. If this materialised, the vessels *Hougomont* and *Ponape* would get the freights since he had ordered both *Winterhude* and *Grace Harwar* to return to Mariehamn. In Cardiff the new captain had taken too much ballast, over 1000 tons in the *Ponape* and Gustaf Erikson wrote very specific orders as to how to proceed with the ballasting depending on the prospects for future employment,

If the ship is half unloaded before any orders for future employment come through and there should not be a guano freight, then we have to think of something else. You should send a telegram when the ship is half unloaded so that I can give orders about ballast. It is much more expensive, as you will find out, if it has to be taken in while lying in the roadstead and that is why we have to know, so the ballast can be taken in at the same time the ship is discharged. It may be back to Australia, up the Puget Sound, to a nitrate port, or worst of all, round the Horn back home.

In the three first cases the ship will do with 850/875 tons of ballast, because to Puget Sound it is only a summer passage and Chile is only just out of the trade winds. To Australia a slightly bigger ballast is perhaps needed when it is going to be winter down south. If going home around the Horn, some more has to be taken in but 950 tons should be sufficient. In any case not as much should be taken in as in Cardiff. This is unnecessary and is throwing away money. Freights have been ordered from Seattle but in that case it will be to go to Victoria, Vancouver or Port Townsend for orders. I mention this so you can get the necessary charts in time, if those are not already on board. In Callao there usually are Yankee schooners and you could get special charts from them if they can not be bought, otherwise you have to send a telegram to New York or London in good time. Please tell this to Captain Sandström [of the *Hougomont*] as well because this goes for both of you.

. . . Don't forget to economise. It is very important now as always, but especially when everything goes badly.

Ponape eventually got the guano freight and went to Isla Guanape for loading, which commenced on 5 May. This was a slow process in the beginning because there were many ships which had arrived before the *Ponape* loading at the same time. In the end it went well enough. Even Gustaf Erikson was satisfied as he pointed out in a letter of 5 June. The *Ponape* sailed on 6 June for Dunkirk via the Panama Canal. The captain had thought of taking a tow in the English Channel and had also written to Clarksons about it, but Gustaf Erikson did not want any tows, he wrote: 'In no cases should towing commence before the Downs, but you have to try to sail as far as possible, because there is no hurry that I know of. You can make a towing contract even at the Downs if it then is necessary'.

The captain answered from the Panama Canal that he would do his best and sail as far as possible. On 17 August 1930, he wrote from Dunkirk to say that he had arrived after a good passage with favourable winds in the Channel. He did not have to take a tow.

Gustaf Erikson wrote to Dunkirk and discussed the future,

The freight market is still impossible and my ships one after another have to come home and be laid up. From that you know that there is no hurry and that you have to economise to the utmost. If possible keep the crew on board so that the ship can be sailed home if no freight is to be got because it is expensive to send out men only for the journey home . . .

The *Ponape* had trouble in discharging the guano in Dunkirk. The deck labour struck and refused to enter the hold until they were paid more. Gustaf Erikson left this matter for Clarksons to settle. He also wrote on 21 August to the captain to say that the outlook was somewhat better than previously, and that he thought that the vessel would not have to be laid up in Mariehamn. Two days later he notified

Ponape's figurehead was of Regina Elena.
R M Cookson

guano. On 28 August Gustaf Erikson wrote to Captain Karlsson in Dunkirk and commented on the crew.

> If the man that you suggest is competent as donkeyman and carpenter he can stay on, but as times are what they are, and there are plenty of idle men, the wages have also gone down, and I ask you to ask him if he does not think that 1000 marks is better than nothing. If you think the man is good then he can have 1100 marks at the most, and tell him that F.Å.A. [The Finnish Steamship Company] has lowered the wages to about a half and are laying up half of their fleet. Hoping that everything goes on normally.

Some of the crew were willing to stay on if they got an increase in wages but most refused. Gustaf Erikson wrote to Antwerp on 11 September

> As regards the crew, may I say just that those who are willing to stay on may do so, the rest shall be signed off immediately, no increase in the wages may be granted, except for those who are promoted, and those who have made one trip as deckboys may of course not advance to AB's. Lehtinen, Vihersalo and Svanfält may thus not get more than 500 marks as Ordinary Seamen. The cook you should try to get for 700 marks, but if impossible then give him what he asks. These concessions are only to save travel money for the crew, because there are men enough here since the North Sea and Baltic traders have started to lay up.

The men, Lehtinen, Vihersalo and Svanfält, had asked for 600 marks and the cook wanted 750 marks a month, but all but the cook stayed on for the offered amount on the undertaking by Gustaf Erikson that they would get an increase after six months.

An agreement had been made to take a passenger for the next voyage. Gustaf Erikson thought that there would be a free cabin because there was to be no third mate. Bedclothes, etc for the passenger were to be bought in Antwerp. He also notified the captain that he was negotiating the sale of *Ponape* but in his next letter, on 20 September, Gustaf Erikson wrote that the ship was to sail for Port Lincoln. The second mate had signed off and Gustaf Erikson said he was sending a man who had been signed on the barquentine *Estonia* instead. On 25 September he wrote again and confirmed that the captain should send an order to Messrs Appleby in London for provisions and sailcloth. Gustaf Erikson wrote (this was in 1930 when the deepest world trade recession of this century was touching its lowest point),

> May I once more remind you that the times are so bad that the ships can only just be kept at sea and it is with fear that I now send out the ship again. Therefore it is necessary to economise to the utmost, to make ends meet. And you must remember that it is only the crew

Captain Karlsson that part of the guano was to be discharged at Antwerp and that Clarksons had already entered into a contract for towing the vessel there. He continued,

> As I already mentioned the outlook is better now. You have to start getting ready for the next voyage. The ship will be painted and docked at Antwerp. Paint for the bottom is to be taken from International, as well as other paints, especially Danboline for the hold, which now has to be painted and cleaned thoroughly during the next voyage. The provisions are to be taken from Appleby in London, but should not be ordered before the freight is fixed and then should be taken for the round trip.

Ponape arrived at Antwerp on 8 September and immediately started to discharge the rest of the

who are making any money and that if I have to lay up, this source of income will fail. During the journey the hold should be carefully cleaned, especially all rust should be chipped and scraped and all bare spots painted over with red-lead once, and perhaps a second time with a lighter coloured paint, and finally the entire hold is to be painted with grey Danboline.

Also see to it that the decks get enough oil and tar after this last cargo which squeezes everything out that was there before.

A few days later Gustaf Erikson wrote again, now giving a very interesting brief account of the situation of his entire fleet. Despite the letters' gloomy tone things were looking up and the freights quoted were much better than those of the preceding year.

To give you an idea of the present crisis in shipping with sailing vessels I may tell you than only five of my bigger ships are fixed to sail in ballast to load wheat in ports in the Spencer Gulf for Europe, namely *Melbourne*, *Olivebank* at $^{31}/_6$, the latter loading in Melbourne or Geelong though, *Herzogin Cecilie* at $^{32}/_6$, *Lawhill* at $^{32}/_6$, and *Archibald Russel* at $^{33}/_9$. Now the rates have gone down to 30s and all the rest of our nine vessels are not chartered yet. The consequence of this is that I have to take the risk of sending *Ponape* down in ballast and unchartered. You should therefore do your utmost from the beginning to economise on board, not only with the gear but also with the provisions the price of which is rising enormously. Therefore make inventories of the provisions after two months, and a second time after two more months, when the ship is due in Port Lincoln for orders. When the ship is provisioned for twelve months you shall see to it that $^2/_3$ of the provisions are still there after arrival in Port Lincoln. In other words, provisions that are sufficient for 12 months shall not be used up in 9, or the time that is calculated for the voyage to Australia and back. Since there are no provisions on board the *Viking*, and also no stores, you are to give to Captain Hägerstrand at least a barrel of meat and a barrel of pork, and more if there is the need for it and a bigger quantity can be spared, then some paint and oils, rope, sailcloth etc. that is as much as can be spared. The same thing goes for my other ships, they will get the same orders, namely *H.C.*, *Melbourne*, *A.R.* and *Lawhill* to give everything they can spare, and if possible I wish that something can be sent to *Olivebank* in Melbourne.

You should never trust the economy of a steward, carefully follow his doings, especially his inventories. Co-operate, and calculate what the food has cost for two months, which is easy to do when the bills for the goods arrive from Appleby, and from them you can find out the prices for the different goods. If the bills don't arrive in duplicate you have to ask for a copy, or perhaps make a copy of them on board. The total wages for the crew for this voyage will be some 2500 marks less than on the previous voyage, which shows that the company has tried to do its best to make considerable savings. Because the ship had to come to such a bad place as Dunkirk, where the discharging was unreasonably expensive, and had to shift to another country, again with full expenses,

extra towing etc. the result is bound to be bad after all the overheads have been paid. But I am satisfied, though, that it has gone as well as it has.

Ballast. Since you had instructions about taking in too much ballast at Cardiff I hope that this time you will not make the same mistake, but will sail with about 900/950 tons. The ballast has to be placed high in the main hatch so the ship will not become too stiff and get dismasted and be carefully covered by battens so that it will not move to either side.

Since only two mates are going to be taken on this voyage, the cabin of the third mate or the second mate could be given to the passenger, so that you will not have intrusions in your cabin. He has of course to be satisfied with the ordinary food of the Captain and the Mates. Bedclothes, blankets and pillows he has to provide himself but he can have the ship's mattress [this seems to contradict the earlier instruction]. If southerly or SW winds are blowing at the time of departure, there is another way out of the English Channel to use, namely north of Scotland, but since high pressure is now prevailing in Europe northerly or easterly winds should be predominant for some time, and I am counting on the ship being ready to sail Friday or Saturday at the latest, thus using the Sunday to catch up a little on the vessels that have sailed earlier, of which the *Melbourne* left the Danish Sounds on the 24th and *H.C.* and *A.R.* the 20th, all for Port Lincoln.

Hoping for a fast and lucky voyage I sign

Cordially, Gustaf Erikson.

P.S. Observe and do not forget to look out for the Mates' bad habit of not keeping the gaskets tight which results in them tearing the sails, and also to furl the sails in time so they will not be damaged, but at the same time set sails as soon as the wind has dropped, even for only an hour at a time. See too, that the best sails are used only in stormy waters and that they are changed in the trade-winds where only old trade-wind sails are to be used. Also see to it that all the sails that are stowed away are well dried, so that they will not rot in the sail room and also that they will not rot furled during storms in the tropic waters.

On 9 October 1930, the captain wrote to inform the owner that the vessel was ready to leave Antwerp. The *Ponape* had been docked and a Lloyds surveyor had ordered some repairs, especially to the donkey boiler. The ship had taken in 1000 tons of ballast, that is 50 tons more than Gustaf Erikson had strongly recommended, but the captain did not indicate this. He reported that the passenger, a Mr Thornton from England, was on board and very comfortable in the ship. Paying passengers were an additional source of income for the company, and the publicity given to

Right: Ponape *lying deep laden in the River Fal in Cornwall above King Harry Ferry. It was most unusual for a sailing vessel to lie so far up the tidal river when waiting for orders though this is a popular laying-up ground for merchant ships.*

Osborne Studio

the Erikson ships, especially in the British press, was free advertising. Later, probably in 1934, the company even had a booklet printed for advertising purposes, which read as follows:

Short holiday cruises [and] long voyages to and from Australia by the large Sailing Ships owned by Captain Gustaf Erikson, Mariehamn, Åland.
What could be a more delightful change from the ordinary routine of a holiday than a short voyage in one of the few remaining real old-time sailing ships? This can be attained at a very moderate cost by large sailing ships which each year are so prominently featured in the newspapers as competing in the annual Grain Race home from Australia. There are sailings from about the middle of June until about the beginning of August from the English, Scottish or Irish ports (where the vessels discharge their grain cargoes) to Mariehamn, which is the capital of Åland. . . . The voyage from London or East Coast ports usually occupies about ten days, but

may be somewhat longer or shorter, and from the West Coast or Irish ports about two or three weeks, but in all cases depending on wind and other weather conditions met with during the voyage. The fare is a minimum of £9 for 12 days or less on board. No berth can be definitely reserved until the minimum fare is paid . . . The *L'Avenir* has been passed by the Finnish Authorities for carrying passengers, and can, in fact accommodate if necessary about 70 altogether. The famous *Herzogin Cecilie*, *Viking*, *Pamir*, *Passat* etc. have each spare berths for only about eight to a dozen and some accommodate even fewer. No special provision is made for passengers beyond providing the berth, which is made as comfortable as circumstances permit, with the same kind of food as is supplied for the Officers – In other words passengers must not expect the same service and attendance as is found on a first class liner. For that reason it might not be altogether too comfortable for elderly ladies or young children, although several ladies have travelled by these vessels both on the short and longer voyages to Australia, and have generally

expressed themselves as being delighted with the experiment. The vessels not being strictly passenger ships, the passengers are signed on to the ship's articles as members of the crew. They are not expected to assist on board, in any way, unless desiring to do so for their own pleasure and at their own risk.

About the long voyages the booklet said, among other things:

> For those who can afford the time for a long sea voyage, the usual opportunities will be available from Copenhagen to South Australia and return Europe if desired. It is possible that one or two of the vessels may also be sailing direct from British ports to Australia. The vessels leaving Mariehamn for Australia in ballast invariably call at Copenhagen on their way out, either for drydocking purposes, and/or taking on board Sea Stores and Provisions, so that passengers are able to join there. The voyage out to Australia either from Copenhagen or Britain usually occupies from about 90 to 100 days, and the homeward voyage to Europe about 100 to 120 days, depending entirely on the weather met with on the way out or home. . . . The fare is on the basis of 10/- per day for the time the Passenger is actually on board. . . . The voyage outwards by these sailing ships is almost invariably via the Cape of Good Hope, and homewards via Cape Horn . . . on the long voyage the ship's steward and cook have to depend largely on salt provisions and preserved goods which will keep on the long voyage. The voyage is purely intended for those who desire a long sea voyage by one of the few remaining sailing ships, and who are prepared to rough it, taking pot luck with the Captain and the Officers.

There follow some health regulations and two forms to be filled in by the passenger and his or her next of kin or other guarantor, which absolved the shipowner of any kind of claim in case of an accident. This sort of experience is a long way from the kind of sailing cruising provided in the new four-masted schooners built by an Ålander for the West Indies cruise business.

The *Ponape* sailed on 10 October 1930, from Flushing Roads and made a passage of eighty-nine days, north of Scotland into the Atlantic and to Port Lincoln for orders. Far out at sea leaving Antwerp three stowaways were discovered, hiding in the forecastle. The ship was too far out for it to be possible to put them ashore. From Port Lincoln the orders were to load at Adelaide. The loading was started on 27 January and completed on 9 February. The three stowaways, all Estonians, were to sail back to Europe on board *Ponape*, because had they been left in Australia the company would have had to pay £100 per head to the Australian authorities. Mr Thornton also wanted to take the trip back with the *Ponape* and an additional passenger was signed on. Gustaf Erikson wrote to Port Lincoln on

29 November and told the captain that the journey to Dunkirk and Antwerp did break even after all and the *Ponape*'s financial result was far better than that of *Hougomont*.

Ponape's journey back to Queenstown in 1931 took ninety days and was amongst the fastest in the Grain Races that year. She departed on 15 February and following her arrival on 25 May the captain wrote to Gustaf Erikson and told him that nothing of special note had occurred during the passage. The vessel went to London to discharge; the captain wrote that although the calculated discharging time was three weeks he thought it would take less time since they had already discharged 300 tons in one day. On 16 May 1931, Gustaf Erikson wrote to the vessel in Queenstown:

> From a telegram I can see that you have sailed not earlier than 15th of Feb., probably delayed by unfavourable winds or calm. Furthermore I notice that you have two paying passengers and three stowaways on board so there seems to be plenty of people and there is nothing to say about that.
>
> Until this day there is no employment for the future and if nothing turns up you have to come to Mariehamn for a while after the ship has been discharged and dry docked.
>
> You have to economise to the utmost, nothing except the utmost necessities are to be taken on board and you have to keep on crew for sailing the ship home. I think it will be impossible to get rid of the stowaways in discharging port without giving them money for the journey home. It is best to keep them on board and then we can pay their fares home from here, if the ship comes here. They can then pass for one man each when so many more have been discharged, otherwise I suppose we have to give them a ticket and some clothes, they cannot expect anything more.
>
> I have made a deal with Messrs. John Marshall & Co. for delivering fresh meat and vegetables in Bristol Channel ports, so if the ship goes there this firm has to be used.
>
> In order to get material for comparison of the journeys of the different ships, I have introduced so called track-charts, of which one is enclosed. You should mark the round trip on the chart and return it to me. The points need not be made more than every 7th or 10th day, observing that more important points will show on the chart. Remarkable events shall be noted in the margin and the prevailing winds between the points.

Gustaf Erikson concluded his letter by once again stating that the times were bad and that it was of the utmost importance to economise. He also wrote that half the North Sea and Baltic traders fleet would remain at home laid up for the first half of the summer sailing season. On 2 June he wrote again to the master and asked him to try to send part of the crew to the *Olivebank*, now lying at Cardiff, needing crew for the journey to Mariehamn. She had been out for so long that it was impossible to refuse permission to the crew to sign off. Gustaf Erikson thought that *Ponape*'s crew could not yet demand to be signed off and since there were stowaways on board the ship could manage to get to Mariehamn with a few hands less.

Captain Karlsson had written before to say that the donkey boiler was rusted beyond use and now Gustaf Erikson wrote to ask if it was possible to repair the old one, and at what cost. If a new one was to be ordered it had to have capacity enough for two winches and be of the same construction as one that previously had been installed in the *Archibald Russell*. He then told the captain to take bottom paint and boot topping on board, but that the vessel was not to be drydocked. Except for coffee, sugar, tea and flour, no stores were to be taken on board; they could be bought more cheaply in Mariehamn. Gustaf Erikson admitted that it would be easier to get all the stores on board immediately, but since the future was uncertain, and he had had an unfortunate experience with the *Grace Harwar* which had had to be laid up for a year with all her stores, he did not want to buy stores now. A new donkey boiler was bought in London to be installed in Mariehamn.

During the summer the *Ponape* lay in Mariehamn and in September put to sea again. Uno Karlsson remained as captain, but a new crew of twenty men was signed on in Mariehamn in September 1931 for a period of eighteen months. Only four, including the captain were from Åland. Except for two German apprentices, the rest came from different parts of mainland Finland. The captain was hired on contract at a monthly fee of 3000 marks, the rest of the crew's wages totalled 11,900 marks per month. The total wage bill was lower than it was in 1929 (when the crew also numbered twenty) when the monthly total was 14,650 marks. In 1935 the amount per month spent on the crew was 14,300 marks.

The difficult times to which Gustaf Erikson so often referred in his letters are reflected in the wages of 1931. Gustaf Erikson's 'house historians', Georg Kåhre and his brother Hilding, wrote in *50 years under the flag of Gustaf Erikson 1913–1962* that the wheat freights were at their lowest in 1930, between 20 and 23 shillings per ton, and that they thereafter varied every year, the average in 1931–33 being about 30s, and in 1934–36 25s. In 1937 freights again went up to 30s and in 1938 to over 40s for most of the vessels, a rise probably caused by the expected war.

In September 1931 the *Ponape* sailed from Mariehamn in ballast for Australia. Gustaf Erikson watched the departure from the jetty in the harbour. He wrote to the captain in Copenhagen saying that he thought that the departure went well, except for lack of room in the harbour. Near Copenhagen the *Ponape* was in collision with an Estonian steamer, the *Linda*, and was badly damaged. This incident happened at night and was probably caused by carelessness on board the *Linda* – they had no lookout and the visibility was clear that night. *Ponape*'s navigational lights were, however, found to be faulty. The damage was repaired in Copenhagen. Captain K A Fredriksson, Gustaf Erikson's right-hand man in such matters, went to Copenhagen to inspect the ship and to report to the owner. The matter was settled at a court in Copenhagen in favour of the Estonian steamer because of *Ponape*'s faulty navigational lights.

Just after the collision the captain spoke on the telephone to Gustaf Erikson, but there was only a very short comment on the accident in his letter to Mariehamn of 7 October. He informed Gustaf Erikson that they had started to clean the store room, that it had been painted and that the new provisions had been taken on board. The ship was also painted on the outside, both sides and bottom. A passenger, the same Mr Thornton, was on board and they had adapted the sail room as passenger's quarters.

On 8 October Gustaf Erikson notified the captain that the *Ponape* had been chartered to load wheat at 31s per ton to the United Kingdom, 31s 9d if to a port on the Continent. As usual the chartering went through Clarksons in London and they were sending the charter party to Port Lincoln. After the repairs had been completed *Ponape* got under way but had trouble in leaving the Danish Sounds. Twice she had to turn back because of a headwind, so the captain decided to let a motor tugboat tow them out. The Erikson barquentine *Estonia* and his schooner *Ostrobotnia* were there at the same time and also had difficulty in clearing Danish waters.

On 10 December Gustaf Erikson wrote to Port Lincoln, welcoming the *Ponape* to port. He told the captain about two of his other ships that had had difficulties getting clear of European waters, *Olivebank* and *Penang*, the former having been forced to anchor for a long time at Läsö and the Downs and the latter having nearly run aground on the Norwegian coast. He also, as always, reminded the captain of the importance of economy

because, every penny saved is a great advantage since the exchange rate is today Fmk 245 and will probably rise further. . . . All the previous instructions are still valid and if the stores have to be completed you have to first ask some of the comrades [the other ships in P. L.] if they have something to spare before one buys something expensive ashore.

He also said that he was displeased with the way in which the captain failed to follow orders, but as the collision with the *Linda* was now in the past they had better try to forget it, and hope that no more incidents of that kind would occur.

The *Ponape* arrived at Port Lincoln on 27 January 1932, after an uneventful passage distinguished only by the poor performance of the cook. She departed on 24 February with 3450 tons of bagged wheat, her total expenses in Australia being £1525 16s. After 118 days sailing she arrived in Queenstown and discharged at Rotterdam, the total freight being around £5500.

After discharging and drydocking the *Ponape* sailed to Trångsund, at the eastern end of the Gulf of Finland near Viborg, to load timber for South Africa. Captain Uno Karlsson had had enough and asked to sign off to get some rest. Some of the crew, nine men altogether, signed on for the next round-trip; some were promoted.

The new captain was Hugo D Karlsson who came from the *Killoran*. On 16 August he signed a contract which gave him a wage of 3000 fmk a month. From Trångsund the *Ponape* sailed to Kotka to take in the rest of the timber cargo. Hugo Karlsson sent a drawing of the midships deckhouse on the *Ponape*, suggesting how to convert it into two cabins for passengers but Gustaf Erikson did not comment. In an interview in 1975 Captain Werner Öjst, master of the *Archibald Russell* in 1932–33, revealed that in general captains did not like to have passengers on board for the voyages to and from Australia. He was offered command of *L'Avenir*, but when Gustaf Erikson told him that he was going to install cabins for about sixty passengers Captain Öjst declined the offer. He had had enough of passengers as mate of the *Herzogin Cecilie*. Captain Carl Granith, who was to follow Hugo Karlsson as master of the *Ponape* expressed the same kind of feelings in a letter to Gustaf Erikson written in August 1935 from *Ponape* on passage from Port Lincoln to Falmouth:

The passengers have probably had a good time on board, although they now are impatient while we have been delayed by headwinds and calm on the last leg of the journey. I have taught them the necessities of the navigation we use etc. But on the whole it is a nuisance to have them on board, especially the women. (For a while we thought that there would be a romance on board and that both of the female passengers would become moored in the matrimonial harbour on arrival to

London. But the affection seems to have diminished when we have come to a cooler climate).

After provisioning in Copenhagen in September the *Ponape* sailed for East London, where she arrived after seventy-five days on 8 December 1932. There she discharged part of the cargo and continued to Lourenco Marques to discharge the rest. Clarksons in London had sent orders to proceed to South Australia and the vessel arrived at Port Lincoln on 19 January, thirty-two days from Delagoa Bay. The orders were to load at Port Broughton. On 1 April she sailed for Falmouth and made a passage of 122 days with much bad weather and calm. After discharging and drydocking in London the ship sailed for Mariehamn where Captain Karlsson resigned for personal reasons.

Captain Carl Granith became *Ponape*'s master from the end of 1933; he had previously commanded the *Lingard* in 1926–27, and the *Pommern* in 1927–33. He was more literate than his predecessors and had a useful habit of writing letters to Gustaf Erikson while at sea, stating on the letterhead the vessel's position. His letters are of particular interest as they give a much broader account of events during the voyages than *Ponape*'s previous captains.

4-mast barque *Ponape* on passage to Port Victoria, S.A. Lat. S 40° 00'; Long. E 123° 30', December 28, 1933.

All is well on board. Today we have been 81 days at sea and three more days of average sailing will be enough to take us to port. As known we left at the same time as *Penang* from Copenhagen on October 8 with a stiff and favourable wind. By and by we left the *Penang* astern, but sighted her again in the North Sea. We went north of the Shetland Islands because the visibility was bad and the weather was quite hard. Northwest of Scotland we sighted a 4-masted barque that we thought must have been the *Olivebank*. Just after that we came into a storm. The sea was rough with the ship rolling in a way I have never encountered before. This ship rolls worse than any I have been in. Although we carried more sail than we should have, the ship rolled so much that she shipped water from both sides. I thought that something in the rigging might break, but everything held fortunately. The ballast was too much spread out and made the ship too stiff, although the 1st mate who has been on board for sometime said that they have had it trimmed even lower. We took up 80–90 tons of ballast on to the tween decks and the ship became better, but still rolls abnormally in the seas. . . .

Near the Cape Verde Islands we were accompanied by the *Passat*. For a whole week we sighted each other without either ship gaining on the other. Finally, when we came into the S.E. trades we were separated, because our competitor was higher up in the wind than we were. Near the 'line' we passed the Spanish training ship *Juan Sebastian del Cano* as if she was anchored, and the same

Captain Uno Karlsson and the crew of Ponape *in about 1930.*
Ålands Sjöfartsmuseum

day we passed out of the south tropics we passed and signalled to the schoolship *Favel* of Helsingfors. They had signalled to the *Passat* two days earlier. Then we did not sight any more vessels until yesterday when we sighted a 4-masted barque that we thought was the *Passat*.

We have cut sailcloth for 1 foresail, 2 topsails, 2 royals and one staysail. Painting has been done in the hold, the bilges we have been able to reach have been washed, and the hold has been prepared for loading. If we have the opportunity before we load, we will put in the new timber in the inside bilge, and chip and paint thoroughly where the ballast has been lying because a thorough overhaul is needed there. I apologise for not sending the ship's measurement papers from Copenhagen. I have no excuse but being busy installing and trying out the radio. . . . Hoping to receive a good charter party and that the coming year may be successful for you and finally wishing you a Happy New Year.

I remain,
Cordially

Later that year on 15 October 1934, Captain Granith wrote to Gustaf Erikson while the *Ponape* was still in the south Baltic, outward bound once again for Australia,

We are still here and it is impossible to come any further because of strong prevailing headwinds. Yesterday we reached Bornholm and rounded the Island. The westerly storm reached such a force that we could not make clear of land and had to go in leewards of the same. Although I have rounded the Horn several times I have never been in more wind for a period of two weeks. We have not lost any sails although we have done some hard sailing in order not to run up on the Russian coast. As an example of how difficult it has been, I can tell you that until now we have turned through the wind 36 times and sailed with only the topsails four times – an excellent opportunity for an untrained crew to learn something.

Truly the Baltic and North Sea trades could be as hard as any form of seafaring and four-masted barques were definitely never intended for Baltic sailing.

Eventually the *Ponape* escaped from the Baltic. She took in the usual provisions in Copenhagen and then sailed for Port Victoria on 21 October. Gustaf Erikson wrote on 20 December to Captain Granith in Port Victoria to say that the *Ponape* was unchartered and that the freights for the next season probably would be lower than for the last one. This was because steamers were accepting freights as low as 26s and the Germans chartered their subsidised sailing vessels for 24s 9d. Gustaf Erikson went on: 'As usual I have to remind you about the economy. It is very difficult on a freight of 25/- to cover the costs of the smaller vessels, and if there is something left over then it is needed to cover the losses from before'.

On the journey to Port Victoria Captain Granith wrote to Gustaf Erikson telling him about how the trip had proceeded so far,

> Lat. 38° 00′ South; Long. 127° 20′ East: On passage from Copenhagen to Port Victoria. January 11, 1935.
>
> All is well on board.
> We are closing in on the destination. Today we have been 82 days at sea and have still some 575 miles left before we reach port.
> We left Copenhagen Oct. 21 and reached the coast of Norway without having to go through the wind. There we got headwinds and were in company with *Pamir* and *Pestalozzi*. North of the Shetland Islands we were again in company with *Pamir* but were separated the next night and have not seen them since or the other ships. After 35 days we passed the equator and when we reached the Island of Trinidad we were 5 days ahead of the time made by us on last year's down trip. But shortly after that we were becalmed and had only weak winds that spoiled this journey from being a fast one. When we came close to Tristan da Cunha I decided to sail quite close to it in order to exchange fresh food for us. The natives came out in good time and the trading started. It was decided that in exchange for fresh meat and vegetables they should get the corresponding amount of flour etc. from us. When they went ashore to fetch the goods I let our female passenger and a couple of the crew go ashore for a short visit because the wind was light and the sea was calm.
> The light winds prevailed until we reached the Cape meridian which was during the Christmas feast. The night between December 26 and 27 we got a sudden storm. We had already taken in most of the sails I wanted stowed but four of our sails got more or less torn to pieces. I have cut canvas for 6 square sails and one mizzen and also 2 staysails, they are not sewn together yet.
> During this passage we have done a lot of work in the rigging.

When *Ponape* arrived in Port Lincoln she was still unchartered and the captain himself sought a freight. He wrote to Gustaf Erikson on 30 February 1935.

> The outlook is everything but good. I got the same answer from the different firms I visited. There is still quite a lot of wheat left, but nobody buys it except China and Japan, which is well known back home. Steamers are now loading for 20/- per ton on bulk and that would make in bags 22/6.

Eventually the ship was chartered, the loading in Port Lincoln started on 1 March, and she sailed on 11 April. At the Lizard on 9 August the *Ponape* received orders to continue to London for discharging.

On 15 July Gustaf Erikson informed Captain Granith that the *Ponape* was for sale, he wrote:

> I am offering her for sale but I am not willing to sell for scrap prices, but what I shall do with her I don't know either. If everything was normal she should return immediately to Australia after discharging, but now I don't know. There will probably be no time for coming home. I have sold *Grace Harwar* for scrap.

The *Ponape* lay in London until the middle of September, sailed yet again for Australia, loaded this time at Port Germein and was ready to sail to Europe in the middle of February; the freight was 26s. On 10 December Gustaf Erikson wrote to Captain Granith giving the facts of the fleet's economic situation:

> When all the expenses of my 14 deep sea vessels, including the classification costs of *Lawhill*, *Herzogin Cecilie*, *Olivebank* and *Killoran*, was 170.000 marks higher than the income of the said 14 vessels, the deep-water fleet showed a loss. . . . That is why I want you to get along with the least possible expenses. . . . If it interests you to know how the affairs of *Ponape* stand, there was
>
> in 1933 a loss of   Fmk 45.000
>   1934 a profit of   30.000
>   1935 a loss of   150.000

Ponape had made a total loss of 165,000 marks during the years that Captain Granith had been on board. Gustaf Erikson calculated that since the *Ponape* originally cost him £5500 all the losses amounted to £7500. Clearly the *Ponape*, now more than thirty years old, was becoming too expensive to run.

In December 1935 all the shareholding companies for the Erikson vessels were converted into more modern limited liability companies. According to Edgar Erikson the immediate impetus for this was the loss incurred by the family as a result of claims following a collision involving the barque *Lingard*. But another reason was no doubt that the family had decided to go into more modern steam tonnage and this was a way to get more funds into the company. For instance the statutes of the Ponape Company Ltd allowed a fund stock of 200,000 marks on 100 shares but the sum could be raised to 600,000 marks. Of the original 100 shares Gustaf Erikson had 98 and K A Fredriksson and Hilding Kåhre 1 each. When the *Ponape* eventually was sold in 1936 the company still remained in existence and in 1937 Gustaf Erikson, as chairman, proposed the raising of the stock to a sum of 600,000 marks in order to buy the SS *Argo*. The stock was raised to that amount with the possibility of raising it further, to 1,800,000 marks. These new limited liability companies had, in common with the old-fashioned part ownerships, one ship per company. In 1939 when the shares in the Ponape Co Ltd had been raised to a total of 900 they were owned as follows,

Gustaf Erikson 360
Edgar Erikson 135
Greta Erikson 135
Eva Erikson 135
Gustaf Adolf Erikson 135

In other words, Gustaf Erikson and his four children still held all the shares, as they had done from 1927 when the *Ponape* was bought from Hugo Lundqvist.

After what was to be her final passage from Australia to England the *Ponape* passed Falmouth on 8 June, 114 days out and discharged her cargo in London. Gustaf Erikson had prospective Canadian buyers for the ship, 'Adventurous World Cruises Ltd. in Toronto wants blueprints of the ship. They are planning passenger cruises with a sailing vessel'. From London the *Ponape* sailed for the shipyard in Nystad, acquired by Gustaf Erikson in 1933, to make some repairs and to wait for her fate. Captain Granith had diabetes and had to leave active sea-life for a year. In 1937 he returned, as captain of the *Olivebank*, in which he perished when it became the first war loss in 1939.

Finally in September 1936 a contract of sale was signed by Gustaf Erikson and the Liepajas Kara Ostas Darbnicas (The Libau Marine Port Works). The sum was £3425 and the ship was to be broken up. She was sold with all her inventory except for six winches and the figurehead. Mr Sven Andersson of the Åbo Akademi Maritime Museum had persuaded Gustaf Erikson to donate the figurehead to the new Maritime Museum in Åbo. In the early 1980s it came back to the Åland Maritime Museum in Mariehamn in exchange for another figurehead from a ship which had more connections with Åbo.

Chapter 8

PARMA

In 1902 A Rogers & Co in Glasgow built the steel four-masted barque *Parma* for the Anglo-American Oil Co. Her dimensions were 327.7 × 46.5 × 26.2ft, her gross tonnage 3084 and net tonnage 2882 (when she was registered in Mariehamn in 1931 the tonnage was 3046/2716) and she could carry 5300 tons of cargo. She was built for carrying oil from New York to the Far East and Australia and was first named *Arrow*. In 1912 the Reederei F Laeisz GmbH in Hamburg bought her and renamed her *Parma* and she was put on the nitrate trade. During the First World War she was seized by the British, and bought back by Laeisz after the peace. In 1930 she was laid up in Hamburg. A year later Captain Ruben de Cloux of Åland formed a shareholding group to buy her. The original group of shareholders at the time of the vessel's first registration in Mariehamn on 2 November 1931, was as follows:

Captain Ruben de Cloux	Finström	$^{36}/_{100}$
Mrs Vivi de Cloux	Finström	$^{5}/_{100}$
Mr Åke de Cloux	Finström	$^{5}/_{100}$
Miss Ruby de Cloux	Finström	$^{5}/_{100}$
Shipowner Gustaf Erikson	Mariehamn	$^{20}/_{100}$
Captain M A Gustafsson	Mariehamn	$^{3}/_{100}$
Captain Isidor Eriksson	Mariehamn	$^{10}/_{100}$
Mr Algot Johansson	Mariehamn	$^{4}/_{100}$
Captain John Wennström	Wårdö	$^{10}/_{100}$
Captain Gustaf Manner	Wårdö	$^{2}/_{100}$

Concealed in the $^{51}/_{100}$ths held by the de Cloux family were those of the Australian born, British domiciled, writer and sailor Alan Villiers, who for some time (1931–33) had $^{19}/_{100}$ths in the vessel and was, in fact, the third largest shareholder after Gustaf

Parma.

Erikson, and also those of Mr James William Appleby with $^{10}/_{100}$ths, who was later listed as Percy Appleby with $^{16}/_{100}$ths. Finnish law did not allow foreigners to hold shares in Finnish vessels, so the British interests could not be overt. Alan Villiers has in his books *The Set of the Sails* and *Voyage of the Parma* described how he met with de Cloux (with whom he had sailed in the *Herzogin Cecilie* in 1928) in London, when the latter was in command of Hugo Lundqvist's barque *Plus* and they came to discuss the purchase of a big sailing ship.

On 29 October the shareholders held their first meeting in Mariehamn and established the articles of partnership. The name of the little company became *Rederibolaget Parma* and it was to function according to Finnish sea law rules about part-owned vessels. In order to cover the price of the ship and also to provide some floating capital, every owner had to pay a sum according to his share in the ship, totalling for all shares 500,000 marks. The price of the ship, according to the bill of sale was 34,000 German reichsmarks, 'slightly under £2000' according to Alan Villiers. The total capital of the company, again according to Villiers, was £3000 and a 10 per cent deposit had been paid to F Laeisz on 15 October. The next day or the day after (Villier's account varies between his books) she was chartered to load 5000 tons of bagged grain in Spencer's Gulf at 31s per ton – a charter worth £7750, almost four times the investment in the vessel and enough to cover both that and her operating costs and still leave a net profit. Thus by her first voyage for her new owners the *Parma* eradicated the danger of depreciation.

Captain Ruben de Cloux was an Åland captain of the old school. He was born in Föglö in 1884, and like many other future captains went to sea in a local *galeas* as cabin boy. He sailed in various Åland vessels until he took his masters' certificate in 1909 and then became mate in the barque *Ocean* which was wrecked in 1911. Following this he spent one season with the East Kamschatka Fishery Ltd, and a year on the steamer *Uno* of Helsingfors. During the First World War he worked on the American tugboat *Slocum*. In 1919 he was given command of the *Lawhill* which he held until 1921, when he became master of the newly bought *Herzogin Cecilie*. It was while he was captain of the latter that, largely due to Alan Villier's writings, he became famous in the British press and the fast passages that he made with her became well known to a large audience. He was then for a much shorter time, master of the *Viking* and then the *Plus* before he formed the shareholding group for the *Parma*.

At the first meeting of part-owners all the shareholders were represented, Gustaf Erikson by his employee Captain K A Frederiksson. Captain Isidor Eriksson was elected managing owner for 1931 and the following year but in fact went to sea and was almost at once replaced by John Wennström of Wårdö, uncle of Ruben de Cloux. Captain Ruben de Cloux was elected master of the vessel for a monthly salary of 5000 fmk. It was also decided that Captain de Cloux should insure the ship against total loss against a premium of five per cent. At the meeting Captain de Cloux formally told the other shareholders that the vessel had already been chartered with grain from South Australia at 31s per ton. In November 1931 de Cloux was in Hamburg taking over the ship. He wrote to the managing owner shortly before the *Parma* was to sail.

> I send in this letter copies of the shares that I have accepted for Messrs Appleby and Mr Villiers . . . As you already know Gustaf Erikson has paid his share to us. . . .
>
> You suggest that we should transform the ownership of *Parma* to a limited liability company, but I think that it can wait for now, because if we do it now it is not impossible that Gustaf Erikson might try to get hold of the majority of the stock, and that I do not want to happen.
>
> I have insured the *Parma* through Clarksons, London, against total and constructive total loss, including collision liability ($^4/_4$ths Running Down Clause), as can be seen from the enclosed letter from Clarksons, for 6 per cent. So I think we don't run any further risk. Furthermore Gustaf Erikson is not taking part in the insurance, but in the presence of witnesses has refused. So the insurance will be divided on $^{80}/_{100}$ at £3000. . . .
>
> I have got 6 apprentices who pay Fmk 1000 each and one who pays 300, 60 Fmk monthly until 300 is paid.

> These payments have been a great help for me to pay the large expenses here.
>
> I am sorry that we did not dare to buy the *Pamir* but let Gustaf have it, if we had been a little more determined when I was home she would now have been ours. Gustaf got her for 42000 Fmk which I think very cheap, but it is now too late to regret that . . .

It is interesting to notice that there must have been some healthy business rivalry between some of the owners of the *Parma* and Gustaf Erikson. He was let in to the ownership with quite a substantial share, $^{20}/_{100}$, but on the other hand de Cloux was afraid that he might want to take over the whole ship. The above also illustrates the importance of the apprentices' fees. They could sometimes mean the difference between having to sell a ship as unprofitable and continuing in business.

The *Parma* sailed in ballast from Hamburg to South Australia, arriving at Port Broughton on 2 February 1932, eighty-three days from Hamburg. On the first muster roll, taken in Mariehamn on 31 October 1931 it is stated that the crew of the vessel was to consist of at least twenty-two men, the master, and first, second and third mates, making twenty-six altogether. The complete crew list for the first passage is as follows:

	mk
Captain Ruben de Cloux, Finström	5000
1st mate Gustaf Manner, Wårdö	2000
2nd mate Torsten Simons, Mariehamn	1400
3rd mate Olof Blom, Wårdö	900
Steward David Eriksson, Wårdö	1500
Cook Runar Ekblom, Föglö	750
Ordinary Seaman Mauri Vass, Raumo	450
Ordinary Seaman Johan Olof Westerlund, Finström	450
Ordinary Seaman Johan Hugo Österman, Finström	450
AB Algo Olof Blom, Wårdö	550
AB Algo Karl Birger Strömberg, Wårdö	550
Carpenter Walter Lindholm, Wårdö	850
Ordinary Seaman Åke Jansén, Hitis	400
Donkeyman Holger Mattsson	800
Deck Boy Nils Johansson, Eckerö	300
Ordinary Seaman Dan Erik Eriksson, Wärdö	550
Deck Boy William K Mansen, Finström	350
Apprentice Heinz Meisel, Germany	—
Apprentice Hans Pfeffer, Germany	—
Apprentice Johannes Riecke, Germany	—
Apprentice Heinz Tennhardt, Germany	—
Apprentice [name unreadable], Germany	—
Apprentice Heinz Sperling, Germany	—
Apprentice Helmut Lenk, Germany	—
Ordinary Seaman Horst de Wolff, Germany	450
Ordinary Seaman Willi Hammerich, Germany	450
Deck boy Sven Cavén, Åbo	100
Deck boy Johannes Rehn, Germany	300
Ordinary Seaman Rolf Christensen, Germany	450

cont.

Above: Karl Karlsson captioned this photograph, 'A study in curves; courses bellying to the good South East Trades, S.V. Parma, 1934–1935.'
Karl Karlsson

Parma, *wet work on deck.*
Helge Österberg

AB [name unreadable], Germany	550
AB [name unreadable], Germany	550
	15.100

The first seventeen on the roll were signed on in Mariehamn on 31 October, the Germans and the mainland Finn, Sven Caven, in Hamburg on 7 November 1931. If we compare the wages of *Parma*'s officers and crew with *Ponape*'s for the same year it is obvious that the captain of the *Parma* has a much larger salary, though we must remember that Uno Karlsson in the *Ponape* was quite young and inexperienced. But on the whole the officers of the *Parma* had higher wages than their opposite numbers in the *Ponape*. The steward of the *Ponape* was better paid, as was the carpenter, while the able and ordinary seamen had about the same wages. Quite a

lot of the crew, seven men, came from Wårdö, probably brought to the ship by John Wennström of that community. John Wennström, Ruben de Cloux's uncle, was a shipowner of the old tradition with much experience as a shareholder in vessels. Thus *Parma* provides another example of how important the ties of kinship were in the old-fashioned shareholding groups in Åland.

In Port Broughton the *Parma* loaded 5220 tons (62,650 bags) of wheat and sailed on 18 March for Falmouth. It was to be a very difficult voyage. Able seaman Birger Strömberg recalled in an interview in 1968, 'It was the worst voyage I have been on, after about a month or so we were at the Horn. We had to sleep in the sail-locker because everything was filled

Parma, *shifting the upper topsail on the mizzen.*
Helge Österberg

Thirty-five-year-old Karl Karlsson, centre, standing in suit and white-topped cap, with the crew of the Parma *at Port Lincoln, Australia, in 1935. The crew at this date included many young Germans.*
Karl Karlsson

with water, we slept among the sails, and it was snowing . . .'. The *Parma* arrived at Falmouth after 103 days and was ordered to discharge at Cardiff. She came to Mariehamn as usual for the summer, and sailed again on the 30 September 1932. Some of the crew had signed off already in Cardiff, among them Alan Villiers and his first wife who had been on the mustering-roll, he as an AB, but without any wages stated. Alan Villiers implies in his autobiography *The Set of the Sails* that he was in the *Parma* for every voyage under the Finnish flag until the summer of 1933 when he left her in Mariehamn. The records preserved in Mariehamn show him as a crew member only for the first homeward passage in 1932.

The Germans who had been apprentices on the first round-trip were now ordinary seamen; the number of men signed on in Mariehamn on 28–30 September 1932, was twenty-seven, all hands told. This time there was only one apprentice, Clive Parker from Wolverhampton, England. On the way out the *Parma* was drydocked and provisioned in Copenhagen. At the Burmeister & Wain yards the bottom was cleaned and painted from the keel to the lightline with a coat of anti-corrosion and anti-fouling. The rest of the hull was painted with two coats of Holzapfels International composition. On 10 October the ship left Copenhagen and sailed through the English Channel with some difficulty, and out into the Atlantic. Ninety-seven days after leaving

Denmark the *Parma* anchored at Port Victoria. She was fixed at 28s 6d per ton and the South Australian Farmers Co-operative Union Ltd loaded 62,863 bags of wheat in her and she was ready to sail again on 1 March. Her freight totalled roughly £7400. As she had already paid for herself, the net profit on this second voyage must have been in the order of £2400. On 26 February 1933 Captain de Cloux sent a departure letter from Port Victoria to his uncle, John Wennström, managing owner of the ship. According to Finnish sea law the master of the vessel should have been formally re-elected, but since the ship had already left, the managing owner proposed 'that Captain de Cloux should receive the gratitude of the part-owners because of the good result achieved during the first voyage of the ship and also the wish from the part-owners that he would remain master of the *Parma*'.

In a letter from Port Victoria Captain de Cloux wrote, 'I see from the letter received from you of Jan 17, that you know that we have arrived here after a long passage, but we have not lost any time though, since we should not have been able to be loaded any sooner, even if we had arrived earlier'.

Åland master mariners. Standing (left to right), Captain Donner of Lemland and Captain Jansson of Listersby, Wårdö. Seated, Captain John V Wennström, managing owner of Parma, *of Wårdö and Captain Victor Karlsson of Wårdö.*

Edward Wennström

Parma's next passage from South Australia to Britain in 1933 was to be the fastest ever in the history of the Grain Races. After eighty-three days at sea she anchored at Falmouth; she was ordered to discharge at Hull.

The annual meeting of the shareholders took place in Mariehamn on 14 December. They were notified that the board had appointed Captain de Cloux's brother-in-law, Karl Victor Karlsson, master of the vessel – another example of the importance of family connections in the tightly knit shareholding groups. Karl Karlsson was only thirty-three years old, but already had vast experience in sailing vessels which has been recorded by one of the authors in the National Maritime Museum's Monograph No 55, *Karlsson, The Life of an Åland Seafarer*. He had previously been in command of the four-masted schooner *Atlas* in which he held 5/100ths.

Captain de Cloux was paid a sum of 5000 marks as

gratuity for his services to the highly successful owning syndicate and in the autumn he took the *Parma* to Söderhamn in Sweden to load a cargo of timber to London. There he left her and Karl Karlsson stepped into his place. The outbound journey to Port Victoria took ninety-three days. The passage was an unlucky one because the ship lost a man in the English Channel on 9 October. Ordinary seaman Birger Ekström from Åland was hit by a block and fell overboard. A lifebuoy was thrown, but since the ship was sailing very fast in force 8, and she was on a lee shore, nothing could be done to save him without too great a risk for the ship and all in her.

After loading in Port Victoria *Parma* sailed for Europe and after a passage of 138 days was ordered direct to Birkenhead to discharge. From there the ship sailed to Kotka to load timber and after that to Raumo where the cargo was completed. She was to discharge the timber in East London and Beira.

After discharging, with long delays, the *Parma* sailed in ballast to Port Victoria, a forty-five day passage. She loaded about 5000 tons of bagged wheat in Port Victoria and sailed on 28 April for Falmouth. This time she had one of the longest passages for the season and took her orders after 136 days at sea; she

A Parma *reunion at a Buffalo Lunch in 1983. The group includes Captain Karl Karlsson, second from left, Jarl Mattsson, chief mate, Justo Häggblom, second mate, Viktor Andersson, third mate and Karl Gunnell, a mess boy.*
Karl Karlsson

discharged at Barry Docks. During this slow journey there was another accident, Åke Ulriksson from Pargas, fell from the rigging and was killed.

Now it was late in the season and the *Parma* was to sail directly to South Australia without going to Mariehamn. After a troublesome start on 21 November she had to be towed back to Barry Docks for some repairs to the windlass. After that she made a fast passage to Port Victoria of seventy-three days. Meanwhile in Mariehamn the shareholders decided to transform themselves into a limited company from 30 January 1936. Captain John Wennström became chairman of the board, Gustaf Erikson and M A Gustafsson ordinary members and Algot Johansson and Isidor Eriksson supplementary members. The shareholding groups had become outdated and the decision was quite in line with what was done with the other Åland sailing vessels at the time.

After loading she returned via the Cape of Good Hope to Falmouth in 117 days. Arriving at Falmouth on 15 July 1936, Captain Karlsson received two letters from the managing owner in which the possibilities of selling the *Parma* for scrap the

following year were discussed. The vessel was due for reclassification in 1937.

Captain Karlsson wrote back to John Wennström sending a list of the necessary repairs that had to be made in order to keep the vessel in sailing condition. Finally the orders came and on 31 July the vessel was towed to Glasgow. The tugs *Warrior* and *Thunderer* were to take her in, the *Thunderer* aft to steer her clear in the bends and to slow down the speed if necessary. At the inlet of the Princess Dock the *Parma* hit the pier head and the watchtower. The tugs pulled her free and finally got her to the quayside in the dock. Both the pier and the ship were damaged. Her stem was broken and several bowplates damaged. The captain blamed the whole affair on the pilot and first tug. He wrote to John Wennström

> The freight market being what it is it was a pity in many ways that we hit the pier. But from our side there was nothing to be done to avoid the accident. Who was responsible for the accident is difficult to say, but my opinion is that both the pilot and the fore tugboat are to blame for what happened. Any compensation from one or the other is not possible to get as far as I can see.

The cost for repairing the ship and the pier was estimated to be at least £485. Although the ship was insured it did not cover accidents like this. It was decided in Mariehamn that the *Parma* was to be sold and Clarkson & Co were commissioned to try to do so. They received a few offers of about £2500 from Clyde shipbreakers and one from a Hamburg shipbreaker of about £3500. On 8 August the board of the *Parma* Co Ltd wrote a bill of sale according to which the firm Kohlbrandwerft Paul Berendsohn was to buy the vessel for £3300. Since there were some difficulties about the payment from Germany the Parma was put under the British flag, which is why the name of Messrs Barnett Brothers appears on the bill of sale in England. This procedure cost extra which was why the *Parma* had to be sold for £3300. But, as Clarkson put it in a letter, they were 'still able to obtain more than the Scotch shipbreakers were willing to pay'.

Gustaf Erikson became interested in acquiring *Parma*'s sails when he learned that the vessel was to be sold for scrap. He wrote to Karl Karlsson and asked him to make a list of all the sails and state in what condition they all were. Immediately after receiving the letter Karlsson replied, offering the left over provisions to Erikson. Whether any deal was completed is not clear from the records.

Killoran *under the British flag.*

Abo Akademi

Chapter 9

KILLORAN

by Brigadier I R Ferguson-Innes

On 30 June 1900 the *Killoran* was launched from Ailsa Shipbuilding Company's yard at Troon. She was named by Miss Corsar of Arbroath, who was possibly a member of the Corsar family who owned the Flying Horse Shipping Line. It has been stated that *Killoran*'s launch attracted great interest locally, because she was the biggest sailing ship ever launched at Troon. The only evidence of 'interest' that I have been able to find however, is a very short paragraph in the *Ayr Advertiser* of 5 July 1900, simply reporting the event. Her builders, when still in existence, had no records of her whatsoever. Both her British owners went out of business over fifty years ago, and only very fragmentary information about their activities and the ships they owned exists.

Killoran was registered at Glasgow on 15 August 1900. *Lloyds Register* records that the ship was owned by The Killoran Barque Company and was managed by Messrs J Browne of Glasgow. It was a common practice in those days to register one-ship companies, usually in the name of the ship. This system of registration ensured that a claim in respect of one ship could not be made against others of the same fleet, since they were each owned by a separately named company. According to *Lloyds Confidential Index* all *Killoran*'s sixty-four shares were held by James Browne.

Killoran was a single deck steel barque with fully raised forecastle and poop. The vessel measured 1523 net and 1757 gross registered tons and her cargo capacity was reckoned at 3100 tons. The principal dimensions of the vessel were 261.5 × 39.5 × 22.7ft. The cabin deck measured 46ft in length and the forecastle 30ft. Her rigging was more lofty than that of most of her contemporaries. The main yard measured 90ft in length, the main royal-yard was 48ft. She was furnished with halliard winches but the yards were braced on the old and time-honoured principles.

Killoran was, without question, built for carrying capacity rather than for speed. Nevertheless, she was a very neat barque, crossing royals over double topgallants. Her topsides were dark green, with white boot-topping and a yellow 'ribbon' running round her hull at the top of the bulwarks. Her saloon was panelled in birdseye maple and teak, and her upper works were white. Obviously she did not have the sheer line of some of her more famous sisters of earlier days. In spite of this her sail plan gave her an attractive appearance which did credit to her builders and designers. She could be fairly said to uphold the claim which has often been made: that the most beautiful of man's creations was the full- or square-rigged ship. In contrast to the many mechanical and architectural monstrosities which man has contrived, sailing ships stand out as objects of great grace and beauty perhaps matched only by nature's creation, the thoroughbred horse.

The origin of ship's names is a fascinating subject, the *Killoran*'s has always been a bit of a mystery. Opinion in Glaswegian shipping circles seems to favour that she was named after Kiloran Bay on the Isle of Colonsay. In support of this view is the fact that her sister ship *Kildalton*, also built at Troon, was without doubt named after a parish on the adjacent Island of Islay – but a discrepancy arises. Kiloran Bay has always been spelt with one 'L', the ship always with two. Another possibility, is that the ship's name is linked to three small hamlets in Eire called Killoran, though a connection between a ship whose origins are so strongly linked to the area of Clydeside and a remote Irish village seems unlikely. One other source, however, does provide possible support for a link with Eire. Captain Alex Bone, who was an apprentice on *Killoran* on her maiden voyage, has recorded that her figurehead was a golden haired Irish colleen. There is no doubt that her figurehead was that of a beautiful maiden, and it was acknowledged to be an outstanding example of a wood carver's art. When I was familiar with the lady, she had aged somewhat since the day when her lips had first tasted the salt spray of the oceans. But I certainly cannot recall any shamrocks or other artistic features which would connect her with the Emerald Isle. Of course over the years she had endured many facelifts by way of the ships' paint locker, and had become a brunette. In my opinion she could just as well have been a bonnie highland lass instead of an Irish colleen. The mystery of her name's origin is likely to remain.

Killoran was one of the few iron or steel barques built at the turn of the century. She was employed in the general tramp trade wherever the freight market dictated. She had no notable passages to her credit and apart from two minor collisions, had an incident-free career. It is therefore unreasonable to expect that her story should be well recorded.

On 8 September 1909, *Killoran* was sold to Messrs J Hardie and Company of Glasgow. Her green topsides were now changed to the then well-known Hardie colours of a dark hull with black and white ports. The founder of this firm was the famed Captain John Hardie, one of the foremost seamen of the day. Hardies was one of the biggest and best sailing vessel owning shipping firms, owning several well known ships. All of those actually built for them were named after battles in the Peninsular War. They were one of the last owners to maintain investment in sail tonnage. *Killoran* was to remain with the Hardie fleet until 1924.

In December 1920, she sailed from Dublin on her last voyage under the Red Ensign. From Liverpool she proceeded to Port Lincoln where she loaded grain for the United Kingdom, calling at the Azores en route. The voyage ended at Sunderland on 29 November 1921. After this she was laid up until 7 February 1924, when she was bought by Gustaf Erikson for £2650. At this time she was one of the three last big steel square-rigged vessels to be registered at, and sail from, a home port in the United Kingdom. The other two were *Hougomont*, which was also sold to Captain Erikson on 28 January 1925,

Scots lassie or Irish colleen? The figurehead of Killoran.
Brigadier Ferguson-Innes

and *William Mitchell* which was broken up in 1927. *Hougomont* was a four-masted barque, and *William Mitchell* was a full-rigged ship. As *Killoran* lasted until 1940, she must therefore receive the honour of being the last British built barque to survive. She was lucky to have been included on Gustaf Erikson's 1924 'shopping list' of desirable vessels for purchase. Otherwise there is not the slightest doubt that her very last voyage would have been that which ended in November 1921, for it was then that the world wide abandonment of sail began in earnest.

The details of her voyages under the British flag (see pp 154-55) have been supplied by The Memorial University of Newfoundland and Strathclyde Regional Archives. In some cases dates are not complete, but no log books or other documents exist.

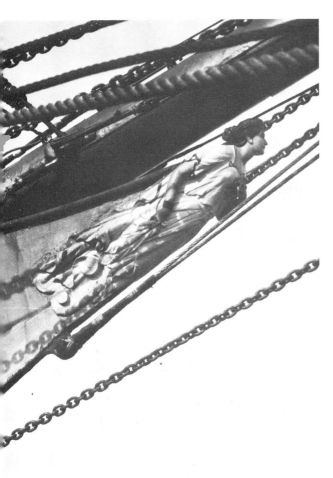

During her days under the British flag she was employed almost entirely trading to ports in North and South America and Australia. She was continuously at sea throughout the First World War, and must have had more than her fair share of luck as for most of the time she was sailing in the North or South Atlantic, certainly not a safe area for a rather slow-sailing ship.

When in April 1916 she lay in Ellesmere Port on the Manchester Ship Canal, the number of sinkings had already begun to increase. Sometime around the end of April and beginning of May the *Killoran* sailed in ballast, her destination Pensacola. One day she was lying becalmed about a hundred miles south-west of Fastnet when excitement rose upon hearing gunshots from the seaward direction. Finally, the wind picked up and darkness came upon them. After some hours of brisk sailing cries of distress were heard and they hove to. The gangway and lifelines were lowered over the side, whereupon no less than seventy-five terror-stricken Arabs climbed on board. They were the survivors from the SS *Trevean* which had been sunk when *Killoran* heard the shots fired. In addition, a handful of Europeans, officers of the same vessel, finally clambered up from the boats. Fortunately, all were transferred some days later to one of the New Zealand Steamship Company's steamers that was on its way to Europe – otherwise the feeding problem on board the sailing ship would have been hard to solve.

Killoran *under tow*.
Åbo Akademi

One of these Atlantic voyages was very nearly *Killoran*'s last, not due to any wartime action but rather because of the forces of nature. She encountered an especially savage cyclone, and to save the ship a sea-anchor had to be put out on the starboard bow and oil-bags placed in the forward heads, whilst only one forestay-sail could be carried. It took a long time to restore the ship to good shape.

Towards the end of the war the ship sailed for Santos and from there to Wallaroo for a cargo of wheat. Her destination was now Dublin and she arrived there in March 1919 after, so it was said, a relatively good voyage, in any case it was well within a hundred days. Imagine the jubilation of the crew when they heard that the war was at last over.

In December 1920 *Killoran* loaded in Dublin and sailed for Australia but at this point her luck ran out. In Irish waters she encountered very heavy weather, lost a whole suite of sails, and had to turn back. An attempt was made to get into Liverpool but she went aground in the Mersey.

Killoran was refloated, fitted out again, and sailed

Killoran's Voyages under the British Flag

Voyage	Commenced	Ports of Call	Ended
1.	20 August 1900 Ardrossan	Montevideo – San Francisco	15 September 1901 South Shields
2.	9 November 1901 South Shields	San Francisco	31 December 1902 Fleetwood
3.	13 January 1903 Fleetwood		19 January 1903 Cardiff
4.	12 February 1903 Cardiff	Acapulco – Tocopilla	5 April 1904 Dunkirk
5.	29 April 1904 Dunkirk		4 May 1904 South Shields
6.	14 November 1905 Hamburg	San Diego – Seattle – Port Townsend	11 March 1907 Liverpool
7.	23 April 1907 Liverpool	Melbourne	18 January 1908 South Shields
8.	15 February 1908		26 February 1908
		Sold to Messrs J Hardie and Company	
9.	December 1909 Liverpool	Sydney – Chanaral – Tocopilla – Queenstown	March 1911 London
10.	May 1911 London	Port Adelaide – Melbourne – Geelong – Plymouth	April 1912 Swansea
11.	May 1912 Swansea	Rio de Janeiro – Astoria – Portland – Astoria – Falmouth	July 1913 Cork
12.	August 1913 Cork	Barry – Montevideo – Newcastle – Caldera – Iquique – Falmouth	February 1915 Rotterdam
13.	March 1915 Rotterdam	Weymouth – Valparaiso – Tocopilla	April 1916 Ellesmere Port
14.	June 1916 Ellesmere Port	Pensacola	November 1916 Liverpool
15.	January 1917 Liverpool	Gulf Port – Buncrana	June 1917 Greenock
16.	September 1917 Greenock	Buncrana – Santos – Wallaroo – Hampton Roads – Plymouth	February 1919 Dublin
17.	March 1919 Dublin	Cardiff – Buenos Aires – Rotterdam	December 1919 Antwerp
18.	February 1920 Antwerp	Montevideo – Bahia Blanco	August 1920 Dublin

for Port Lincoln. From here she made a long passage of 157 days to Sunderland, where she was laid up for a year. Subsequently she was transferred to the River Blackwater where she lay for a further two years. It was here that Gustaf Erikson acquired the vessel. In March 1924 he paid £2650 for her and took her to Grangemouth for a survey.

The vessel's new master was Captain K J Erikson, and it was he who was in charge of *Killoran* for her first voyage under the Finnish flag, from Grangemouth to Antofagusta and return to Liverpool. From there she sailed to Restigouche in Canada and took on cargo for Buenos Aires where she arrived on 25 September 1925. On 15 December she sailed and made a good passage of fifty-six days to Port Lincoln. She now loaded a cargo of coal in Newcastle, New South Wales and departed on 1 April for Callao. On this part of the voyage she nearly met her doom. She was caught in a full gale and suffered severe damage. She was pooped and lost her helmsman, her wheel and her binnacle overboard. Her cargo of coal shifted and under normal circumstances she should have been lost.

It says much for the seaworthiness of the old ship and the skill of her crew, that she eventually made port under a form of jury rig. In those days she

Voyage	Commenced	Ports of Call	Ended
19.	December 1920 Dublin	Liverpool – Port Adelaide – Port Lincoln – Azores	27 November 1921 Sunderland

Laid up until 23 February 1924 then sold to Gustaf Erikson.

20.	25 April 1924 Grangemouth	Antofagasta	26 February 1925 Liverpool
21.	11 April 1925 Liverpool	Restigouche – Buenos Aires – Port Lincoln – Newcastle – Callao – Sydney – Port Lincoln – Falmouth	25 June 1927 Rotterdam
22.	3 July 1927 Rotterdam	Norrköping – Vestervik – Port Adelaide – Ylo – Don Martin Island	24 September 1928 London
23.	20 December 1928 London	Port Lincoln – Ylo – Santa Rosa Island	5 October 1929 Antwerp
24.	22 November 1929 Antwerp	Newport – Venezuela – Falmouth	1 July 1930 Helsingfors
25.	14 July 1930 Helsingfors	Trångsund – Kotka – Copenhagen – Lourenco – Marques – Port Lincoln – Wallaroo – Lizard	15 August 1931 Gravesend
26.	19 September 1931 Gravesend	Port Augusta – Falmouth	13 June 1932 Sunderland
27.	20 September 1932 Mariehamn	Copenhagen – Port Lincoln – Falmouth	22 June 1933 Tyne
28.	26 July 1933 Tyne	Mariehamn – Oskarshamn – Port Victoria – Queenstown	20 June 1934 Belfast
29.	13 September 1934 Mariehamn	Helsingør – Port Germein – Falmouth	28 June 1935 Belfast
30.	1 September 1935 Mariehamn	Gothenburg – Port Victoria – Port Germein – Falmouth	12 August 1936 Ipswich
31.	19 September 1936 Ipswich	Port Victoria – Falmouth	7 June 1937 Hull
32.	9 July 1937 Hull	Fredrikstad – Oslo – East London – Port Victoria – Port Germein – Falmouth	14 July 1938 Tyne
33.	13 August 1938 Tyne	Mahé – Auckland – Port Lincoln – Queenstown	29 November 1939 Cork
34.	27 February 1940 Cardiff	Buenos Aires Sailed on 15 June for Las Palmas. Did not arrive.	Sunk at 15.39 hrs on 10 August 1940 in Lat. 33.06 North Long. 34.19 West.

steered from the after end of an open poop, some time later she was fitted with a wheelhouse which came from *Hougomont*'s wreck in 1932. The structure did not enhance *Killoran*'s appearance, but no doubt successive helmsmen were duly grateful for the shelter it provided.

Under Gustaf Erikson's ownership she kept her Hardie colours for a time, but at various times afterwards her hull was black, dark grey, light grey, and white. It is clear from illustrations which have appeared in several publications that in this respect she followed the pattern of other ships in the fleet. It was vital that costs were kept as low as possible. Conditions at sea were hardly better than those during the nineteenth century. I speak from personal experience, having spent a year at sea on *Killoran* in the 1920s. Hard tack was still very much the order of the day. Accommodation and the standard of general comfort was virtually unchanged. In bad weather men lived in their wet clothes and slept on wet beds just as generations of the predecessors had done in another day and age. Members of *Killoran*'s former British crews would have felt very much at home! The wage bill was no doubt the smallest that could have been achieved. A captain received about £20, an able seaman £3 and a junior rating £1.50 a month. None of the above are intended as unkind criticisms. Gustaf Erikson, a remarkable man, deserves a very deep debt of gratitude for his tremendous achievement of operating the world's last fleet of big steel square-rigged sailing ships. The incredible fact is that he did it so successfully and for so long.

From 1927 until 1939, *Killoran* was employed mostly in the Australian wheat trade. During this period she made ten voyages in the so-called Grain Races, taking on average, 125 days from Spencer Gulf to Falmouth/Lizard/Queenstown for orders, thereafter discharging at ports as far apart as Belfast and Rotterdam. This average time meant that she was always nearer the bottom of the list than the top for the fastest passage in terms of days.

In general, however, the *Killoran* carried more varied freights than Erikson's larger vessels did. Every now and then the vessel was fixed in a different market. For example, in 1928, under the command of Captain R Lindholm, she made a round voyage from Adelaide to Ilo, Peru, and on this occasion achieved the very good time of forty-six days. Thereafter she took a cargo from Don Martin Island to London and passed through the Panama Canal – one of the very few sailing vessels that took that route. In the next year she again crossed from Adelaide to Ilo, now taking a cargo of guano from Santa Rosa Island to Antwerp, so that she once more had to pass through the Panama Canal.

In 1930 the *Killoran* visited Newport, Puerto Caballo, Tucacas, Falmouth, Helsingfors, Copenhagen and Delagoa Bay. She lost one man on the passage to Puerto Caballo – and a lifeboat. The lifeboat was picked up by a steamer – and the re-insurance rate rose by forty per cent.

On 13 July 1939, having been much delayed by grounding in the Seychelles and consequent dry docking in Auckland where she discharged, *Killoran* sailed from Port Lincoln to Falmouth 'for orders'. She was ordered to Cork where she arrived on 29 November. This was the last pre-war cargo of Australian grain to reach Europe under sail, but this voyage had a greater significance. Firstly, it ended the era of the world's last fleet of merchant sailing ships. Secondly, it brought about the effective extinction of the 'windjammer', and the end of the sailing ship as a carrier of world trade and commerce, in which, in one form or another they had been engaged throughout the centuries. For although *Viking*, *Pamir* and *Passat* made the odd voyage after the end of the war, the story of the merchant sailing ships had really come to an end. It was indeed fitting that this significant voyage was made by the last British-built barque, under the house flag of the last great Åland sailing shipowner.

However, there was no intention of letting the *Killoran* remain idle. It was hoped that, in some degree, it would be possible to repeat the very profitable voyages of the sailing vessels in the First World War. At the beginning of January 1940, Eriksons were advertising for crews for the *Killoran*, the *Pamir*, *Lawhill* and *Archibald Russell*. The three first-named had managed to get their crews on board before the Germans occupied Norway and had then sailed, *Pamir* and *Lawhill* to Australian waters, where they went into service between the American west coast, or Africa, and ports in Australia or New Zealand. At the end of 1941 they were commandeered where they were then lying.

On 18 January 1940 *Killoran* left Cork in tow for Cardiff where she arrived on 21 January. She loaded coal for Buenos Aires and sailed on 27 February. She arrived on 28 May. On 15 June, loaded with 2500 tons of maize and 500 tons of sugar she sailed for Las Palmas. She never arrived.

During the morning of 10 August, a fine sunny day with a flag calm sea, she was sighted at about 29,000 yards by the German armed merchant cruiser

Killoran *from the forecastle head.*
C S Cooper-Essex

Poop and main deck of Killoran, *Falmouth, 1937.*
C S Cooper-Essex

Widder, commanded by Korvetten-Kapitan von Ruckteschell. The German ship closed and at 13,000 yards identified a barque under full sail and flying the Finnish flag. She was steering 144 degrees – south east towards the Canary Islands. At 4000 yards two shots were fired across her bow and she was ordered to heave to. *Widder* then came up on *Killoran's* lee side and sent a boat across. Captain Karl Leman accordingly went on board the German ship but did not take any papers with him. He was questioned about his destination, his cargo, its consignors and consignees. Subsequently, a German officer went on board *Killoran* to examine the ship's papers and to verify Leman's statements.

There is no doubt that von Ruckteschell was far from satisfied with Leman's explanation. He was greatly influenced by the fact that all the arrangements for her cargo had been negotiated and financed by the British firm Messrs H Clarkson – who were of course Erikson's agents. He also believed that there was a possibility that the cargo might be transhipped or ordered elsewhere after arrival at Las Palmas. It is quite clear from the general wording of his report that he felt there was something fishy about the whole business. He finally concluded that the ultimate destination for her cargo, one way or the other, was England. He decided therefore, that in accordance with the laws on contraband, *Killoran* must be sunk.

One time-bomb was placed in the bows, another aft, and one on either side amidships. They were all sited some two feet below the water line, and set with seven minute fuses. The demolition party left *Killoran* at 15.26 hours; the charges went off at 15.36 hours. The explosion must have ripped *Killoran's* sides apart for she sank at 15.39 hours, and settled some 2700 fathoms down. The German captain records the position in his log as 33.06 north, 24.19 west. This account of her sinking is taken entirely from von Ruckteschell's official report. There seems no reason to doubt its accuracy.

It may seem strange that von Ruckteschell decided to sink *Killoran*. She was flying a neutral flag, was sailing between two neutral ports, and at this time both Argentina and Spain were more than favourably disposed to the Nazi cause. But there is no doubt that he believed he was right to do so. Captain Leman and his crew were on board *Widder* for about six weeks. They were later interned in France and in January 1941 they were repatriated to Finland.

Lloyds had posted *Killoran* 'missing' in November 1940, but her fate was only confirmed when later that

Killoran *sinking*.
Dr David Papp

month a German officer stationed in Finland gave Gustaf Erikson a copy of the German newspaper *Deutche Allgemeine Zeitung* and he saw in it a picture of a sinking sailing ship which he recognised as *Killoran*.

In spite of Finland's officially 'friendly' status the German authorities gave them no information on the sinking, or about the captured crew, until people in Mariehamn got in touch, via the Ministry of Foreign Affairs, with the German authorities. It was on the 9 October 1940, that the *Killoran*'s crew were landed in St Nazaire, but it was not until 16 January 1941 that they began their homeward journey to Finland.

So ends *Killoran*'s story. In one sense her end was not such a bad one. She sank gracefully with all sails set and she was at least spared the indignity of the breakers yard, or ending her days as a coal hulk.

Several facts emerge from *Killoran*'s story which show that she justifies her place in the record books. Firstly, she was the last surviving British built steel barque. Secondly, in 1939 she carried the last pre-war cargo of grain from Australia to end the era of the last fleet of merchant sailing ships. It was this voyage which also saw the end of the big steel built square-rigged sailing ship as a carrier of world trade. Thirdly, in her forty years of service she sailed over 800,000 miles. (The figure cannot be more precise since none of her log books survive.) Lastly, the abstract of her voyage shows that she spent nearly all of her service trading to Australia and the west coasts of North and South America, in the course of which she rounded Cape Horn no less than thirty-five times – and survived. *Killoran* was a fine tribute to the men who built her, to those who sailed her, and to the seaworthiness of the old ship herself.

Although the facts and figures in the second and third points cannot be claimed as records, it is reasonable to assume that there can be few, if any, sailing ships which remained in service for so long, or logged such mileage.

Chapter 10

INGRID

Between fifty and sixty years ago a big black auxiliary barquentine occasionally used to visit Fowey Harbour in Cornwall to load china clay for Rouen. She was much larger than any other of the quite numerous British schooners and the two or three barquentines which were still profitably employed in Britain's home trade in the final years of the 1920s. She was a beautiful ship with a handsome hull and flaring bows of the kind that used to be associated with Canadian-built vessels, and a lovely rounded transom counter. Although the foremast was in three parts and she had staysails between the main and foremasts, she had no yards crossed, though there were a couple of yards lashed down on deck on the port side.

Her registered managing owner was a local, Miss Annie Stephens, but the vessel's affairs were actually handled by Thomas Stephens, her brother. They were children of the great John Stephens of Fowey who, between 1867 and his death in 1902, had been the managing owner of thirty or so small schooners, principally employed in the very tough trade of carrying salt preserved codfish from Newfoundland to Mediterranean and west European ports. These vessels were the property of shareholding groups which operated in very much the same way as those in Åland. John Stephens was constantly buying and selling shares in vessels.

After their father died Annie, Thomas, and their brother Edward had continued in the shipping business. In the late 1920s, at the period when the Grain Races were just beginning, their schooner *Jane Banks* completed a series of voyages on government contract to Bermuda, bringing back cargoes of Admiralty stores. They also owned the *Waterwitch*, a classic old barquentine which had begun her life in the 1860s as a collier brig and which was destined to become the last square-rigged merchant vessel to operate from a home port in the United Kingdom. This was very appropriate, for she, like her Åland contemporaries, *Kristina*, *Frideborg*, *Sigyn*, was far more representative of the ordinary merchant sailing vessels of the preceding three centuries than were the great steel Grain Racers.

The Stephens' black barquentine had the odd name of *Rigdin* and her port of registration on her stern was not Fowey but Southampton. Her master was Captain George Beynon of Fowey, a veteran of the Stephens' fleet in the great days of the Newfoundland trade. In 1985 I talked with John Cockle, a professional sailing ship seaman who had served in the *Rigdin* as a boy, and whose father had been a seaman with the Stephens' fleet in the Newfoundland trade. John Cockle told me about life in the *Rigdin* between fifty and sixty years ago.

> She was a beautiful vessel and very well fitted out. She needed only about ten minutes pumping each watch, much better than the barquentine *Frances and Jane* in which I had served immediately before. *Rigdin*'s forecastle, as I knew her, was below deck, but it had bunks for twelve men. Originally she had a deckhouse forecastle for eight men. We handled her with only six. Aft, she had a long poop cabin sunk into a shallow poop deck. The poop house was on the main deck, Scandinavian style, not below decks with cabins and messroom as in all British-built vessels of this class. There were cabins for the chief engineer, the steward, the master, two mates and two storerooms, as well as the big messroom where we all ate together in the democratic way we did in the merchant schooners.
>
> It wasn't easy to get work in those days and I cycled over to Fowey from Truro, where I lived with my

parents, to try to get a berth. Captain Beynon took me because my father had served with him. I cycled back home and got my gear and took a train to Fowey which cost me two shillings. She was lying off Bodinnick on buoys. She had only just been bought by the Stephens and she had been refitted at Benjamin Tregaskis' yard at Par. They had given her the square rigged foremast in three parts – she had been rigged as a fore and aft motor schooner without any yards before and the idea was that as she earned money she would be fully rigged as a barquentine. This was because Captain Beynon was used to the rig, his last command had been the barquentine *Lydia Cardell* for the Stephens. But it didn't work out that way. They had sent on board the future lower topsail yard. We rigged it up as the foreyard and bent the topsail as a square sail, on the first passage from Fowey to Rouen with clay. In Rouen it was cockbilled to clear the cranes and when we went into Dover, with engine trouble, on the passage from Rouen to London we sent it down and lashed it on deck and left it there. As she was rigged, without square sails, she would not handle under sail, she fell off all the time when she was on the wind. She was dependant on the engine to keep her going to windward, and the engine was a four cylinder hot bulb diesel which gave us endless trouble. You didn't dare let go a mooring or haul up the anchor until the engine was well and truly running.

We took silver sand from Rouen to Greenwich and had a cracked cylinder head, so we lay two months to the buoys of Tate & Lyle's refinery at Canning Town waiting for the spare part from Denmark, where the engine had been made. We took cement from Greenhythe to Liverpool and Runcorn and then loaded coal in Garston for Fowey. These were good passages and we sailed a lot with the wind abaft the beam. But the next passage to Aberdeen with clay and back to Blyth to load coal for Fowey was a different story. With the engine playing up all the time, we had to put in to a number of places to work on it. In Fowey we lay six weeks. We put her up on Mixstow Beach and scraped and painted her on one side a couple of tides and then did the other side a couple of tides.

All this was very good for me. Captain Beynon was like a father to me and with Jimmy Jack, the mate, you were learning seamanship all the time. He had great patience with us two boys and would show us how to do things again and again. She was a happy ship and a fine training ship for a youngster. They were wonderful men. Beynon's whole life was the ship and the crew. These were caring men, they looked after us like they looked after their ships. The only trouble with the *Rigdin* was that she had been rigged at some time as a motor schooner and yet the engine, although it wasn't very old, was no good – or perhaps our engineers just didn't understand it. And, of course she was too big for the home trade.

John Cockle was perfectly right of course. The *Rigdin* was a small deep sea vessel and the days when a sailing vessel of her 400–500 ton cargo capacity could be profitably operated on deep water routes had finally disappeared with the end of the post First

Master shipbuilder Eric Söderström and his wife.
Captain Göte Sundberg

World War boom. In the home trade, with very hard work and expert management, there was still money to be made in the 1920s with sailing and auxiliary vessels of 150–250 tons cargo capacity, or even less, and some men, like the Slades of Appledore were doing quite well at the time. Of the Appledore men John Cockle said

> The Bar crowd [Appledore Bar lies across the mouth of the twin Taw and Torridge rivers] were family. They were clannish, close, they worked on a different basis, they were all related, it was a tribal set up. They made money because they worked like that. The secret of success with these last sailing vessels was family operation, that and a good engine driving a screw. That's how the Bar men did it and that's how the Dutch did it with their motor coasters which had the additional advantage of a bigger capacity on a smaller draught than the old sailing vessels.

Rigdin fell betwixt and between. Too deep for the tidal berths the small vessels used and too big to be operated economically, she could not make enough money to justify the new engine she really needed. Tom Stephens had bought her for only £400 and she was a real bargain at that price. He had purchased her from Southampton, where she was laid up, to give Captain Beynon a ship after the *Lydia Cardell* had been lost in collision, but, bargain as she was, the acquisition was a rare error of business judgment, uncharacteristic, but probably partly sentimentally inspired. John Cockle went on,

> We took silver sand again from Rouen to Sunderland and because of the engine we took fourteen days over it,

The Ingrid *was built by twenty farmers and farmers' sons working under Eric Söderström as master shipwright. Here are nineteen of the building gang with the growing vessel behind them.*

Mrs Karlsson, Geta

so there was a hue and cry for us, and when we got in the press were waiting to meet us. We took coal back from Blyth to Fowey and had a real smoker from the east. We went into Plymouth, it was a horribly dirty night. The skipper told me, 'just you go up there and stow that main gaff topsail'. I went up and I rode it down. I didn't have time to be frightened, but I was when I thought about it afterwards. After we discharged in Fowey she was put on the buoys. I stayed with her for some time, but after a while the tug *Gallant* put her up on the beach at the entrance to Pont Pill and there she stayed.

She slowly fell into disrepair in the way laid up wooden sailing vessels always did. The next time I saw her, in 1937, her masts had been taken out of her and she filled on every tide. I called on Tom Stephens and after several hours of talking about the vessels his family had owned and the way they had managed them I asked him what he was going to do about the *Rigdin*? 'Boy', he said 'You can have her for £15!' Two years later she was patched up and towed away to Plymouth to be broken up, and even that can scarcely have been a very profitable venture for the people who bought her.

The letters in *Rigdin* can be reshuffled to read *Ingrid*. Her documents recorded simply that she was built at Geta, Åland's northern parish. My determination to find out more about her led in due course to my friends at the Cape Horners' lunch greeting me with, 'Hello you! How are you and your girl friend *Ingrid*?' But they were very helpful in unearthing her story, which turned out to be most interesting. She was a twentieth century anachronism – a perfect, and very late, example of the Åland farmer–shipowner–shipbuilder pattern of building and operation common in the 1860s and 1870s. *Ingrid* was the only Åland-built vessel to be bought by British owners and operated from a home port in the United Kingdom. She was, moreover, owned for some years principally by Gustaf Eriksson.

During the years of secondhand sailing tonnage, in the 1890s and early 1900s only four big vessels were built in Åland; the barque *Helmi* of 1892 (her forecastle and galley are now preserved in the Åland Sjöfartsmuseum where, showing the living conditions in the wooden vessels, they form a most valuable display), the three-masted schooner *Witus* built in 1900, the barquentine *Adonia* of 338 tons built in 1911, and the schooner *Ingrid*. The *Ingrid* was a true throwback to the old days in Åland of rural shipbuilding, shipowning and ship management in extended trading. Her passages about the seas of Europe and across the Atlantic were adventures in which most people in the community of Geta, where she was built and owned, were involved in one way or another.

When the ice breaks up in the Gulf of Bothnia and drifts south each spring it crashes against the pink granite shores of Geta. From Geta Bergen, one of the highest points in Åland, you can see most of the parish with its farms and wood lots and *fjärds* penetrating the land. Here stands a granite monolith with the inscription *Se Gud i Naturen* – literally 'See God in Nature', though perhaps better translated 'Heaven lies around you'. This was a great shipbuilding and shipowning area and many surviving big farmhouses still give evidence of the prosperity of the district a hundred years ago.

In the winter of 1905–06, during the years of secondhand tonnage, long after the great days of farmer–shipowning, a group of men and their wives assembled in the big parlour of one of the farms and the wood burning stove was specially lit for the occasion. Such social gatherings were part of the pattern of Åland rural life and had their own rules, with the women just listening and talking at one side of the room and withdrawing fairly early, to leave the men to drink and talk far into the night. These were hard times with no market for timber and poor crops. Eventually, it appears, someone proposed that they should seek to solve their own problems and do as their fathers had done, build themselves a ship with their own timber and sail her themselves.

Though few big vessels had been launched, smaller vessels, *galeaser* and *jakter*, had been built steadily, an average of one a year for the preceding ten years in Geta Community itself. Eric Söderström was a local farmer–shipbuilder whose family had lived on the site of their farm, Norrgårds in Olofsnäs, since the 1600s. Born in 1835, he was forty-two years old when he built his first vessel, the schooner *Evert*. Previously he had been a blacksmith at the building of a number of vessels and 'forced by necessity in the summer of 1866 during the bad years' (as Georg Kåhre puts it in his history of Åland shipping under sail), he had sailed in the brig *Aura*, built in Geta in 1864 and lost in the Kattegat in 1879. Eric Söderström's biggest ship was the barque *Helmi*, built in 1892 of 490 tons.

A day or two after the party in the farmhouse, in early 1906, Eric Söderström was asked by representatives of the group of farmers to build a large schooner for trading to Britain and western Europe. It had been a long time since he had built a big vessel and he took the half model of a *galeas*, the *Emelia* which he had built in 1889 for a farmer in Hammarland, scaled it up and lengthened it, giving the new model a relatively long uniform midships section. From the new half model Eric Söderström made a set of drawings, a pencilled draft drawn out on squared paper, a sheer plan, body plan, and half breadth plan. The half model of the *Emilia*, the half model of the new schooner and the drawing are now all preserved in the Ålands Sjöfartsmuseum in Mariehamn.

The building site was at Knutnäs, a quarter of a mile or so from Eric Söderström's farm. Here there are open stretches of grass, leading down between birches and pines to the edge of the Kalvfjärd, with relatively deep water off the narrow beach. In this beautiful place Eric Söderström laid his keel blocks, set up his sawing stage (for there was no question of digging a sawpit in the pink granite of Knutnäs) and a blacksmith's shop and with the aid of some twenty farmers he began work on building a 140-foot vessel.

Her ownership was to be divided into a hundred shares and it is still said that 'almost everyone in Geta had something in the *Ingrid*'. In fact originally, it appears, thirty men provided the material for building her and each had from one to six shares in her in return. The shares changed hands fairly frequently, even while she was building, and about the time she was launched there were thirty-eight shareholders, all from Geta except the master, Erik Malmqvist, who had $^1/_{100}$th. The first *huvudredare*, or managing owner, was farmer Johan Fridolf Jansson of Knuts Farm, Olofsnäs, who had $^6/_{100}$ths. The original documents of vessel property were issued, some for cash, some in return for timber cut on farmer's wood lots and hauled to the building site, some in return for labour as well as for other materials for the building of the vessel. The notebook in which Eric Söderström recorded the deliveries of timber and other materials to the site by the thirty original shareholders still exists. The timber came from the local woods on each side of the *fjärd* and it was all soft wood, pines, spruces, and birch of various kinds. With these materials the vessel might be expected to have a normal working life of perhaps fifteen years. The ironwork was made up by Eric Söderström himself from secondhand material purchased from scrap merchants in Stockholm.

The launch was a great occasion. In 1976 Eric

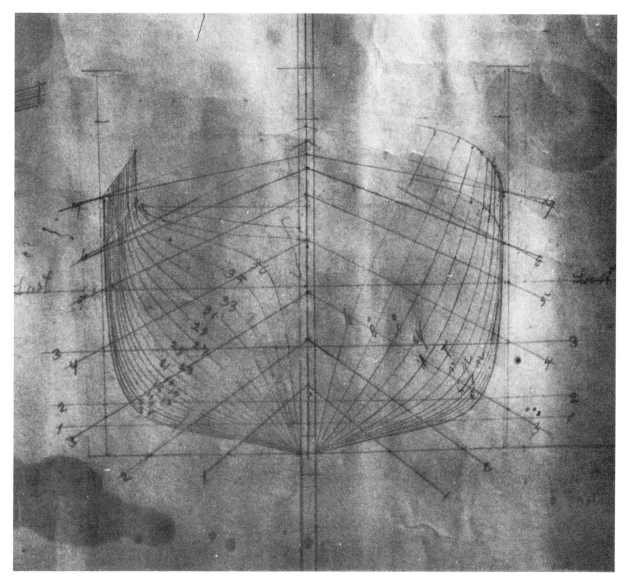

The body plan drawing prepared by Eric Söderström for the building of the Ingrid.
Ålands Sjöfartsmuseum

Söderström's grandson told me that as a small child he was allowed to be present, but not to be on board, as his elder brother was. He remembered the growing tension as everybody waited for his grandfather to begin the process of knocking in the wedges which would free the vessel to slide into the water. The new schooner, named *Ingrid*, went down the slip at a great pace and the boy hoped that she would go right over to the other side of the *fjärd*, but the check ropes stopped her and she floated proud and high. There was only just enough water for her, light as she was with the minimum of fittings on board. She was towed down the *fjärd* to deeper water, where the masts were stepped and she was rigged and fitted out for sea. Her sails were made by an old sailmaker called Sundqvist from drafts drawn by Captain Malmqvist.

The new schooner was first registered at Mariehamn on 16 May 1907. She was give a Bureau Veritas certificate of classification for nine years from May 1907. Research has revealed no hint of the source of her name, except that *Ingrid* is more commonly used in Geta as a girl's name than in any other community in Åland. She was rigged as a three-masted schooner with double topsails and topgallant on her fore topmast. She had very tall topmasts and a considerable area of canvas. She began her working life with a passage May to June 1907, from Mariehamn to Umeå (on the Swedish coast on the Gulf of Bothnia) to begin picking up a cargo of timber offcuts for Lorient in western France. For the next seven years her career was that of a very successful vessel, continuously employed, except during the winter lay ups, and her voyage record, which has been compiled by Mr Lars Grönstrand (see pp. 170–72), shows her sailing all over the Baltic, south to western France, west to the west coast of Ireland and north to the White Sea. She visited Britain, loading china clay at Fowey, coal at Swansea, and bringing timber from the sawmills of the Swedish coast of the Gulf of Bothnia to Middlesbrough, Lowestoft, Littlehampton, Grimsby, London and Dover.

During these years she was run as a communal venture. Her annual fitting out was on a basis of contributions in kind from each shareholder. Her provisioning was similarly arranged. Each farmer contributed meat, flour, salt and sugar. The butter sent by each shareholder was coloured differently, so that the crew should know from which farm it had come. The hard durable bread was made up in ring-shaped loaves about ten inches in diameter and one inch thick. After baking these *rågbrödkakor* were taken out of the farm ovens and were hung on poles, and slung from the kitchen ceilings for drying. They were brought on board in sacks, hundreds of them, and the last ones to be eaten in the autumn were as hard as flintstones.

In 1911 Captain Erik Mattsson, also a shareholder, from Åkerlund Farm in Geta, took over command and it was he who took *Ingrid* to the White Sea in 1913. Erik Hugo Mattsson was born in 1884 and at the age of twenty-five was already a veteran of merchant sailing ships. He fixed the vessel's cargoes and agreed the freights, he navigated her and employed the crews and supervised her maintenance. He had great responsibility and his position was very influential.

When he came home at the end of the sailing season in December 1913 it was in Erik Mattsson's home at Åkerlund, where his family had lived for four centuries that the shareholders' meeting was held. The shareholders congregated in the great drawing room with huge red plush sofa, great round woodburning stove and carved wooden decorations – which all still exist. Here the farmers inspected their accounts, tried to quiz him a little, then drew their share money in cash which he doled out from a cash box as he sat on the sofa; then he locked the box and put it under the sofa. What was left was his by right, and it included the *kaplake*, the five per cent of the freight money which went to the master and could become the foundation of his fortune.

In 1914 Captain Mattsson married Selma Maria, a very attractive twenty-three-year-old who had lived in the United States. Together they sailed from Sundsvall in Swedish Bothnia to Dover. On a second passage with timber to Dover, made in July–August 1914, Captain Mattsson saw a good deal of floating wreckage and guessed that the threatened war had broken out. Finland including Åland was part of Russia; Germany, at war with Russia, controlled the Baltic and there was no way home. *Ingrid* was laid up in Rochester. Some of her crew found their way to the United States, some eventually to Scandinavia. Eric

Mattsson had his freight money, which he had drawn in Dover in new gold half sovereigns (dated 1913 and 1914). He made a bag out of sail canvas, filled it with the half sovereigns and strapped it inside his right thigh. Then he made his way across to Norway and across Sweden to the coast. There was no service across the Gulf of Bothnia and no trade, so he bought a 20-foot fishing boat and sailed it across the Åland Sea to the wharf nearest his family farm. The half sovereigns were duly distributed at a shareholders' meeting and some of them are still in the proud possession of Geta families.

The Baltic was closed and most Åland vessels caught there were laid up for the duration of the war. Communication with those vessels which had been outside the Baltic on 4 August 1914 was very difficult. Many of them were at first laid up in foreign parts,

The original of this photograph is entitled, in Swedish, in what appears to be contemporary handwriting, 'Ingrid on arrival at Littlehampton 8 October 1910'. The record of the vessel's movements shows her in Littlehampton in October 1911. The caption of the original photograph therefore remains a mystery.
Ruben Jansson

while their owners waited to see what would happen to freights and war risks. By 1915 prospects were improving and the *Ingrid* was moved to London from Rochester to have her bottom caulked and to be fitted out. An Åland crew reached her by devious routes and she made three voyages under Captain Mattsson. According to a letter written by Gustaf Erikson in 1919 these consisted of 'one from Canada (Montreal) to Brest and a third from Jamaica with log wood to Bordeaux, and a passage in between with pitch pine from Gulfport to France'.

On 27 October 1916 *Ingrid* was insured, through Clarksons, against freight and war risk from Canada to 'West Coast Great Britain or East Coast Ireland'. She was similarly insured on 28 April 1917, the freight for £3300, and the vessel for war risks, to cover her passage from Jamaica to Bordeaux. The transatlantic freights were indeed very high and these passages paid very well. But when she reached Bordeaux at the end of the third voyage she was laid up again. She had run out of her Bureau Veritas class, it was difficult to arrange repairs and after early 1916 increasingly difficult to get a new crew of eight men out to her from Åland. In 1917 the all-out submarine blockade was at its height, but freights were also very high and shipowners with vessels earning money at sea outside the Baltic were looking for outlets for investment. Among these was Gustaf Erikson, whose *Tjerimai*, and other vessels were making a great deal of money.

On 8 January 1916, Gustaf Erikson started to buy shares in *Ingrid* from the Geta farmers and on 2 August 1916 the vessel was again registered at Mariehamn, with him as *huvudredare* and largest single shareholder owning $30/100$ths. On 14 June 1917 Gustaf Erikson telegraphed to Clarksons in London, 'intend to buy *Ingrid*, telegraph freights Canada or Gulf to Buenos Aires freshwater places present previous'. And then, exactly a fortnight later, he telegraphed again, 'owners ordered first June lay up *Ingrid*. Bought whole ship today. Ask Matsson or Chief Mate Lindgren go Master otherwise recommend others and expenses classification Bureau Veritas, docking, painting'.

In Mariehamn on 2 November 1917, Captain Mathias Emil Nordberg of Lemland and a crew were issued with passports to go through Sweden to Bordeaux, but they do not seem to have made the journey and it was not until September 1918 that a crew of six went out to Bordeaux from Åland on a single joint passport. Captain Hugo Lindblom was appointed to take charge of *Ingrid* at 1000 finnmarks a month, (or, as Gustaf Erikson wrote 'the same salary that I pay to the Master of *Grace Harwar*') and to sail her, with a small cargo of gunpowder, to Martinique to load sugar. She was again insured through Clarkson's on 19 February 1919 against war risks and missing for £4000 (valued at £8000) for a passage from Bordeaux to Martinique. The freight was insured for £4000. Captain Lindblom was instructed by Gustaf Erikson in the first of the series of his inimitable letters that,

the ship needs: the foremast repaired and the bottom caulked and painted with anti-fouling composition, and its classification at French Veritas should be renewed if possible.

The foremast is partly rotten and a section must be scarphed in, though it might perhaps last a trip or two. So inspect her carefully. The mizzenmast will also be bad, but since this is less serious it may be good enough for now – I will leave you free to judge however, and also to renew it. Since so much work is called for, the classification may be granted without costs. You must be specially careful to paint the bottom as often as required with the best recommended bottom-paint, and give the bottom at least two coats, even three at the bow if necessary, in order to protect her from being afflicted with worm. The vessel is weakly built and sea-soft, so it is most advisable to sail cautiously, especially in high seas and headseas, etc. Incidentally the vessel sails well and has been quite watertight except in storms when she has leaked more. If the opportunity arises, strengthen her with more iron knees wherever she most seems to need it in future. The vessel is among the most advantageous there are at 292 tons net, loading 55/600 tons deadweight, according to trades, summer or winter storms, 200/220 standards cut wood from the Baltic etc. sails with a crew of 8 men in all and has a light and easily-handled rig.

Make up an inventory right away and send home. You will find good fittings on board, a set of good sails, of which a number are new and unused, and almost a set in poorer condition. Captain Sjölund from Föglö kept watch all the time until a few months ago, and now a Frenchman has been engaged by the broker Balguerie, who has also been in charge of the vessel and has in his possession about 8000 francs in cash which was left to him by Captain Erik Mattson when he laid-up the vessel and went home.

Captain Lindblom proved a somewhat unreliable correspondent. On 4 January 1919 Gustaf Erikson complained:

It is noteworthy that some other letters have not been received, nor have the accounts covering the half-collected freight, expenses in Brest and the vessel's repairs and Classification. Cabled asking Clarksons when sailed and the balance remitted and was told that your departure took place on the 18th ult, but no prospect of remittance. Hence 127,000 francs was used in Brest, corresponding to about 200,000 Fmk.

On the other hand, one does not know what repairs to the bottom of the hull have been made, possible strengthening with more iron knees etc. etc. Is the vessel now in first class shape and condition in respect of its hull, rigging, fixtures and fittings, and has it been granted four years first class in ...

But the next letter he received was dated 1 March and addressed from Falmouth. It reported a casualty:

With this I have to report the disagreeable news that we arrived here at Falmouth yesterday in damaged condition. After having been at sea for a month, with storms and bad weather from the SW, we lost all three topmasts on the 19th February, in the morning. It was a heavy sea, so the vessel rolled violently the whole time we were out. It began, three days after we left Verdun Roads, with a storm from the southwest which went on day after day, though we had one storm from the ESE, and so were able to slip away from the land a little. We ran before the wind for two days, one day under bare rigging only, so it was very fresh for a vessel such as *Ingrid*. She began to leak as soon as we put to sea and the heavier the sea, the worse it got, to that we often had over a foot of water above the ceiling when the pumps stopped during the times we were shortening sail, which seldom took more than an hour. Sails were blown to pieces before us, for they were rotten after having lain for so long, backstays parted, bolts snapped in the deadeyes, the deadeyes cracked apart, lanyards were torn away, though we managed to repair them afterwards as it turned out, and the mizzen and fore-gaffs broke – these we fished.

We managed, however, against a greater or lesser degree of adversity, until the morning of the 19th February, when, in a heavy roll, the mast yoke broke away from the foremast. On the next roll, the topmast went overboard, together with the yards, taking with it the main and mizzen topmasts, the foreyard broke in two pieces which came down on the deck, the top and the trestle-trees on the foremast broke up, and the gaff, the gaff-foresail and the stay-foresail were torn completely apart. Everything was left hanging from the fore-rigging towards the starboard side and on the forestay, and it began to cut hard into the side, so we were afraid to haul it in.

However, we managed to get everything cut away successfully and with hardly more than a little chafing on the rail and the side. Thereupon we rigged up new forestays and got headsails bent, so we got the vessel to fall away and we began to steer northwards to look for a port of refuge. We were then at about Lat 40° 33′N, Long 14° 39′W, by dead reckoning. During the time work was in progress to clear the rigging from the vessel, two men were put to work pumping the water which was slowly rising in the hold, so that at 2 pm all hands had to be called to the pumps, and they worked for two hours with both pumps before we had her pumped dry.

Over the nine days it took us to reach here after losing our rigging, the pumps have had to be in action constantly. On top of everything else, the mate went crazy the day after our misfortune. He began to brood, thinking we would never reach port so he was no use on

deck. Although, happily, we managed to get here in the end, I suppose on many occasions the outlook was black nevertheless. The vessel is not yet any more watertight, since we had 32″ of water above the ceiling this morning, from a period of 12 hours. The cargo we have inside has also become wet; a third of our ballast was pumped up during the time we were at sea. Now awaiting reports from London as to what is to be done with the vessel. She will never be watertight, unless she gets a new bottom, or is sheathed, since her bottom is just like a honeycombe eaten up by worm. There are few places where her planks are thicker than half an inch.

The Falmouth shipbuilder R S Burt, in a long estimate dated 14 March 1919 found the vessel was extensively damaged and concluded by writing:

It is very probable when the keel is ripped out a number of the floors if not all will be found broken, but at present it is impossible to ascertain, moreover a number of the ends of the futtock timbers at the bilge may be broken and I should say they were, and to repair same, it would be a very expensive way of building a new ship.

Gustaf Erikson had thought of having the vessel partly repaired in Britain and sailing her home to Åland under jury rig to be sheathed over and put in the Baltic trade, but in a letter to Clarksons he concludes, 'I wonder if we might get a higher price if the vessel were to be auctioned without the costly outfit supplied by Mathieson in Bordeaux for 30,000 francs, which could then be taken ashore'.

Mr Burt, after surveying the vessel, estimated the cost of putting her in good condition again at £6650. The vessel had been insured with the Marine Assurance Union of Finland. They considered that the greater part of the total repair costs related to damage incurred on the open seas, and since the insurance covered the vessel only against damage by stranding or collision they stated that they were not liable for the greater part of the claim. The matter was referred to an average adjuster who supported the insurance company in his conclusions, but Gustaf Erikson was not satisfied and submitted the matter for decision by arbitrators, arguing that the vessel had not sprung a leak in the open sea, which would indicate that she was sent to sea in an unseaworthy condition,

but through a great part of the rigging going overboard to remain hanging on the foresail stay, and then commencing to strike hard again the outside of the vessel. If this circumstance was compared with the schooner *Ingrid* being only twelve years old and being classified for the whole time, and that the vessel underwent just before the commencement of the voyage, comprehensive repairs, and after such reconditioning was again classified, and that upon survey after the damage it was ascertained that 600 feet of side planks had been damaged by the fallen rigging, then it becomes apparent that the marine damage did not arise on account of the state of the vessel, which before the fall of the rigging did not leak to any appreciable extent, unless the vessel had struck a floating object, and in that case according to the Marine Assurance Union's own condition as well as general practice, it is dealt with as for cases of stranding.

On these grounds Gustaf Erikson claimed that he should be awarded full insurance cover as for total loss and found,

it to be proved that the schooner *Ingrid* before its departure from Bordeaux underwent comprehensive repairs in that place, and that according to the classification certificate of 15 January 1919 received Class in the Bureau Veritas, from which fact *Ingrid* must be regarded as having been in a fully seaworthy state upon departure ... and that the reported leak in schooner *Ingrid* must be accepted as having arisen by reason of the rigging which went overboard commencing to strike partly against the outside of the vessel.

On these grounds the arbitrator granted the full insurance claim to Gustaf Erikson and his fellow shareholders. Erikson at that time had $^{90}/_{100}$ths in the vessel, Axel Melander, his cousin, $^{3}/_{100}$ths, Captain Malmqvist still had $^{4}/_{100}$ths and Fru Rotz $^{3}/_{100}$ths. The insurance money was shared between them on 9 June 1920. On 15 July at a meeting in Mariehamn the company was formerly dissolved and the affairs of *Ingrid* wound up.

She had already been sold through Clarksons on 8 December 1919, for £2200 (which went to the Marine Assurance Union of Finland) to Allen Adams and Co Ltd at Southampton, who were shipbrokers and dealers in chandlery and stores. She was taken out of the Finnish register on 20 August 1919 and the next formal record of the vessel is her registration as a British vessel, No 23 of 1921, at Southampton under the anagram name of *Rigdin* (changed by authority of a Board of Trade minute of 12 March 1921) official number 145343, signal letters KJHP. She was registered as an auxiliary motor schooner of 294 tons net with a Danish-made semi-diesel auxiliary of sixty-five nominal horsepower built in 1920. Although no record has been found of the repairs made to *Ingrid* during the eighteen months or so between the cancellation of the Finnish register and her re-registration as a British vessel it is evident that a great deal of money had been spent on getting her into condition to be granted a load line and registered as a British merchant ship. Thereby she had been given a second life, after the end of her natural working life of fifteen years or so.

A new suit of sails was made for her by Penrose Canvas Products Ltd of Truro. The drafts of these have survived and from them it is apparent that she was re-rigged as a schooner without yards on her fore topmast but with three jib headed gaff topsails on fore, main and mizzen, (a *slätskonare* or *slätoppere* as the Ålanders would have called her). She would appear to have been somewhat under canvassed, and there was no doubt intended to be operated as a motor schooner with the engine in fairly constant use.

The firm of Allen Adams & Co Ltd was finally wound up in April 1924 and no references to the *Rigdin* have been found in surviving accessible records concerning the company. In the three years she was registered in their ownership she made only one, but rather remarkable, voyage from Falmouth (where it is evident that her rebuilding had been carried out) to the West Indies via Hull and back to Swansea. For this she signed on a crew of twelve, a master, a mate, six seamen, two engineers, two cook/stewards. She would have to have had a very good freight to pay a crew of this size – when the Ålanders employed her on Atlantic voyages when she was a fully rigged schooner with an extensive area of square canvas on her foremast she had a crew only of eight.

The rest of the story is more intriguing still. She sailed from Falmouth to Hull and back to Falmouth again, finally clearing Falmouth on 29 May 1922. She arrived at Hamilton, Bermuda, on 10 July, after a slow passage of six weeks or so. She left Bermuda on 28 July and arrived at St Thomas on 10 August – perfectly good sailing time. She left on 14 August and arrived at Port of Spain, Trinidad, on 19 August, leaving on the 8 September. She then disappeared until the 3 November when she arrived at Horta, Fayal, in the Azores 'for small repairs' following deck and engine damage sustained in a hurricane between Puerto Rico and Hispaniola. At this stage she discharged two of her crew, including the oldest member, on the grounds of ill health. On 13 November, she sailed for Swansea arriving on 1 December – an average length passage from the Azores for a vessel of her class. She was reported as having a cargo of asphalt.

I described this voyage and the general circumstances of the *Rigdin*'s history to a senior officer of the United States Coastguard. His comment was that you could pay a crew of twelve and take two months to get from Trinidad to the Azores via Puerto Rico in a vessel known to be a fast sailer with a

The derelict Rigdin *ex* Ingrid *lying in Pont Pill opposite Fowey, Cornwall, in 1937.*
Basil Greenhill

relatively powerful auxiliary engine if you went via the coast of New Jersey. The pitch would have made good ballast for a cargo of rum, picked up during visits to various islands. Such a voyage was perfectly legal for a British ship during those years of Prohibition, since the vessel never entered US territorial waters. There was a danger of highjacking, but a big crew could help to discourage that. Many vessels were employed in this particular business at the time and though the risks were high, so were the potential profits. For obvious reasons rum-running in the 1920s was almost undocumented and remains a largely unstudied trade.

The *Rigdin* cleared Swansea towards Southampton on 31 December and arrived in Southampton on 3 January. She had a normal-size crew of seven including the master's wife and nine year old daughter engaged for the voyage at £5 each for the run. Then she was laid up, Allen Adams and Company Ltd were wound up a year later, and the *Rigdin* was sold. It appears that she remained laid up in the neighbourhood of Southampton for six years, latterly at least at Woolston on the River Itchen. When she was surveyed by Tom Stephens he found no worm in her. She was in fact in very good order and must have been unusually well looked after during the lay-up period. In September 1929 she was registered in the name of Miss Annie Stephens of Treglines, Par, Cornwall, spinster, shipowner. Tom Stephens told me 'We had lost the *Lydia Cardell* and we had to have a new vessel for Annie'. For her delivery voyage of two days the *Rigden* had a crew of ten, veterans of famous British merchant schooners of the late 1920s, the *Lydia Cardell*, the *Mary Barrow*, the *Jane Banks*, the *Katie*, the *Snowflake*. Tom Stephens himself went as a nominal purser. His last vessel had been the Stephens' schooner *Natalla* in 1917.

Rigdin lasted for almost exactly one year in the home trade under Stephens' ownership but the American stock market had collapsed and the world plunged into depression and unemployment. Early in 1931 Edward Stephens made some notes regarding his finances and his will. These notes concluded

Then the *Waterwitch*, the *Jane Banks*, and the *Rigdin* will all be free. *Rigdin* had better be laid up until times alter. Keep *Waterwitch* and *Jane Banks* going to

Falmouth. There is the coal there all the time, a steady job, it is the best paying freight in the market.

Rigdin lay for eight years in the mouth of Pont Pill opposite Fowey until she was towed away to Plymouth to be broken up.

There is a postscript. In John Cockle's words

Once in the North Sea with the engines stopped gently sailing on a lovely moonlight night I was at the wheel. The mate, Jimmy Jacks, said, 'I'll go down to have a cup of coffee'. When he was below I looked along the deck and on the starboard side I saw a man by the main rigging in a little round hat. He walked aft on the starboard side. Looked into the binnacle, walked forward and before he reached the steps down from the little poop he disappeared.

Captain Beynon told John Cockle that he had seen the ghost of William Ready, a Par man who had served in *Rigdin* as ordinary seaman during the West Indies voyage and had subsequently committed suicide.

Ingrid's Voyages 1907–1931

Year	Commenced	Ports of Call	Ended
1907	Mariehamn 23 May	Umeå–Holmsund	Sundsvall 14 June
	Sundsvall (Capt Malmqvist)	Mariehamn 22 June	Lorient 22 July
	Lorient		Middlesbrough 19 August
	Middlesbrough 26 August	Helsingfors 2 September	Trangsund/Viborg 7 September
	Trangsund		Aarhus 10 October
	Aarhus	Copenhagen 2 November	Helsingborg
	Helsingborg 18 November		Kotka 3 December
1908			Lowestoft 9 June
	Lowestoft 30 June		Odense 15 July
	Odense		Mariehamn 8 August
	Mariehamn		Sundsvall 13 August
	Sundsvall	Marihamn 3 September (in Mariehamn Capt A Abrahamsson took over) passed Copenhagen 18 September	London 1 October
	London		Fowey 22 October
	Fowey		Räfsö 26 October (discharge at Raumo)
1909	Mariehamn		Flensburg 22 May
	Flensburg		Räfsö 18 June
	Räfsö (Capt Malmqvist)		Littlehampton 3 August
	Littlehampton 18 August		Sundsvall 1 September
	Sundsvall 22 September	Mariehamn (Capt E Fahlen took over)	
	Mariehamn 27 October		Jersey 23 November
	Jersey		Grimsby 23 December
1910	Grimsby 31 December		Höganäs 5 January
	Höganäs		Sundsvall 14 April
	Sundsvall 4 May	Mariehamn 11 May	Tralee Bay 1 June
	Tralee 17 June		Swansea 23 June
	Swansea 4 July		Trelleborg 28 July
	Trelleborg 9 August		Brahestad 23 August
	Brahestad 9 September		Littlehampton 8 October

Year	Commenced	Ports of Call	Ended
	Littlehampton 20 October		Fowey 31 October
	Fowey 14 November		Swinemunde 2 December
	Swinemunde 21 December		Mariehamn 24 December
1911	Mariehamn 25 April		Räfsö 29 April
	Räfsö 11 May		Lowestoft 28 May
	Lowestoft 13 June (Capt E Mattsson)		Nederkalix 29 June
	Nederkalix 15 July	Pass Helsingfors 20 July	Boulogne 10 August
	Boulogne 26 August		Umeå, Holmsund 7 September
	Holmsund		Mariehamn 3 October
	Mariehamn 5 October		Gravesend 19 October (Discharge Northfleet)
	London 8 November		Stockholm arrive Sandhamn (Archipelago of Stockholm) 12 December
1912	Furusund (custom place in Archipelago of Stockholm) (Capt E Mattsson)		Sundsvall 6 May
	Sundsvall 22 May		Tralee 24 June
	Tralee 8 July		Fowey 18 July
	Fowey 31 July		Stockholm 14 August
	Stockholm 31 August		Skellefteå 4 September
	Skellefteå	Ursviken 25 September	Northfleet 19 October
	London 29 November	Pass Holtenua 8 December	Stockholm 12 December
1913	Norrtelje 19 April (Capt E Mattsson)		Dover 7 May
	Dover 17 May		Middlesbrough 22 May
	Middlesbrough 2 June		Mesane, White Sea 23 June
	Mesane 17 July		Southampton 18 August
	Southampton 4 September		Räfsö 29 September
	Räfsö 11 October		Northfleet 10 November
	London 24 November	Karlskrona 15 December (refuge)	Ystad 7 December Laid up at Ystad
1914	Ystad 17 April (Capt E Mattsson)		Sundsvall 27 April
	Sundsvall 9 May		Dover 28 May
	Dover 21 June		Sundsvall 2 July
	Sundsvall 17 July		Dover 14 August

Laid up at Rochester. Moved to London for caulking and fitting out, 1915.

Year	Commenced		Ended
1916	Three voyages across the Atlantic 1916		
	London		Darien
	Darien 18 April		Brest 4 June
	Brest 27 June		Montreal
	Montreal		Brest
	Brest		Jamaica
	Jamaica		Bordeaux

Laid up in Bordeaux until January 1919.

Year	Commenced	Ports of Call	Ended
	Partly refitted and departed bound towards Martinique. Put into Falmouth with weather damage.		
1922	Falmouth 5 May		
	Hull 12 May		
	Falmouth 29 May		Hamilton, Bermuda 10 July
	Hamilton 28 July		St Thomas, BWI, 10 August
	St Thomas 14 August		Port of Spain, Trinidad 19 August
	Port of Spain 8 September		Horta, Fayal, Azores 3 November
	Horta 13 November		Swansea 1 December
1923	Swansea 31 December		Southampton 3 January (Master George Reginald Langmaid)
	Vessel laid up in Southampton until 1929		
1929	Southampton 5 September		Fowey 6 September (Master George Beynon)
	Vessel refitted and rerigged as barquentine at Fowey		
1930	Fowey 25 March		Rouen 29 March
	Rouen 5 April		London 10 April
	London 7 June		Liverpool 14 June
	Liverpool 25 June		Runcorn 25 June
	Runcorn 29 June		Garston 1 July
	Garston 10 July		Fowey 15 July
	Fowey 15 August		Aberdeen 26 August
	Aberdeen 8 September		Blyth 22 September
	Blyth 9 October		Fowey 4 November
	Fowey 19 December		Rouen 22 December
1931	Rouen 4 January		Dover 7 January
	Dover 7 January		Sunderland 20 January
	Sunderland 26 January		Blyth 26 January
	Blyth 18 February (Master George Beynon)		Fowey 4 March

Vessel laid up until 1938 when towed to Plymouth for breaking up.

Chapter 11

AFTER THE GRAIN RACES

Steamship owning in Åland goes back a good deal further than is usually supposed but the early experiments were short-lived and usually under-capitalised. Not until Hugo Lundqvist's Rederi Ab Alfa of 1928 was the era of continuous steamship owning really inaugurated.

Åland's first steam vessel was the *Osmo*, built at Grangemouth in 1900 and bought in 1911 by a shareholding group in Mariehamn, which included Erik Nylund who was later to become prominent in this field of shipping. He was mate of the vessel, but the venture lasted for only a year and the *Osmo* was resold. A year or two later a little wooden steamer named *Algot*, built in Sweden in 1884, was bought, but after a few trips in the middle Baltic she too was sold, at a loss, a few months before the outbreak of the First World War.

Åland's first successful steamer was the *Agnes*, an old British collier launched as the *Domino* at Newcastle in 1877. She made money during the First World War through a contract with the British government running coal from Britain to France. She was not sold outside Åland until 1922. In 1920 Gustaf Erikson, in the post-war boom, with capital accumulated during the war, bought two new steamers built in Finland, the *Edgar* of 331 tons gross, named after his five-year-old elder son, and the *Rigel* of 978 gross tons. The investment turned out to be unwise because the vessels proved unstable carrying deck cargoes in the timber trade and uneconomic as regards fuel consumption, so they were sold the following year. Gustaf Erikson's next investment in steam tonnage took the form of his purchase of shares in the Rederi Ab Alfa seven years later.

During the First World War boom period of 1917 onwards a small fleet of wooden sailing vessels, barques, barquentines, three- and four-masted schooners was built in Åland. In many cases, notably those of the two barques, *Fred* and *Carmen*, vessels were designed and built with a view to conversion to motor power as soon as they had earned enough to buy the engine. Unfortunately the majority of them were not only very slowly but also badly built with the result that they were too late for the war and post-war booms and uneconomic in the hard years which followed. Though many of them lasted even into the 1930s they were never very profitable and the installation of motors was delayed, or never took place. But during the same period, and in the 1920s, a number of good secondhand steam and sailing vessels, all of wooden construction and mostly small, were bought from mainland Finland and elsewhere abroad. Some of these were operated, under the peculiar Åland conditions of management and manning, very profitably. In 1928 Ålanders owned twenty-one iron and steel sailing vessels, four wooden barques and no less than eleven small, wooden steamships (except for the Alfa company's *Thornbury*), and thirty-five *galeaser* and *jakter*, making a total of 105 vessels.

The 3000-ton *Thornbury* was a success from the start, proving stable with the big timber deck cargoes and economic in fuel consumption. She was soon followed by the *Charterhague* of over 4000 tons. She had been built in England, at Chepstow in Gloucestershire, in a short-lived wartime yard, as the *Silverway* in 1920. She too, was a success and was followed by the *Hildegaard*, the *Dagmar* and the *Pandi*, all 3000–4000 ton vessels which comprised a well kept, well run and profitable fleet which has continued to develop in various ways ever since.

Erik Nylund developed his steamship interests with the 5000 ton *Yrsa* and the Dutch-built *Yildum* of 5600 tons. Among other vessels he was the chief shareholder in the wooden motor vessel *Torborg*, built in Finland in 1921, which loaded about 600 tons. Arthur Andersson, who has been mentioned several times in this book, disposed of his fleet of sailing vessels to buy the 3000 ton steamers *Asko*, *Asta* and *Asturias*. The flagship was named *Atlas*, after the great four-masted schooner Arthur Andersson had owned. She was smaller, with a cargo capacity of about 1500 tons. These were all secondhand vessels, but after the Second World War Andersson's company purchased newly built tonnage.

A phenomenon of the post Second World War era was the rise of the Sally Company founded by Algot Johansson, a returned emigrant from the United States of America, who began his shipowning career with his shares in *Parma*. In the 1930s and 1940s the Sally Company bought a score or so of old coal and oil fired steamers at little more than scrap prices, choosing vessels suited to timber carrying, and running them as earlier generations had run old sailing vessels. The company prospered during the Korean War and the tanker boom and later in the development of the great Baltic ferries. Today the old tradition of Anglo–Åland business co-operation is carried on in the Sally Company's development of the port of Ramsgate and the Ramsgate–Dunkirk ferry service, an ultimate consequence of the financial success of the *Parma* venture.

An interesting episode of the 1930s was the transference to the Finnish flag and Mariehamn registration of a dozen old coal-fired steamers owned in Sweden. Now Åland companies are 'flagging out', but in the 1930s Åland was 'flagged into' to avoid high Swedish operating costs. These vessels were of 3000–6000 tons and five of them were managed by Captain Paul Kåhre, formerly master of *Mozart*. Most of them, together with a number of other steam vessels mentioned here, were lost in the Second World War, others, as they were replaced by new motor driven tonnage, were sold to Italian or Greek owners and operated under the Panamanian flat, or sold for scrap.

What then happened to the Erikson shipping concern after the Second World War and the last of the Grain Races? Two wooden motor ships, the *Vera* and the *Sweden*, had already been purchased in 1933 and operated successfully in the timber trade to Britain and western Europe. More steamers and motor ships followed in the 1930s. The last sailing vessel ever to be acquired was the auxiliary three-masted schooner *Sirius* in 1942. In 1947 the company's first new ship, the oil-burning steamer *Kungsö*, was built in Turku (Åbo). In 1950 Edgar Erikson entered the business of running small refrigerated ships, called 'reefers', sailing principally to the Mediterranean. The *Kallsö*, a small Dutch-built vessel of only 450 tons deadweight, was the first of these ships, purchased with the aid of credits from Dutch banks. This reefer fleet has been continuously modernised and renewed and today comprises some ten or so vessels most of which are operated from Mariehamn under the flag of Cyprus. There are also four other reefers under Erikson management.

For many years these reefers were operated through a pool established in Hamburg under the name of International Reefer, but today they are operated directly from the Erikson office in Mariehamn. These vessels are of up to 2000 tons deadweight and their management is a highly specialised business. Even today, in the depth of the greatest shipping depression of all time, the operation of reefers is perhaps a less discouraging form of shipping business than many others and in the Erikson offices plans for new tonnage are under way.

However, the company's main business since the Second World War has always been the latter day equivalent of the old Baltic timber trade, the mainstay of Åland's merchant fleet since the great days of the 1860s – the carriage of timber and forest products, not only from the Gulf of Bothnia but nowadays from North America as well. The *Styrsö* was converted from a war damaged steamer to a motor ship for this business at Nystads Varv during the war. She was named after the island south of Mariehamn owned by the Erikson family where Gustaf Erikson built his summer home and where he was to die in 1947. Since then all Erikson vessels have been named after Åland islands, with names terminating in the 'ö' which is indicative of an island. The *Andersö* and the *Balderö*, of nearly 17,000 tons each, and, in the mid 1980s the ultimately sophisticated *Degerö* were all built for the carriage of forest products in various forms.

When Finland and the Soviet Union signed peace terms in 1944, war reparations of over 300 million United States dollars were required from Finland within six years. Finland paid them in full, and on time, and must be the only nation to have done so in modern history. In the years of the Grain Races, from 1928 to 1939, Finland had built a total of fourteen

Above: the stern of Erik Nylund's wooden motor ship
Torborg. *She was discharging timber in Penzance in 1935.*
The pole-masted schooner lying inside the tug is the Hetty,
built at Devoran in 1878.
Basil Greenhill

Below: the steamship Alden *was owned by the Gustaf*
Erikson Company from 1943 to 1958.
Rederi ab Gustaf Erikson

Kungsö *was the first ship ever to be built for the Gustaf Erikson Company. She was launched in 1947 in Åbo.*
Rederi ab Gustaf Erikson

merchant ships of over 100 tons gross with an average size of 1600 tons gross. Between 1945 and 1952 the country launched 581 vessels totalling 365,155 gross registered tons, an achievement as incredible as it sounds. In the course of doing so she turned herself into a modern industrial nation. Erikson's Nystads Varv got its due share of this new construction, specialising in composite fishing boats and river barges. After the reparations had all been paid the yard continued with ordinary construction orders for the Soviet Union as well as for other buyers, including the owners of the yard, for whom the *Norrö*, the first Finnish vessel with hydraulic deck cranes, was built in 1954. In 1957 the first reefer to be built in Finland, the *Fiskö* was launched for the Erikson's at Nystad.

For many years the Lundqvist companies, the Asta Shipping Company and the Gustaf Erikson Company joined together to operate United Lines in the Baltic forest product trade. But this successful operation was dissolved when new building became necessary to replace older tonnage in the late 1970s.

Under present conditions and with Finnish law as it stands the investment would simply not have continued to be profitable. The company is still family owned and there is a spread of investment into banking and other industries in mainland Finland and North America. Edgar Erikson believed that in the middle 1980s world shipping is in its worst state in modern history. With running costs at western European levels and the high wage levels prevailing in Finland he considered that ship owning by the private sector is in danger of vanishing from the world scene. Even the *Degerö* in her first months of operation was covering her day to day costs but not providing funds for her own replacement. In the second half of the 1980s the Åland shipping industry is in the greatest danger it has been in since it began in the years after the Crimean War. The following words of Justus Harberg, managing director of the Åland Shipowners Association, appeared in the *Baltic Shipping Gazette*:

In the Åland Islands, like the whole of Scandinavia and other high cost regions in the northern hemisphere, we have been forced more and more into confrontation with an unpleasant reality – our traditionally operated shipowning industries are threatened with extinction.

Such trends and future prospects are without any

Above: Sommarö *was built in Holland for the Gustaf Erikson Company in 1959.*

Rederi ab Gustaf Erikson

Below: Tersö, *one of the Gustaf Erikson Company's modern reefers.*

Rederi ab Gustaf Erikson

historical counterparts in the majority of traditional shipping regions. Wars and other exceptional circumstances have occasionally brought about various temporary disturbances, recessions and interruptions in the shipping industry, but the prerequisites for carrying on international maritime trade on a national basis have always emerged again, and the industry has recovered. This has been the case in the Åland Islands too, both before and after we obtained our partial autonomy. Primarily for geographical reasons Åland bears a great resemblance to Norway in its dependence on the sea and shipping. But mainland Finland too is often compared to an island from the aspect of marine transportation.

If Åland is compelled to give up carrying on maritime trade, the consequences for our Islands will be tangible. Almost half of Åland's gross regional products now derive from the shipping business, and many activities and jobs, particularly in Mariehamn, are connected with the operations of marine transportation. The majority of persons directly working in the shipping industry are ship's officers and crews, and the effect upon Åland would be extremely serious if the trend towards abandoning sea-faring professions should continue.

As regards the future of shipping, we in Åland, together with the whole of Finland, Scandinavia, Great Britain and other countries, are confronted with a challenge that is unprecedented in modern times. The problem is really a global one; for some length of time ahead it will clearly be impossible to increase world production and trade to such an extent as to provide work for all ships. . . .

One question that may be of crucial importance to the future Nordic and European Shipping Industry is whether in the long run we may completely lose grip of marine transportation operations in our countries, if our national sea personnel drastically declines in numbers or vanishes altogether. That risk exists.

This gloomy picture does of course extend outside north west Europe and is part of a world pattern. There are many signs that the Ålanders are at last being forced to seek some alternative outlet for investment in industries other than ordinary merchant shipping. There is, in the great ferry companies, an outlet that is not totally remote from traditional shipping. They continue to prosper and grow through the deepening gloom of the international shipping business. In the early 1960s a large ferry running between Finland and Sweden could carry 1000 passengers, only ten to twenty per cent of them in fairly spartan cabins, and 150 cars. Today's giant ferries carry up to 2500 passengers, virtually all in cabins, and up to 600 cars. From the simplicity of the 1960s today's ferry has grown to resemble a huge floating conference hotel. They are more luxurious in terms of comfort, interior decoration, service and food than in any other form of scheduled travel. At the same time the carriage of cargo by regular scheduled ferry services in the Baltic region has increased spectacularly.

Finland's seaborne trade, excluding coal and oil, in 1965 was worth roughly 7700 million finnmarks and of this just over 8 per cent was carried in regular ferries. In 1983 the value of Finland's seaborne trade ran at 87,780 million finnmarks of which no less than 40.9 per cent was carried in the ferries. The answer to the question 'why and how?' rests, of course, in the development of the roll-on roll-off transport of cargoes in lorries. The ferry industry, in which Åland shipowners have investments of scores of millions of pounds, continues to grow and there are good prospects for a buoyant future. Although there is a vast difference between *Mozart* and *Mariella* or *Ponape* and Mariehamn's 21000 gross registered ton ferry *Birka Princess* which runs on the Stockholm–Mariehamn service, the new ships are in direct line of descent, in terms of Åland as a shipping community.

The new ships are even further removed from the old way of life of the farmer–seafarer with their *galeaser* and *jakter* and their farms. Sometimes, however, you can still get just a glimpse of that old way of life. One autumn day in the early 1980s Kalle Karlsson then aged eighty-four, invited my wife and me to visit Långskär, one of the outer islands of Wårdö community, to see some stone bread ovens left there by the Russians after the Little Northern War of 1742. Karlsson was formerly master of the *Atlas* and the *Parma*, and had worked in seventeen sailing vessels and steamers from 1913. Långskär was where, in his youth, Kalle's family took sheep in sailing farm boats to live off the sparse grazing of the stunted bushes during the summer. We went in his fine sixteen foot wooden motor boat on a very breezy day with a rough sea running. The conditions were marginal and the French-built motor gave trouble at critical moments. At times it looked as if our friends from the Mariehamn base of the coastguards might be looking for us the next day, and we calculated the chances of a cold, wet night in the open on the exposed skerry, or, worse still, in the boat drifting northwards in rising wind and sea into the Gulf of Bothnia. We were reminded of the reality of the lives of the Cape Horners in their youth in the 1920s and 1930s, of life on small farms and in open boats, of the coming winter, with the dark, the deep, deep, cold and the driving snow.

In the end, encouraged by an odd mixture of English as spoken in the forecastles of merchant sailing ships in the First World War, Wårdö dialect and impeccable modern English and Swedish, and

The huge Baltic ferry Viking Saga *seems ready to gobble up her ancestor, the little* galeas Astrid, *still earning a living as a cruise vessel, as they lie in Helsinki's South Harbour.*
Basil Greenhill

with a little help from me, Kalle Karlsson brought the erring French motor to life and in the gathering dusk we nursed her back through ten kilometres of the labyrinth to his boathouse at the back of the lovely bay of Östervik. My wife noticed the flurry of skirts behind a bush as Kalle's wife, anxious for her eighty-four-year-old husband, (who had never wavered or hesitated throughout this little adventure), withdrew from her lookout place before he saw her.

Kalle died almost a year later and there were then only three 'Albatrosses', (former masters of merchant sailing vessels in the Cape Horn trade), among the survivors of the Grain Race at the monthly lunches at the Nautical Club in Mariehamn. Here they still gather, with the relics of a great seafaring history in the museum downstairs and the busy ferries coming and going outside the windows, just down the harbour from the statuesque *Pommern*.

It has been a great privilege to know them.

Edgar Erikson on board the Tamar ketch barge Shamrock *at Cotehele Quay, Cornwall, in May 1985. With him is Peter Allington, master of the vessel.*
Basil Greenhill

Date of Ownership	Type of Vessel	Name of Vessel	Dead-weight Tonnage	Material	Date Built	Builder	Place Built
1913–1925	3 bk	TJERIMAI	1550	Composite	1883	J F Meusing	Amsterdam
1913–1914	4 bk	ÅLAND ex Renee Rickmers	3300	Iron	1887	Russell & Co	Port Glasgow
1914–1916	3 bk	FREDENBORG	600	Wood	1881	Johan August Henriksson	Isaksö, Geta, Åland
1916–1917	3 bk	BORROWDALE	1850	Iron	1868	W H Potter & Co	Liverpool
1916–1935	S	GRACE HARWAR	2950	Steel	1889	W Hamilton & Co	Port Glasgow
1916–1923	3 bk	PROFESSOR KOCH	2350	Steel	1891	Russell & Co	Port Glasgow
1917–1919	3 Sr	INGRID	650	Wood	1907	E Söderström	Knutnäs, Geta, Åland
1917–1919	3 bk	SOUTHERN BELLE	850	Wood	1871	J Mulcaha	Church Point, Digby, Nova Scotia
1917–1942	4 bk	LAWHILL	4600	Steel	1892	W B Thompson & Co	Dundee
1917	4 bk	MARGARETA ex Craigerne	3100	Steel	1889	R Duncan & Co	Port Glasgow
1919–1924	3 bk	WOODBURN	2600	Steel	1896	Russell & Co	Port Glasgow
1921–1936	4 bk	HERZOGIN CECILIE	4350	Steel	1902	Rickmers A/G	Bremerhaven
1922–1933	3 bk	LOCH LINNHE	2200	Iron	1876	J & G Thomson	Glasgow
1922–1953	4 bk	POMMERN ex Mneme	4050	Steel	1903	J Reid & Co	Glasgow
1923–1924	4 bk	CARRADALE	3300	Steel	1889	A Stephen & Sons	Glasgow
1923–1941	3 bk	PENANG ex Albert Rickmers	3250	Steel	1905	Rickmers A/G	Bremerhaven
1924–1939	4 bk	OLIVEBANK	4400	Steel	1892	Mackie & Thompson	Glasgow
1924–1940	3 bk	KILLORAN	3050	Steel	1900	Ailsa SB Co	Troon
1924–1934	3 bk	CARMEN	850	Wood	1921	Lemlands Varv	Granboda, Lemland, Åland
1924	4 Sr	POLSTJERNAN	1600	Wood	1920	Skinnarviks Varf	Dragsfjärd
1924–1939	4 bkn	BALTIC	750	Wood	1919	A/B Baltic	Vasteranga, Lemland, Aland

NOTE: The vessels in this list are those in which Gustaf Erikson was at one time or another the largest single shareholder. The list does not include a number of vessels in which he had shares (see Appendix II). It does not include fully powered steam and motor vessels which were not dependent on sails in any way.

Gross Ton-nage	Net Ton-nage	Dimensions (ft in)			From Whom Bought	Price	Notes
		L	B	D			
976	827	188 3	36 7	21 1	N Tarasoff m fl, Lovisa	Fmk42,500	Lost in collision with Dutch trawler in the North Sea, 22 August 1925.
2135	2064	283 0	40 5	24 6	Rickmers Reismullhlen, Rederei & Schiffbau, AG	£6500	Stranded on the coast of New Caledonia in August 1914.
435	431	131 8	31 2	15 4	Alandskt rederi	£300	Sold in 1916. Broken up shortly afterwards.
1268	1191	226 4	36 4	22 0	August Troberg, Marie-hamn	Fmk300,000	Torpedoed in 1917 in North Atlantic.
1816	1564	266 7	39 1	23 5	Rederi A/B Delfin, Helsingfors	Fmk940,000	Sold for breaking up, 1935.
1453	1357	236 2	36 2	21 7	August Troberg, Marie-hamn	Fmk750,000	Condemned at Montevideo after collision with iceberg, 1923.
305	291	132 0	27 0	13 0	Ålandskt rederi		Sold to British owners in 1919 fitted with auxiliary engine and used in West Indies and home trades under the name *Rigdin*. Broken up 1939. Only Åland built vessel to become British.
	588	146 0	31 4	18 8	Ålandskt rederi		Sold for breaking up, 1919. Part of masts and rigging incorporated in new barque *Carmen* (qv).
2816	2540	317 4	45 0	25 1	August Troberg, Marie-hamn	Fmk2,500,000	Condemned by Prize Court, 1942, in South Africa. Fell to pieces at Laurenco Marques.
1873	1748	270 2	40 0	23 6	August, Troberg, Marie-hamn	Fmk1,100,000	Torpedoed March 1917 in the Irish Sea.
1552	1445	242 0	37 5	21 8	A Blom, Nystad	Fmk2,900,000	Sold and reduced to a coal hulk, 1924.
3111	2584	314 8	46 3	24 2	French Government	£4250	Wrecked Salcombe, South Devon, England, 1936.
1460	1175	235 9	37 1	22 1	C Lundstrom m fl, Nystad	Fmk400,000	Wrecked in the Åland Islands, 1933.
2376	2114	294 8	43 4	24 5	Greek Government	£3750	Preserved intact as a merchant vessel at Mariehamn.
1967	1881	285 7	41 0	23 7	Rederi A/B Aura, Åbo	Fmk417,000	Sold for breaking up, 1924.
2019	1743	265 7	40 2	24 3	John Nurminen O/Y, Raume	Fmk540,000	Missing on passage from Port Lincoln towards Cork for orders, 1940.
2795	2427	326 0	43 1	24 5	Skibs A/S Ostra, Kristiansand		Sunk by a mine in the North Sea, 1939.
1817	1523	261 5	39 1	22 7	J Hardie & Co Glasgow	£2650	Sunk by enemy action, August 1940.
558	445	176 1	33 9	12 9	Ålandskt rederi		Abandoned near Bornholm, 1934.
1028	733	202 9	40 3	16 0	Dragsfjärds Rederi A/B	Fmk150,000	Sold, March 1925.
451	354	171 4	33 7	11 3	A/B Baltic, Lemland	Fmk163,500	Sold, May 1939.

Date of Ownership	Type of Vessel	Name of Vessel	Dead-weight Tonnage	Material	Date Built	Builder	Place Built
1924–1949	4 bk	ARCHIBALD RUSSELL	3950	Steel	1905	Scott & Co	Greenock
1925–1932	4 bk	HOUGOMONT	4000	Steel	1897	Scott & Co	Greenock
1925–1935	3 bk	LINGARD ex Wathara	1600	Steel	1893	Fevigs Jernskibsbygerri	Arendal
1925–1934	3 Sr	OSTROBOTNIA	800	Wood	1919	J Lundqvist	Jakobstad
1925–1944	3 bk	WINTERHUDE ex Mabel Rickmers	3250	Steel	1898	Rickmers A/G	Bremerhaven
1926–1928	3 bk	LALLA ROOKH ex Karhu ex Effendi	1450	Iron	1876	R & J Evans & Co	Liverpool
1927–1936	3 bkn	ESTONIA	800	Wood	1921	A Wammus	Gutmannsbach
1929–1932	4 bk	MELBOURNE ex Gustav ex Austrasia	4250	Steel	1892	Russel & Co	Port Glasgow
1929–1939	Aux 4 Sr	MADARE ex Fox III	900	Wood	1919	Arveskjobings Skibsverft	Arveskjobing
1929–1951	4 bk	VIKING	4000	Steel	1907	Burmeister & Wain	Copenhagen
1929–1936	4 bk	PONAPE ex Bellhouse ex Regina Elena	3500	Steel	1903	Bacini	Genoa
1931–1951	4 bk	PAMIR	4500	Steel	1905	Blohm & Voss	Hamburg
1932–1936	4 bk	L'AVENIR	3650	Steel	1908	Rickmers A/G	Bremerhaven
1932–1951	4 bk	PASSAT	4700	Steel	1911	Blohm & Voss	Hamburg
1933	Aux twin screw 4 Sr	ODINE ex Astrella, ex Odine ex Pauline	1600	Wood	1917	McEachern Ship Co	Astoria, Oregon
1933–1937	3 bk	VARMA	1400	Wood	1922	Nystads Slip	Nystad
1933–1943	3 bk	ELÄKÖÖN	1400	Wood	1920	Nystads Slip	Nystad
1933–1939	Aux 3 Sr	VELLAMO	550	Wood	1919	Nystads Slip	Nystad
1933–1943	Aux 4 Sr	VALBORG	1500	Wood	1919	Cholberg Shipyard	Victoria BC
1934–1937	3 bk	KYLEMORE ex Suzanne	1900	Steel	1880	J Reid & Co	Port Glasgow
1934–1937	3 bk	PESTALOZZI ex Claudia	1600	Iron	1884	Blohm & Voss	Hamburg

Gross Tonnage	Net Tonnage	Dimensions (ft in) L	B	D	From Whom Bought	Price	Notes
2354	2048	291 3	42 9	24 0	J Hardie & Co Glasgow	£5500	Sold for breaking up, 1948.
2074	2084	292 4	43 2	24 1	J Hardie & Co Glasgow	£3500	Dismasted and presented to Waratah Gypsum Co for use as a breakwater, at Stenhouse Bay, Spencer Gulf, Australia, 1932.
1039	882	213 0	33 9	17 7	James Bell & Co, Hull	£2200	Sold in Gothenburg in 1936 after collision damage. Preserved as museum ship at Oslo but broken up in the late 1940s.
500	434	163 9	32 8	15 2	Jakobstads Varv & Rederi A/B	Fmk150,000	Hulked at Nystad, 1934.
1972	1709	267 2	40 5	24 1	French Government	£1950	Sold to German Navy, 1944.
824	741	196 5	31 8	19 6	Werner Hacklin, Räfso		Sold for breaking up, 1928.
481	414	151 5	33 9	13 6	T & S Oates	N Kr12,000	Wrecked in Baltic, 1936.
2691	2525	305 1	44 0	24 7	Hermann Engel, Hamburg	£4000	Sunk in collision off Irish Coast, 1932.
544	366	155 9	34 6	16 1	R Boxberg, Helsingfors	Fmk750,000	Sequestrated in Bremen after collision and sold.
2670	2154	293 8	42 5	23 2	De Forenede Dampskibs Selskab	£6500	Preserved at Gothenburg, Sweden, in much altered state.
2342	1974	283 8	42 5	23 2	Hugo Lundqvist m fl, Mariehamn	£5500	Sold for breaking up, 1936.
2798	2365	316 0	46 0	26 2	F Laeisz, Hamburg		Sold to German owners and lost at sea in 1957.
2754	1871	278 2	44 8	26 5	Belgian Government	£2820	Sold to German owners and lost at sea in 1938.
3130	2585	322 0	47 2	26 5	F Laeisz, Hamburg	£6500	Preserved at Travemünde, Germany, in much altered state.
1723	1349	248 2	44 5	19 7	Erik Nylund, Mariehamn		Rigged down and sold at the Nystad yard, motors transferred to *Valborg*. She appears to have been bought for her motors and gear.
718	649	201 7	35 0	17 2	Undenkaupungin Laiva O/Y, Nystad		Condemned and sold to German owner, 1937.
827	756	209 5	36 0	17 1	Undenkaupungin Laiva O/Y, Nystad		Sold 1943 to Finnish owners and converted in 1945 to a motor vessel. Hull still in existence 1977 as bridge between two islands in the Finnish Archipelago.
337	201	139 4	28 6	12 2	Undenkaupungin Laiva O/Y, Nystad		Sold to Finnish owners in 1939.
964	472	197 5	40 0	16 5	Hugo Lundqvist m fl, Mariehamn	Fmk225,000	Fitted with engines from *Odine* on purchase. Sailed on Norwegian coast during WWII. Condemned after fire, sold to Norwegians.
1229	1001	226 2	36 4	22 1	H Marechal, Havre	£800	Sold for breaking up, 1937.
1046	851	206 6	34 1	19 6	H Marechal, Havre	£800	Sold for breaking up, 1937.

Date of Ownership	Type of Vessel	Name of Vessel	Dead-weight Tonnage	Material	Date Built	Builder	Place Built
1934–1935	4 Sr	REGINA	1000	Wood	1919	G Kyntzell	Borga
1934–1942	4 bkn	DIONE	1000	Wood	1923	B Donner	Jomala
1935–1947	4 bk	MOSHULU ex Kurt	4900	Steel	1904	W Hamilton & Co	Port Glasgow
1942–1946	Aux 3 Sr	SIRIUS ex Bjerkvik ex Marten	180	Wood	1901	E Norstom	Västervik Sweden

Appendix 2

LIST OF SAILING VESSELS IN WHICH GUSTAF ERIKSON HAD A FINANCIAL INTEREST

Date of Share ownership	Type of Vessel	Name of Vessel	Vessel No	Parish of Registry	Number of Shares	Notes
1903–1912	bkn	DEO GLORIA	3	Lemland	$^4/_{100}$	wrecked
1893–1898	bkn	ADELE	96	Lemland	$^3/_{32}$	wrecked
1901–1905	bg	KAROLINA	113	Lemland	1901, $2 \times {}^6/_{192}$; 1902, $^2/_{32}$	wrecked
1917–1928	bkn	NEPTUN	166	Hammarland	1901, $^1/_{20}$; 1902, $^1/_{80}$	wrecked
1891–1900	bk	MATHILDA	167	Lemland/Wårdö	1891, $^1/_8$; 1894, $^{10}/_{80}$	ship sold
1901–1903	bk	KALEVA	182	Lemland	$^1/_{40}$	ship sold
1901–1902	bk	HILDA	199	Lemland	$^1/_{16}$	wrecked
1901–1902	Sr	ALMA	203	Lemland	$^4/_{32}$	wrecked
1903	bg	RAKKAUS	204	Lemland	$^1/_{40}$	ship sold
1916	bk	NORDEN	218	Geta	$10 \times {}^1/_{80}$	wrecked
1892–1899	bk	GESSNER	219	Lemland/Sund	$^{10}/_{80}$	wrecked
1903–1907	bk	ROXANE	230	Lemland	$^2/_{100}$	ship sold
1894–1911	bk	OCEAN	303	Lemland	1894, $^2/_{100}$; 1905, $^4/_{100}$	wrecked
1898–1928	bk	MONTROSA	319	Lemland/Mariehamn	1898, $^3/_{100}$; 1915, $^1/_{10}$, $2 \times {}^5/_{100}$	ship sold
1899–1906	bk	EUROPA	322	Mariehamn	$^2/_{100}$	wrecked
1899–1910	bk	DUGUAY	325	Jomala/Lemland	$^2/_{100}$	broken up
1899–1903	f	VANADIS	329	Mariehamn	$^2/_{100}$	wrecked
1902–1913	bk	WOLFE	363	Lumparland	$2 \times {}^2/_{100}$	ship sold
1900–1901	bk	CUBA	364	Mariehamn	$^2/_{100}$	wrecked
1915–1916	bk	ASIA	369	Finström	$10 \times {}^1/_{100}$	lost
1909–1915	bk	CHRISTIANE	370	Lumparland	$^1/_{100}$	ship sold
1901–1911	bkn	CERES	376	Lemland	$^2/_{40}$	ship sold
1901–1911	bk	AUGUSTA	385	Lemland	$^1/_{40}$	wrecked
1902–1906	bkn	IDA	404	Lemland	$^4/_{40}$	wrecked
1902–1903	bk	HOLME-STRAND	408	Lemland	$^4/_{100}$	wrecked
1905–1915	bk	ISABEL BROWNE	416	Lemland/Wårdö	$^1/_{100}$	war loss
1903–1908	f	ALBANIA	419	Mariehamn	1903, $^3/_{100}$; 1906, $2 \times {}^1/_{100}$, $^3/_{100}$, $^2/_{100}$	sold

Gross Tonnage	Net Tonnage	Dimensions (ft in) L	B	D	From Whom Bought	Price	Notes
681	545	182 0	34 5	16 2	A Ekbom m fl, Mariehamn	Fmk35,000	Lost in the Baltic by fire, 1935.
502	428	160 2	33 0	13 2	O Engman m fl, Mariehamn	Fmk95,500	Sold to Finnish owners, 1942.
3120	2696	335 3	46 9	26 6	Charles Nelson Co, San Francisco	US$12,000	Preserved at Philadelphia in much altered state.
116	72	93 5	23 0	8 5	Karl J Fremling, Lemland		Sailed on Norwegian coast during Second World War. Sold to Norwegian owners, 1946.

NOTE: Gustaf Erikson also held shares in *Southern Belle* before he acquired control of her in 1917, and in *Parma* (see text).

Date of Share ownership	Type of Vessel	Name of Vessel	Vessel No	Parish of Registry	Number of Shares	Notes
1916–1936	bk	PROMPT	475	Wårdö/Mariehamn	1916, $^5/_{100}$; 1917, $2 \times {}^1/_{100}$, $2 \times {}^1/_{100}$; 1919, $^1/_{100}$	ship sold
1910–1917	f	PERA	499	Wårdö	1910, $^1/_{100}$; 1916, $^2/_{100}$, $^1/_{100}$	war loss
1916–1918	bk	CONCORDIA	510	Jomala	$^1/_{20}$	ship sold
1916–1926	bk	PARCHIM	531	Wårdö	1916, $^1/_{100}$; 1917, $3 \times {}^1/_{100}$, $^3/_{200}$	ship sold
1916–1917	bk	LUCIPARA	557	Mariehamn	$^5/_{100}$	war loss
1913–1916	f	FRIEDA	560	Vårdö	1913, $^2/_{100}$; 1916, $3 \times {}^2/_{100}$, $2 \times {}^1/_{100}$	wrecked
1943–(1972)	g	ENSE	581	Jomala/Saltvik Mariehamn	$^{10}/_{100}$	?
1942–(1972)	g	SAGA	621	Mariehamn	$^{20}/_{100}$	?
1919–1930	g	NÄSBORG	634	Saltvik	1919, $^1/_{40}$; 1920, $^4/_{40}$	sold shares
1920–1927	3 Sr	ESPERANZA	636	Hammarland	$^{10}/_{100}$	wrecked
1926–1929	bkn	VINETA	649	Mariehamn	$^5/_{100}$	wrecked
1920–1934	bk	FRED	674	Finström	$^{50}/_{100}$	wrecked
1920–1937	3 Sr	LINDEN	676	Mariehamn	1920, $^{10}/_{100}$; 1923, $^5/_{200}$; 1928, $^5/_{100}$	ship sold
1923–1929	3 Sr	BALDER	685	Mariehamn	1923, $^4/_{40}$; 1925, $^1/_{40}$	wrecked
1926–1935	3 Sr/aux	VESTA	694	Mariehamn	$^5/_{100}$	ship sold
1926–?	3 g/aux	VIDAR	708	Saltvik	1926, $^{10}/_{100}$; 1938, $^5/_{100}$	?
1931–1935	bkn	MOZART	728	Mariehamn	$^1/_{100}$, $^2/_{100}$	ship sold
1943–1947	g	HELENA	744	Mariehamn	$^5/_{100}$	ship sold
1929	bk	THEKLA	746	Mariehamn	$^{25}/_{100}$	ship sold
1926–1933	3 Sr	HILDUR	789	Mariehamn	$^{10}/_{100}$	wrecked
1933–1937	3 Sr/aux	JOHANNES	808	Saltvik	$^2/_{100}$	ship sold
1929–1942	3 Sr/aux	GUSTAF	820	Mariehamn	$^{45}/_{100}$	ship sold
1930–1936	3 g	JENOLIN	594	Mariehamn/Sund	$^{10}/_{100}$	wrecked

Index

Following the Swedish language practice, words beginning with the Swedish letters Å, Ä and Ö, are placed, in that order, after Z. Figures in *italic* refer to illustrations.